HEALING INVISIBLE WOUNDS

Transfiguration by Raffaello Sanzio. *Courtesy of the Vatican Museums*

HEALING INVISIBLE WOUNDS

*Paths to Hope and Recovery
in a Violent World*

RICHARD F. MOLLICA, MD

HARCOURT, INC.
Orlando   Austin   New York   San Diego   Toronto   London

Requests for permission to make copies of any part of the work
should be submitted online at www.harcourt.com/contact or mailed
to the following address: Permissions Department, Harcourt, Inc.,
6277 Sea Harbor Drive, Orlando, Florida 32887-6777.

www.HarcourtBooks.com

Library of Congress Cataloging-in-Publication Data
Mollica, Richard F.
Healing invisible wounds: paths to hope and recovery in a violent world/
Richard F. Mollica.—1st ed.
p.   cm.
Includes bibliographical references and index.
1. Political refugees—Mental health.   2. Political refugees—Counseling of.
3. Posttraumatic stress disorder—Treatment.   4. Psychic trauma—Treatment.
I. Title.
RC451.4.P57M65   2006
616.85'21—dc22   2006004785
ISBN-13: 978-0-15-101036-3   ISBN-10: 0-15-101036-6

Text set in Minion Cyrillic
Designed by Lauren Rille

Printed in the United States of America
First edition

K J I H G F E D C B A

To my parents,
FRANK *and* IRENE MOLLICA

CONTENTS

Prologue   1

Chapter 1: Striking Out on a New Pathway   7

Chapter 2: The Trauma Story   34

Chapter 3: Humiliation   62

Chapter 4: The Power of Self-Healing   88

Chapter 5: Storytelling as a Healing Art   110

Chapter 6: Good Dreams and Bad Dreams   134

Chapter 7: Social Instruments of Healing   157

Chapter 8: The Call to Health   188

Chapter 9: Society as Healer   214

Epilogue   241

Acknowledgments   249

Endnotes   253

Bibliography   261

Index   269

Healing Invisible Wounds

PROLOGUE

A LITTLE ITALIAN BOY about nine, with wild and curly hair, rushed along the tenement streets of Harlem to meet his father at his fruit and vegetable store. This little boy admired his father, Carmelo, who seemed special to him with his beautiful red mustache and bright blue eyes. None of his Italian friends had a father so handsome. He hoped he would grow up to look exactly like Carmelo.

As the little boy came around the corner near the store, he saw a huge crowd of people gathered around the boxes of grapes and oranges. They were not buying anything but were shouting fearfully in Italian. He pushed through the thickening crowd. In front of the vegetable boxes he found his father lying on the ground, with blood the color of his mustache pouring down his face. He had been murdered. The boy would never know by whom.

A few years later when the boy was thirteen, he contracted meningitis. The illness did not kill him, but it did impair his vision so badly that he was declared legally blind. Shortly thereafter his mother died. These were tragic losses, but what was remarkable was that as he grew up, the boy chose not to let these events rob him of the joy of life. He owned a bicycle shop in Harlem and did everything a sighted person could do. He married and raised four children. He built a sailboat and sailed it around City Island. He repaired and drove cars, and lived life with such delight and vigor that his children were hardly aware of his past pain. Instead, they grew up hearing stories about a grandfather with a big red mustache and developed a strong visual appreciation of the world passed down to them by a man with limited sight. This extraordinary man was my father, Frank Mollica, son of Italian immigrants, and the way he lived his life taught me many valuable lessons about reality.

From my father, I learned that we create our own reality, and often there is more than one to choose from. In some ways my father made my family, our friends, and our relatives all forget that he was nearly blind. Only when he declined to drive at night or when he asked to use my stethoscope to listen to a car engine—almost always making the correct diagnosis—was I reminded of his limited vision. He loved drawing and painting and helped my siblings and me make the most beautifully designed and colorful projects for school. His automotive garage was more like an artist's loft than a repair shop, his tools arranged on color-coded boards. There was a harmonious arrangement to the usual automotive riffraff: barrels of oil and grease were placed just so; old mufflers were organized by make and size. My father was obsessed with "seeing," and this obsession extended beyond the visual world. As he always told us, "See reality clearly, but never give up your dream." No matter how terrible our life might become, we could always do something valuable with it.

Years later, when he was failing from cancer of the lung that had spread to his brain, in a rare lucid moment he said, "Son, I want you to know that the saddest thing that ever happened to me was the death of my father. I have missed him my entire life." He cried gently, a few hours passed, and he died.

Although my father's early life was full of tragedy, he always approached his adversities with a sense of humor. One of his favorite expressions was, "Don't worry, it's going to get worse." I never appreciated the extraordinary irony of this comment until I shared it with some Indo-Chinese colleagues, all of whom had experienced extreme violence. Their universal reaction to my father's wisdom was to laugh. Later they inscribed his words in Khmer on the wall of the health clinic in a Cambodian refugee camp. My father fashioned a hopeful reality out of tragedy that most traumatized persons can relate to. Such people have a choice about how they want to see the world and construct a life for themselves out of their hurt and pain, and about how much of their pain they will share with others.

More and more the individual trauma stories of ordinary citizens are being reconfigured into a collective victims' voice. The shouts of horror from the media, aid workers, and politicians are getting louder and louder. After the tsunami catastrophe of December 26, 2004, a front-page photograph in a major American newspaper introduced the reader to the disaster by showing a woman in total emotional collapse.[1] She is sitting on a bare hospital floor in Nagappattinam, India, surrounded by the bodies of tsunami victims, many of them her own children. The children in front are lying naked, while the feet of others protrude from a white gauze blanket. This image allows little response other than extreme fear and hopelessness, as well as a sense that we have intruded insensitively into a private experience. Journalists are debating amongst themselves whether the final screams of a person being beheaded should be broadcast to the general public. For those of us viewing these daily images of horrible events, the major question is how to handle them without turning away in impotent despair.

My father's trauma story and the thousands of trauma stories I've heard over the past twenty-five years as a doctor caring for survivors of extreme violence seem incomprehensible and impossible to imagine. Yet the stories are usually gentle in tone and full of nuance. Within an individual, the trauma becomes transformed into something radically different than anyone could have predicted. The tsunami survivor who was exploited in the newspaper photograph will, with quiet dignity, convert her unspeakable pain into the energy for survival. This not-so-mysterious force, which lies within her and within all of us, is the biological, psychological, and social power of self-healing, that innate capacity possessed by all human beings to restore their physical and mental self to a state of full productivity and quality of life, no matter how severe the initial damage.

The trauma stories in this book will illustrate how evolution's great healing power is activated when violence threatens survival. The stories may sometimes feel exotic and exceptional, yet such extreme situations are relevant to all of us in our everyday lives. We can be filled with joy as we celebrate the heroic lives of those who have overcome life's tragedies. Yet we can also forget that a tragic dimension exists in every life, especially if our pain is caused by other human beings. Every one of us is eventually called upon to pass through one of these crises, whether physical injury, disease, family violence, or the death of a loved one. This book reveals the healing power that resides in each of us, which is capable of aiding our recovery from terrible life experiences. Those who have been through extreme violence such as war and torture can serve as our guides, teaching us how to cope and thrive in a more ordinary and conventional world. "If they can do it, we certainly can do it." We can also learn how to cope with violence in our global society.

While public discussions of the psychological impact of extreme violence, including natural disasters, are now commonplace in the media, twenty-five years ago they were almost nonexistent. In fact, they were almost taboo. In the mid-1980s I was denied a meeting with the United Nations High Commissioner for Refugees because he firmly believed that refugees did not have emotional problems or psychological distress associated with their displacement and homeless state. At that time it was impossible for international and American policymakers and humanitarian relief agencies to accept the invisible psychological wounds affecting traumatized persons throughout the world. Today there is instead a demand for scientific methods and practices to help heal those wounds.[2]

Violence creates in people a new kind of historical space, formed when a crack in the "cosmic egg" of ordinary life occurs. All that was fairly mundane and predictable suddenly is thrown into a radically new and different place. Such shifts are historical because they reflect an upheaval in social and political relationships that has major consequences, not only for individuals but for the world itself. These spaces are often created by violent events, sometimes at the individual level, but mostly at the community level. Within these situations, revelations can and do occur as new truths emerge. Perpetrators and those in the media who exploit the horror of violence focus only on the point at which a new reality is cracked open. Unfortunately they do not stay around to see what unfolds afterward. Those transforming revelations are told through the lives of the storytellers in this book. Tragedy and pain cannot be avoided in our ordinary lives, but they can take on new meaning as they are integrated into a broader healing framework.

Chapter 1
STRIKING OUT
ON A NEW PATHWAY

ALTHOUGH WE ALL KNOW that suffering is a universal human experience, the modern world still does not know how to speak about and understand the terrible experiences that human beings inflict on each other every day. Because of the horror and disbelief associated with human-on-human violence, it is easy to slide into a cynical attitude that nothing can be done to prevent this violence or to recover from it. One reason for this is that the major harms caused by human aggression are invisible wounds. While physical scars can be identified and accounted for by medical science, psychological, spiritual, and existential injuries remain hidden.

I have spent the past twenty-five years caring for people who have experienced human aggression on a societal scale, as refugees, victims of torture or terrorism, and survivors of war. My experiences reveal a new way of thinking about human aggression and the healing of the physical and emotional damage caused by violence. Major insights, which I call scientific epiphanies or revelations, occurred as I interacted with my patients. I proceeded to investigate these conclusions scientifically and, when they were proven valid, to integrate them into my clinical care. These revelations form the basis for the healing practices advocated in this book.

My pathway to this work was a circuitous one. Educated in a technical high school with an engineering curriculum of physics, chemistry, and math, I discovered early on that science does not address the moral and humanistic issues of society. These matters are better addressed by the humanities and arts. Although I had never met a doctor except during routine physical examinations, in college I majored in chemistry and religion, fantasizing that in medicine I could apply my interests in science, religion, philosophy, and the arts to better the human condition. While in medical school in New Mexico, I worked in the remote Hispanic villages of northern New Mexico and the Indian reservations of Zuni and Jemez Pueblo, serving poor patients within a rich cultural and natural environment. Subsequently I undertook residency training in psychiatry while simultaneously pursuing an advanced degree in religion and philosophy. Divinity school provided the moral compass for my medical and scientific skills, as well as for my future work with survivors of extreme violence. My interests in the arts and literature have also informed my work, yielding metaphorical insights to mysteries that are beyond the abilities of science and medicine to explain.

A NEW CLINIC

When I arrived at Harvard as a young doctor in the early 1980s, I knew that I wanted to provide the highest quality of medical and psychiatric care to the poorest people in my community, in spite of financial and political barriers. Looking around the Greater Boston area for those who most needed help, I found that newly arrived refugees from Southeast Asia were both extremely poor and almost totally excluded from the existing public, private, and academic medical systems. With the help of James Lavelle, a young idealistic social worker already working for the refugee community, we decided to set up a small free clinic for them in the Brighton section of Boston, initially called the Indochinese Psychiatry Clinic, later the Harvard Program in Refugee Trauma. Our little group unknowingly became one of the first refugee mental health clinics in America.

During this time, medicine and psychiatry were still color- and gender-biased, in spite of the work of individuals such as my mentor, Fritz Redlich, a Yale professor of psychiatry. Redlich showed in a study in the early 1950s that although mental illness was more prevalent in the poor, they received a radically different type of psychiatric care than middle-class and rich patients.[1] Poor patients were often given drugs and rarely psychotherapy because they were considered incapable of psychological insights into their mental health problems. Psychiatrists rarely treated these patients; instead they received treatment primarily from paraprofessionals, that is, mental health workers with limited clinical training. Twenty-five years later, I revealed in a follow-up study that treatment biases toward the poor and African Americans remained unchanged, in spite of enormous efforts by the federal government to rectify the situation by providing easy access to community mental health centers. Newly arrived Southeast Asian refugees were still thrown into a large group of low-status patients receiving a low level of health care and mental health care, because they were poor, overwhelmed by social problems, nonwhite, and unfamiliar with American mental health practices, especially psychotherapy.

All refugees entering America have a basic health screening in a government-funded primary health care center. Tens of thousands of Southeast Asian refugees, victims from the war in Vietnam, were flooding through these centers to start their new lives in America. Our team of medical pioneers was waiting in the Brighton clinic to help them with their emotional distress, which was often readily apparent to the primary care doctors who referred them to our clinic. Our staff included Jim Lavelle; Ter Yang, a Hmong chief from the animistic tribes of Laos; Binh Tu, a Vietnamese ex-soldier who had been the "Frank Sinatra" of the Vietnamese army; and Rosa Lek, a young Cambodian woman whose job was drawing blood in a medical laboratory.

The mental health clinic was initially open one half-day a week. Our services were free and none of us were paid. Referrals came flooding in from our medical colleagues at the rate of sometimes twenty refugee patients in a single afternoon. The refugees did not have to be convinced of the value of the clinic; they immediately felt comfortable being greeted by a medical doctor, a social worker, and respected members of their own communities. Our Indo-Chinese colleagues were never used as interpreters; they always functioned as integral elements of our treatment team, in a bicultural partnership that was key to our clinical success.

As I listened to the story of Leakana, an elderly Cambodian woman who was one of the first patients in our clinic, I realized that the conventional psychiatric tools I had been taught would not be sufficient to help her:

> During the year of the snake, the God of the Sun came to stay in my body. It made my body shaky all over—and I fainted. Upon awakening, I can remember as I opened my eyes that it was very dark. I then went to the rice fields to find someone to ask them what time it was. A voice shouted 10 o'clock. Suddenly, the owls began to cry and all the animals that represented death were howling all around me. I could also barely see a small group of

people whispering to each other in the forest. I became so frightened that I tried to calm myself by praying to all the Gods and the angels in heaven to protect me from danger. I was so paralyzed with fear that I was unable to walk either backward or forward.

I came to settle in east Boston near the ocean. Now when I dream, I always see an American who dresses in black walking along the sea. One day when I was in my sponsor's house, I had this vision. This year, the year of the cow, I would like the American people to help me build a temple near the seashore. Since the Pol Pot soldiers killed my children, I am so depressed that all I can think about is just to build a temple—that is all. God appeared to me again the other day, and he told me to build a temple. Please help me make my dream come true. If not, I do not think I can live any more.

Leakana had survived the Khmer Rouge labor camps that killed five daughters and four of her ten grandchildren. After fleeing Cambodia into the Thai refugee camps, she and a remaining son and daughter were resettled in America. Psychologically, she was full of fear, anxiety, and despair. Her main medical complaint was that she was dizzy and chronically on the verge of fainting.

At that time I was unfamiliar with Leakana's culture and language and the extent of the atrocities committed by the Khmer Rouge. Few Americans were then fully aware of the genocide in Cambodia between 1975 and 1979, when more than two million people, out of approximately eight million, died of starvation and murder in the labor camps.

In order to help Leakana, I worked very closely with the Indo-Chinese members of my group. Although they were not medically trained, they were able to contextualize for me the past history and suffering of these patients. They also provided insights into the cultural manifestations of suffering in different Southeast Asian societies. My elderly Cambodian patient was a deeply religious Buddhist widow. She believed her spirit was possessed by the god of the sun, who caused her to faint and accompanied her to a place with animals and people who represented death. Spirit possession is common in Cambodian culture and can, as in this patient's case, be dangerous. Once the spirit has entered a person's body and mind, it can cause serious illness and even death if it is not quickly eliminated. This patient was extremely depressed because the Khmer Rouge had killed most of her children and grandchildren. Through her request for help in building a temple, she was telling us that the solution to her extraordinary grief and despair was not to be found in the counseling and medication we offered her. Her pain was so great that it could only be relieved by building a Buddhist temple.

In a conventional psychiatric setting Leakana would have been diagnosed as having a psychotic illness because it seemed that she was out of touch with reality by claiming to be possessed by the god of the sun, hearing voices, and having hallucinations. She would have been given drugs and denied access to psychotherapy. Her request for help in building a temple by the sea would have been interpreted as grandiose and delusional. But this assessment would have been inaccurate. In her understanding of my role as a doctor to keep her healthy, it was legitimate for her to ask me to help build this temple, because she felt she was going to die. I agreed to her request, having no idea how I could honor it. The solution we came upon was to speak to local Cambodian authorities, who allowed Leakana to enter the local monastery as a Buddhist nun. Although she was never able to build a temple herself, she could still devote her life to Buddhism. Leakana visited me every month for the next fifteen years until she died, never indicating to me any disappointment in not being able to achieve her dream.

In the early 1980s American psychiatrists and psychologists had little capacity for identifying and treating psychological problems in non–English speaking populations such as Leakana's. Furthermore, a deep belief existed in medicine and psychiatry that patients who had experienced horrific atrocities, including rape and other forms of criminally inflicted traumas, could not be rehabilitated. It was generally thought that Holocaust survivors in particular expressed their upset through physical and bodily complaints and illnesses. Medicine believed that these traumatized patients were not "psychologically minded" and their capacity to resolve their trauma-related problems was therefore limited.

These beliefs were found to be wrong as our clinic successfully treated more than ten thousand survivors of mass violence and torture over the next two decades.

INVENTING A NEW CLINICAL APPROACH

From the beginning of our clinical experiment I was concerned with correcting the trend that our Indo-Chinese patients were either neglected or primarily given drugs because of their low status in the health care system. We had to come up with an effective alternative. The English psychiatrist Douglas Bennett offered us a different way of treating these patients. After serving as a glider pilot in World War II, Dr. Bennett began working in the infamous Bedlam Hospital in London, where he struggled with rehabilitating the seriously mentally ill.[2] These patients had been abandoned by medicine and psychiatry and were now warehoused in a mental hospital. They were called the "objecting" and "objectionable" patients of English society, because they fiercely resisted psychiatric treatment and often were physically unattractive as a result of poor living conditions and personal hygiene.[3] Dr. Bennett looked for "gold in other people's dustbins." His approach, a commonsense philosophy of clinical care, rejected and transformed traditional psychiatric practices that forced drugs upon patients and demanded their dependency upon the psychiatric system, thereby hindering their successful integration into society. He labeled his approach "upside-down psychiatry,"[4] and believed that no patients were hopeless—all could have socially productive work that provided them with an income, no matter how serious their psychiatric impairment. Focusing on the concrete realities of everyday life, Bennett was a pioneer who moved mentally ill people—previously abandoned in the horrible idleness of the mental hospital—to community living and factories where they worked for a living, sometimes achieving self-employment.

Like Bennett's patients, the Harvard clinic refugee patients were the poorest members of the local communities. If they sought help in an emergency room for serious emotional distress, they ended up being committed to a mental hospital against their will, and were strongly advised to take psychotropic drugs without counseling or social rehabilitation. During the first few years of the clinic, we rescued hundreds of refugees from the mental hospital. At our clinic we provided them with all of the material (for example, housing) and emotional support (such as counseling in their own language) they needed to obtain a job, live independent lives, and care for their families. Similar to Douglas Bennett's experience in London, most succeeded in being self-sufficient; few ever needed psychiatric hospitalization.

THE PHENOMENOLOGICAL METHOD

After the clinic was established and started attracting Indo-Chinese patients, we had to discover the true nature of their clinical problems and the best way of helping them cope with their emotional upset. The answer came from the phenomenological method, which had been developed and widely applied in Europe and embraced by America's greatest psychologist, William James. The basic principle of this method is that a fresh approach to human behavior and relationships can be obtained by the psychologist or doctor by abandoning all currently held theories, opinions, prejudices, and biases. To best help patients, the healing professional has to let go of all of his or her assumptions and "see" what is actually present. It is extremely difficult for practitioners to reject everything they have learned because they've come to depend on conventional labels and diagnostic pigeonholes. But when I began treating Indo-Chinese patients, I wanted to make my own discoveries about how best to help them without being blinded by the observations of previous medical providers.

We therefore made a list of conventional psychological beliefs, then proceeded to intentionally disregard them when they were proved not to be valid over time. The beliefs we abandoned included the views, posited by conventional psychiatry, that torture survivors and other patients who had suffered extreme violence were untreatable; that traumatized people would not readily talk about their traumatic life experiences; and that patients from non-Western countries primarily expressed their depressed feelings through physical complaints. Over the past twenty years, many such standard assumptions have been proven false. The capacity of persons to recover from violent events and to engage in self-healing is, in fact, the major discovery celebrated in this book.

EXEGESIS: THE MEANING OF WORDS
Another major breakthrough in our approach was an intentional focus on culture and history as revealed in the words that our patients

used to describe their traumatic life experiences. We could not take the words of these traumatized persons for granted, because language can hide their true experiences. When refugees say they became "homeless," they may mean fleeing their village before armed men arrived, or they could mean watching aggressors rape and murder their daughters in their own home before it is burnt to the ground and they are forced to leave their village. The phrase "sexual abuse" can have many different implications in different societies, from rape or standing naked in front of others to different degrees of societal stigma and ostracism, such as divorce or the killing of the raped women.

Divinity students learn a critical approach to interpreting texts called the exegetical method or exegesis.[5] An exegesis is an explanation or critical interpretation of a text, aiming to make as explicit as possible the precise meaning of a passage, usually in the Bible. Connotations of the words and concepts in the passage are explored and placed into the author's historical context. Using this method, biblical scholars try to get closer to the original meaning of the words and phrases used by God and Jesus in the Old and New Testament.

As an example, in the following passage in the Gospel of St. Mark (7:24–30) a Syro-Phoenician woman begs Jesus to heal her daughter, who is possessed by a demon:

> And he said to her, "Let the children first be fed, for it is not right to take the children's bread and throw it to the dogs." But she answered him, "Yes, Lord; yet even the dogs under the table eat the children's crumbs." And he said to her, "For this saying you may go your way; the demon has left your daughter." And she went home, and found the child lying in bed, and the demon gone.[6]

The translated words in this passage were originally written by Mark in Greek. When Jesus says to the woman, "Let the children first be fed, for it is not right to take the children's bread and throw it to the dogs," Jesus is using the Greek word *teknon [τέκνων]* for *children* because it indicates a child who stands "in relationship to God." In this passage, Christ is asserting to the Syro-Phoenician woman, a Gentile, that Christ has come first to Israel. But Jesus' choice for the word *dog, kynarion [κυναρίον]*, in his reply to the woman is the Greek diminutive, *κυναρίον*, for *little dog*. Elsewhere in the Bible the word used for *dog, kyon [κυων]*, connotes the scavenger sort who haunted the streets and refuse dumps of town and was considered by the Jews to be filthy and vicious. In this passage, Jesus seems to have in mind not the scavenger dogs but the little dogs that can be tolerated. The Gentiles, like "little dogs," will eventually be allowed into the house of God.

My experience with the exegetical method in divinity school had an impact on my approach to work as a psychiatrist. This uncovering process, the seeking of the historical origins and meanings of words and phrases that could bring the reader or, in my case, the doctor, closer to the actual world of the storyteller, is a powerful method of interpretation. We began carefully translating the common terms and words used by refugees to describe their traumatic life events. There are major differences, for example, in the use of the word *torture* in Western and in Asian societies. In Western society, *torture* is derived from the Latin word *torquere*, which means "to cause to turn, to twist" in order to extract testimony and/or evidence to repress opposing religious or political views. Now, torture denotes the use of physical and mental pain to extract legal confessions and suppress an individual's human rights. In Cambodia, however, the Khmer word for *torture, tieru na kam*, is derived from the Buddhist term for karma, defined as the individual's actions or thoughts, often of an evil nature, in a prior existence that affect life in the present. Cambodian survivors often believe that the torture experience is retribution for bad actions in a prior life. Doctors must remember this connection when working with tortured Cambodian patients, and help them overcome their self-condemnation and their belief that they are responsible for the torture and ensuing illness.

Hundreds of examples exist of the insights gained by using the exegetical approach in defining traumatic events in different cultures.[7] For example, the term *brainwashing* was popularized during the Korean and Vietnam Wars as an effort by Communist forces to transform the political beliefs of their captives. After the Vietnam War the Communist victors put South Vietnamese troops into "reeducation" camps where they were brainwashed through psychological and physical abuse. The Vietnamese term for this is *cai fu tao tu tuong,* which means to reeducate someone's ideas or thoughts. Similarly, in Cambodia, the term for brainwashing is *ab ram nae namgoy pla phdu cit gammit* and literally means "guidance through education" in order to change the way a person feels or thinks. In contrast, in Iraq *brainwashing* translates in Arabic as g*haseel mokh,* which literally means to "wash the brain." Within the Muslim belief system, brainwashing is inconceivable. Muslims who have true faith and conviction in their hearts are not vulnerable to manipulations, threats, or deprivation. Devout Muslims cannot be brainwashed because their resistance to manipulation is a moral choice, that is, a commitment to goodness and justice over evil and tyranny. Within current Iraqi society, the term *brainwashing* is a literal translation from English that has no meaning.

Critically interpreting the language a survivor uses allows a doctor to understand the meaning traumatized patients give to their experiences.[8] Words, especially those that denote traumatic events, need to be carefully defined in the life of the patient, family, and community. While the experience of torture is a horrific event everywhere, different cultures regard its causes and consequences in different ways. In some societies torture survivors receive compassion, while in others they are blamed and punished. This understanding can aid in the healing of the survivors and, sometimes, even of society.

MOMENTS OF REVELATION

Our scientific methodology prepared the staff and me for a number of critical scientific insights. These very important outbursts of scientific clarity or enlightenment, although rare, are enormously enriching and productive. Italian philosophers refer to them as *i momenti,* or moments of revelation. When you abandon old ideas, you permit intuition and imagination to lead you to something entirely new. In a flash of insight, I knew to abandon the conventional diagnosis of psychosis in Leakana, the elderly Cambodian woman, so I could feel the deep grief of her depression, and thereby follow her inclination to recovery through her Buddhist faith.

During my time caring for persons affected by extreme violence, I have had a number of moments of revelation that have completely transformed my manner of thinking and working as a medical doctor. It is important to listen to the patient and also to the prejudices and the boundaries of knowledge in your mind. We have to be vigilant to our biases and be ready to receive new knowledge.

FINDING THE KEY THAT OPENS TRAUMA'S MYSTERIES

After five years, the refugee clinic was able to expand from an afternoon to a full-time clinic. Up to this point our patients had not been direct about describing their traumatic life experiences, but only gave glimpses of the atrocities they had experienced or witnessed. Then a public television film director asked if she could interview some of our patients who had been tortured. She was producing a documentary for the series *Nova* on different approaches in major torture treatment centers in Europe, Central and Latin America, and the United States. After some discussion, the team's response was an emphatic no. We naively believed there were no torture survivors in our clinic and, even if there were, they wouldn't want to tell their stories to a filmmaker. While some patients had alluded to the violence they experienced, we believed we were caring for refugees who primarily had been forced out of their villages and homes, rescued, placed in refugee camps through the United Nations, and resettled throughout the world. No one yet had collected any empirical data on the level and type of traumatic events experienced by these refugees. In our clinic, I had heard about only a few cases of torture.

We considered it unethical to ask traumatized refugees to describe their experiences to a filmmaker. The filmmaker insisted we were wrong. Still convinced that we were right, we compromised by inviting two patients to be interviewed on camera. Much to our surprise, both patients agreed to tell their trauma stories. Both had been tortured and both were eager to tell the world what had happened to them.

We waited in trepidation, concerned with exposing the patients to a painful interview, but they came well prepared. Both were beautifully dressed in traditional costumes; they forcefully delivered their personal stories with grace and dignity, and in their own languages. They were almost defiant as, for the first time, they fully revealed their torture. One patient spoke about her entire family being executed by the Khmer Rouge, after which she was beaten and thrown unconscious but still alive onto a pile of corpses—her family and relatives.

My staff and I were shocked to hear these gruesome stories. How could someone share such terrible events publicly and not be emotionally devastated? The filmmaker was not surprised, having also captured stories of torture from survivors in El Salvador, Chile, Argentina, and many other violent places in the world.

This event was a turning point for the clinic, forcing us to confront our reluctance to acknowledge that many of our refugee patients had been tortured, as well as our Western bias that victims don't want to talk about their experiences. If these two survivors could publicly share their torture experience, why shouldn't we ask our patients if they wanted to do so in the privacy of our clinic? So we started asking, and the patients started sharing their stories, with relief. Because of the filmmaker, the patients' trauma stories became and remain a centerpiece of the healing process.[9]

The trauma story is a personal narrative told in the person's own words about the traumatic life events they have experienced and the impact of these events on their social, physical, and emotional well-being. It is not someone else's interpretation of events, although it may contain observations on the reactions of family members and the local community. The storyteller may tell the story to others for many reasons, including the desire to receive benefits or medical care. Similarly, the survivor may have many personal and social reasons for keeping the nature and history of their traumatic events a secret (for example, in the case of rape trauma).

Conducting an interview that helps patients tell their trauma story is difficult and takes practice, which is why it was possible for us to treat refugee patients for years and not know they had been tortured. At that time, doctors did not know how to treat the psychological effects of torture. Also, as all therapists know, traumatic life histories can be very elusive. Often, when the therapist is ready to listen to the patient's story, the patient is not ready to tell. And when the therapist is not prepared, the patient is often on the verge of full disclosure. This lack of synchronicity between therapist and patient is a mysterious obstacle in the healing process. Because the trauma story is so loaded with meaning and so closely associated with the essential worldview of the traumatized person, it can only be presented to someone else in an oblique way. The emotions and events that are the most important to you are difficult to tell directly to other people.

The trauma story itself remains hidden until the patient finds the opportunity to reveal just a fragment. Maybe this reluctance exists because the survivor fears rejection, or, worse, because he or she fears the intended listener has no interest or curiosity in the story. Understanding the trauma story demands a considerable amount of skill from the listener, not just to share the emotional feelings but also to enter into an examination and appreciation of the historical, cultural, and personal meaning of the events. This well-rounded approach allows even the most severe torture events to be told.

DISCOVERING THE HEALING POWER OF SELF-CARE

Of all the moments of discovery enjoyed in our clinic, here is the most surprising and revolutionary: patients have the ability to heal themselves. Medical doctors are trained to identify illness and apply a basic approach that primarily emphasizes the use of medications. Psychiatrists learn the bio-psychosocial approach, which attempts to examine the physical, psychological, and social causes of illness. Divinity school trains students to consider the historical and cultural influences revealed by language. But the person whose life has been transformed by traumatic life experiences is not asked, by any of these professionals, to play an active role in healing. As a doctor caring for a Cambodian widow in her late thirties with two elementary-school-age and two high-school-age children, I found what I was missing: the power of self-healing.

Sovannary suffered from depression. For eighteen months she was treated with medication and psychotherapy. An hour each week I sat quietly in a room with her and my Cambodian colleague and asked her to share her struggles with adjusting to life in America. Together we strived to alleviate her problems. One day she stopped her medication, saying it could not help her. She told me that she had to speak to me privately. I was shocked as she made this request in perfect English, though up until this point her therapy had been conducted entirely in Khmer with the assistance of my Cambodian colleague. I had never heard her speak English. Sovannary stated that she specifically learned English so that she could tell me her story directly. For the first time, she then revealed her secret, in graphic detail.

As a teenager she had been in love with a young man, but her parents refused to allow the marriage and arranged for her to marry a husband of their choosing. This rejection of her boyfriend broke both of their hearts. Many years went by uneventfully until the Khmer Rouge came to power. Her husband was executed by Pol Pot's soldiers, and she was sent to a concentration camp with her children. While in this camp Sovannary met her childhood sweetheart for the first time since her youth. Instead of helping her, at the first opportunity he raped her and, while he was doing so, a Khmer Rouge soldier came upon them and put a bullet into his head.

As Sovannary told me her story, I could sense her guilt for thinking she had caused the death of her childhood boyfriend. She still had strong positive feelings for him, even though he had raped her. Maybe he had become violent because he felt she had betrayed his love many years ago. Sovannary felt terribly proud that she had learned English in order to share with me this memory that had been burning in her mind. Her secret was now out in the open, within the privacy of our relationship. She later told me that since talking about her experience, she no longer felt hopeless to do anything about the effects of this episode in her life. I told her I was honored to be her doctor and proud to have such an active and powerful patient who could master a difficult language in order to tell her story.

The mutual respect that developed between us in counseling rekindled in this patient her self-worth as a human being. Her memories of the tragic event gradually faded. Her mind was liberated to think positively about herself and her children. Sovannary's serious depression soon lifted; her entire life expanded as she became more involved in helping her community and helping her children adjust to school. Twelve months later she moved her family from Boston to be with her sister in California. I did not hear from her for a while until I received an enigmatic phone call. My staff told me that a Cambodian woman was calling from California requesting that I attend her wedding. It turned out to be Sovannary. Not only was she marrying, but she had also established a mental health clinic in her community for Cambodian survivors of the Pol Pot genocide.

Sovannary showed me the power that all patients hold for self-healing. For most traumatized persons, repairing the destruction of their normal lives is an ordeal more difficult to endure than actually suffering the physical and mental pain of violent acts. We must look carefully for efforts at self-healing and strongly support and nourish them in all who have survived extreme violence.

Self-healing can also be witnessed on the collective level, but here the healing forces are not as easy to identify. The healing power of all individuals within a society too rarely lines up in the same direction. But in Bosnia, efforts at self-healing flourished among the citizens of Sarajevo as a whole. Sarajevo, a beautiful city of Orthodox Christian,

Muslim, and Roman Catholic religions, experienced one thousand days of barbarism unlike anything seen in Europe since the atrocities of World War II. Thousands of innocent and unarmed men, women, and children were subject to bullets and mortar shells raining down from the surrounding hills each day. With no food, no electricity, and no heat, it is incredible that the people of Sarajevo survived while the world passively watched the massacre on television.

Even after this terrible attempted murder of an entire city, Sarajevo's citizens never gave up their fight for survival. One spring day immediately after the war had ended, I was walking along the river, surrounded by mass destruction, wondering how these people survived. And then I came upon an art exhibition. In refugee camps or other places of violence, I always seek out artists and artisans. Their works of beauty hold an inner hopefulness that is often missing from the squalor of their environment. In Sarajevo I read the following statement, written in English on an art-show poster. This artist, C. Boltanski, clarified for me the collective power of self-healing:

> We often ask ourselves: if there would be a catastrophe, if our lives would become full of war and hatred, and if we had to be subject to that, how would we react? Citizens of Sarajevo were not prepared for that: as one would say, happy people, in a town both beautiful and quiet. No poverty, easily established and well kept relations between people; everybody thinking about their own work, their children, weddings and burials as the rhythm to existence; everything is simple, and then the horror happened; it's like when you feel well, and then suddenly a doctor tells you that you have cancer—throwing you, in that way, to the world of illness and death.
>
> What I've seen here, and what they have taught me is that life, the desire to live, is always stronger than barbarism, and that people can go on despite shelling and life without anything, hoping, creating, loving. Sarajevans understood

that if they continue, if they had a coffee on a café terrace during the ceasefire, if they talked about art till dawn, asking themselves if such and such film is interesting or what is the newest rock band in the USA like, they would in that way give the best resistance to the fascists.

I found a similar collective emphasis on self-healing during my work in New York City immediately after the attacks on the World Trade Center. A clinical team including members of my staff, the chaplain at Yale, and a visiting Japanese professor assisted our colleagues at Bellevue in caring for patients affected by this tragedy. The solidarity among New York City residents from different races, ethnic backgrounds, and social classes was extraordinary. As in Sarajevo, everyone was in alignment, each contributing to the safety and security of others.

Studies later confirmed my impressions in New York City that individuals affected by the events of September 11 were primarily seeking help from family members, friends, clergy, and religious institutions. Their general medical doctors and nurses were also actively sought out. An extraordinary level of coping developed. In fact, the Bellevue primary care doctors came to the conclusion that the patients were basically asking them not to take on their social and family problems, but simply to help them cope with their fear and anxiety of future terrorist attacks, and especially how to assist their children and other family members through the crisis.

Traumatized people throughout the world voice the same request for help with self-healing. The healing professions, especially medicine, ignore these requests and tend to act without understanding survivors' real needs. This is partially due to the fact that doctors and therapists do not know what to do with people who want to help themselves. It is also easier to avoid engaging people whose problems seem too overwhelming and impossible to fix by conventional healing practices. The survivor, in reality, is offering us an outreached hand, saying: "Please do not reject me: I'll do most of the work. All I need from you is to acknowledge my efforts and to help me when I go astray."

A LITTLE BIRD ENTERS MY SOUL

Another of the *momenti* that I was lucky enough to experience revealed the importance of getting as close as possible to the survivor in order to promote healing. In 1986, I asked my clinical colleague, Svang Tor, a survivor of the Khmer Rouge regime, to assist me in an oral history project at the Schlesinger Library on the History of Women in America. I asked her to help find ten Cambodian women from different social backgrounds who had resettled in the area. I was looking for volunteers to participate in an oral history of their lives. The women we found over the next fifteen years are from all walks of life: some rice farmers, one a royal dancer, another a princess. None of them had ever before told her life history to anyone. These women, interviewed over the course of more than twelve hours each, were not our patients but simply persons in the community. What emerged from this project is the historical perspective of ten lost and forgotten women who, because of the violence they experienced, have been able to provide us with a greater understanding of trauma and its aftereffects.

Setting out to collect these oral histories, Svang and I had no comparable model to copy. To begin with, we had to determine the proper personal distance between the oral historians and ourselves. We were not their therapists and they were not our patients. We did not expect them to reveal intimate details about their life problems. We were also not journalists writing a story about the lives of

Cambodian women or scholars publishing a book on the social history of Cambodian women. So, to establish a level of intimacy that created a historical dimension in the interviews, we told them: "You are speaking to history through us."

These stories are historical because the storyteller, no matter how poor or ordinary a person, believes that the story is not just about herself but also about her culture and society. It teaches something about how the world worked within her lifetime. All of the women would agree that their stories reveal the nuances of Cambodian culture to those who know nothing about it. They would also agree that their stories are an accurate depiction of the Khmer Rouge.

But, could we fully appreciate the experiences and emotions these women expressed about their lives? Although Svang and I appeared an unlikely pair, our friendship provided a positive environment for the women. Svang had been a victim of the killing fields, but she also worked closely with me in the clinic as a mental health worker. She interviewed these women in Khmer while I listened quietly. Occasionally Svang would stop and interject important points in English. I would make written and mental notations of these points. While we listened I could appreciate the physical communication and body language of the storytellers. Hundreds of hours of listening to a foreign language I could not understand taught me nonverbal ways of understanding their experiences. I could see their expressions, feel their emotions, and visualize the very scenes that they were describing in Khmer. During almost every session a personal connection developed between the woman, Svang, and myself. Our triadic relationships with each other became seamless and timeless.

Though I am neither Cambodian nor a woman, my mind still resounded during the oral histories with these women's voices; I have never heard so loudly or so clearly. When the oral historians cried, I cried; when they laughed, I laughed. It was natural. The gaps in race and culture between us had little impact on my appreciation of their life histories, just as modern listeners can resonate with the beauty of ancient poetry thousands of years later. This project gave us an appreciation of the great capacity for understanding that can develop between people from radically different cultures, experiences, and gender.

The completion of the oral histories, including the preparation of translated transcripts and audiotapes, resulted in a crisis for Svang and myself. The women were very pleased with the entire process; they had spoken to history through us and their job was completed. In contrast, Svang and I were not sure what to do with the stories. It did not seem appropriate to exploit the oral histories for our academic and professional interests. They were not our stories; we had not earned the right to take credit for them. On the other hand, to place them into a library archive waiting for an anonymous audience seemed wrong.

The stories were also very disturbing to read, every volume holding an incredible amount of pain and suffering. We were ambivalent about sharing this with others; at the same time, we could not abandon the work. We wondered if we had spent almost fifteen years on a reckless task because we had never been fully clear on how we would share the end results. But the project had changed us; we were certainly better persons and therapists after having completed this painful task. We knew the oral histories had an inherent capacity to transform still others. But how?

I found a resolution in a Renaissance painting exhibition at the Metropolitan Museum of Art. In a small painting by the Sienese artist Sassetta, Saint Thomas Aquinas is praying to the crucified Christ. And out of Jesus' mouth a glorious and magnificent small bird flies into the mouth of the saint. While looking at this painting, I asked myself what audience could ever see this little bird or appreciate its critical meaning to the saint. In early Renaissance Siena, saints were regarded as heroes different from the classical Greek and Roman heroes of Florence; the saints were to be admired and imitated. This masterpiece was created as an altar painting, intended to be seen up close only by the priests as they were saying mass, to remind them to copy the roles of the saints in their work within their communities. The bird spirit of the crucified Christ is, in fact, not only being incorporated into Saint Thomas, it is flying into the souls of the living priests who witness this painting. At this moment of revelation, I finally understood the function of the oral histories. The "bird spirits" of the Cambodian women were flying into our souls, and into the souls of those willing to get close enough to hear the stories of survivors. This is a metaphor for the healing experience, because the healer has to place himself as close as possible to the pain and suffering of the traumatized person in order to take in the revealed truth. This process becomes the foundation of all healing actions.

PAIN OF THE HEALER

Sometimes healers and their patients can enter the ranks of the ashamed, which include more than those affected by extreme violence. Social stigma and shame can attach itself to patients with cancer, HIV/AIDS, or Alzheimer's disease as well as those patients coping with domestic violence and sexual abuse. The doctor can also be negatively affected by this phenomenon. I did not fully realize this until my sons were old enough to ask me what I did for a living. Many people regard my job of caring for the survivors of mass violence and torture as a heroic act. I could always take pride, especially with medical colleagues, in the strenuousness of the medical task and the unambiguous moral and humanistic nature of the job. But when my children began asking questions, I had to acknowledge that I really did not want to tell them too much because I felt some shame about my work. The healer, I have discovered, cannot wash away the stains of human cruelty that lie before him or her through the healing process. Committed and involved, the doctor accepts, if reluctantly, the silent shame of the inconceivable. It is difficult to share this with a small child.

Visitors can feel this shame when they enter a Holocaust museum or stand in front of the Vietnam Veterans Memorial in Washington, D.C. The initial reaction that holds back emotions leads to uncontrollable waves of tears, which move to anger, followed by that subtle feeling of shame. This process may not be universal, but it is one that many have described and I have experienced. The world of the ashamed is always being populated with new victims because of the endless stream of rape victims, abused children, and other innocents who have become the flotsam and jetsam of human cruelty. The healer and the survivor have committed no crimes, but they almost always feel guilty about something. Thang, a Vietnamese prisoner of war, could not stand to be around friends his own age because of his humiliation. He had become a great man; because of his compassion he had developed a deep forgiveness for those who had tortured him. But he had no forgiveness for himself.

The pain of the patients can penetrate into the deepest level of the mind and feelings of the doctor and linger there forever. The ancient Greek poet Sappho's words describe this process:

> *Pain penetrates*
> *me drop*
> *by drop.*[10]

The act of witnessing violence can be as deeply injurious to the witness as it is to those actually experiencing the violence. What this means is that the doctor pays some emotional price for assisting in the healing experience. This cannot be avoided because the clinic's staff is essentially wedded to the patient in a therapeutic partnership with the goal of producing a positive healing result. How does the doctor or therapist persevere?

After one of the times I worked in the Balkans, I took a trip to Italy to recuperate. I was physically as well as mentally exhausted from all the destruction I had encountered, feeling that human beings were incapable of giving up their savage and barbaric acts. The human race seemed driven to continuously create new victims and patients. And then I walked into the Villa Borghese museum in Rome and experienced a moment of enlightenment. I was standing in front of a large and magnificent painting by Caravaggio that I had never seen before. The painting depicted Mary holding the young Jesus as he steps on the head of a snake.

At first you do not notice it—the large foot sticking out from under the Virgin Mother's dress. It is an enormous and indelicate foot with big fat toes—not the tender and delicate foot you'd expect of Mary. And on top of his mother's foot is Jesus' small child's foot—slowly, firmly pressing down, forcing Mary to crush the snake. Saint Anne, her mother, is watching with a scowl on her face; you can see that she is not happy with Jesus' behavior. Jesus' mother seems perplexed, neither pleased nor displeased. She seems to say, "Child, what are you doing?"

Jesus has determination in his eyes. He already knows of his crucifixion. He is a handsome, youthful boy involved in the present confrontation with evil. He knows what he must do to the snake now, though it will still make no difference to his future. Like many children he is a sage, a wise man in the body of a child.

The young Jesus, my boys, and all our children know exactly what is on God's agenda. My sons know exactly what I do and they silently praise my life's work. They are not afraid. Quietly, they place their feet on mine and sweetly whisper in my ear, "Keep pushing, Daddy. You may be tired and frustrated after twenty years of doing this, but we are with you." Children see the truth directly. They are not full of emotional ambivalence or Byzantine rationalizations. A politician harms millions of people in the Balkans and the newspapers are filled with excuses, historical references, soul searching, lies, denials, testimonies, vilifications, forgiveness…and the distortion of truth goes on and on.

In front of this painting, I closed my eyes and the sublime memories of human devotion and dignity that I have experienced with others filled me with beauty, peace, and love. At that moment I realized that I could persevere.

Chapter 2

THE TRAUMA STORY

*P*HILOCTETES SERVES AS a metaphor for the essential reality of the trauma survivor and his or her story. It is the genius of Sophocles that more than two thousand years ago he wrote a drama that still speaks directly to the enigma of our experience of personal and collective violence.[1] The play ponders the fate of every traumatized person: how can we survive and be made whole again once terrible events place us in painful and unpredictable circumstances and our society either ignores or abandons us?

Philoctetes, the great friend of the deceased Hercules, is wounded by a sacred serpent sent by Hera, causing an incurable injury and unbearable suffering. Hera's purpose is to keep the Greeks from winning the Trojan War by using Hercules's magic bow, which had been given to Philoctetes by Hercules upon his deathbed. Instead of being aided in his injury and pain by his fellow Greeks, Philoctetes is abandoned to the isolated Aegean island of Lemnos. No one listens to his wails of sorrow, which hides the fact that only the bow of Hercules, possessed by Philoctetes, can save the Greeks and end the

Trojan War. After nine years of futile battle, the Greeks finally seek out the hero they abandoned on Lemnos in order to find their salvation. As Odysseus states, "Only his bow captures Troy."[2] Odysseus tries to convince the son of Achilles, Neoptolemus, to lie to Philoctetes in order to steal his bow. Fortunately, Neoptolemus's compassion for Philoctetes spoils Odysseus's plot. This young man cannot betray his father's friend in the face of his suffering. Because of the boy's honesty, the play's secret truth is revealed: The bow is worthless without the survivor. Only Philoctetes can shoot it.

Too often, modern-day listeners try to "steal" the "bow" of the trauma story without realizing that its true meaning cannot be revealed without the participation of the survivor. The *Philoctetes* story is not only about possessing the bow, but about being able to use it. In the case of the trauma survivor, the bow is the full story. Only by listening to the survivor tell the story can the bow's arrows be released and, in the process, the victim and even society can be healed.

Though tellers of trauma stories have layers of knowledge and wisdom to pass along, therapists and theorists tend to focus on the trauma story separate from the teller, in essence saying, "We have the story; we do not need to know the concrete personal realities of the storyteller."

HISTORICAL PURPOSE
OF THE TRAUMA STORY

The trauma story is everywhere. On a given day, try to notice what is being shared by our spouses, relatives, friends, workmates, the media, and from the pulpits of our religious institutions. Usually these stories are very brief, presented in small bits and pieces; sometimes a reaction is solicited and often no response at all is expected. In any small gathering you can find people who have encountered a devastating divorce, sexual abuse, a life-threatening illness, or the loss of a loved one to accident or crime. No one is immune. Emotionally disturbing events happen not only during times of war, terrorism, and ethnic conflict.

Out of our need for healing and survival, human beings have developed a complex array of physical and psychological responses that include language and communication. The latter warn us that dangerous things are happening and that there are ways to cope with and react to the threat. The trauma story can be seen as early in human history as the Upper Paleolithic period cave paintings in France. In Les Trois Freres, a large dancing wizard displays the horns and ears of a deer, the eyes and face of an owl, the beard and body of a man, and the tail of a horse. It can be assumed that this special human being of great supernatural powers was able to protect the people who drew his image from inhospitable weather, lack of food, and aggressive animals. In Egypt's nineteenth dynasty (1314–1650 B.C.) demons appear in the *Amduat* (or *The Book of That Which Is in the World Beyond the Grave*).[3] These demons represent cruel and malignant forces that can possess and destroy a person and his community. Such early artworks tell of humanity's concern for protecting itself from the destructive forces that exist in the world.

Trauma stories today have moved away from tales of supernatural agents to stories of distressing and painful personal and social events. Surviving and healing from violence rely not only on a wizard's magic but on modern personal and professional coping strategies. Linking the word *trauma* to *story* is a relatively modern idea. *Trauma,* which originated from the Greek *traumatikos,* until recently referred to a physical injury and its repair. Today, *trauma* also refers to nonphysical social and psychological injuries to the mind and spirit. These wounds are no longer hidden from view because scientific tools can now identify the psychosocial suffering and disability associated with violence.

Our species demands that we learn how to survive all threats to our human existence, especially those created by our own hands. When violence leads to physical and mental injury, it also engenders a healing response. One aspect of this is the trauma story, whose function is not only to heal the survivor, but also to teach and guide the listener—and, by extension, society—in healing and survival.

Sophocles's *Philoctetes* warns us, however, that the wisdom a trauma story has to offer is often neglected by others. As traumatized people know, whether they are sharing their experiences of a painful divorce or relating the death of a child, many listeners have already established how they will listen and what they will allow themselves to hear. Some listeners will avoid hearing the story because they feel it is irrelevant to their lives; others will not want to experience any emotional upset by listening too closely. A modern tendency is to select out the brutal facts and pay attention only to this aspect of the story. Extreme violence can fascinate our morbid curiosity because it is extraordinary, exciting, and provides an opportunity for experiencing something beyond belief, with little fear of being injured. Out of this thrill there is rarely progress to the wisdom and insight that is available if we truly listened. As in *Philoctetes,* wisdom derived from traumatic events remains known only by the survivor, whether the trauma is due to a tragedy in ordinary life or during a war or natural disaster.

FOUR ELEMENTS OF THE TRAUMA STORY

The collection of oral histories that occurred concurrently with the development of our refugee clinic offered us insight into the structure and content of the trauma story. Early on we discovered that it was easier and more informative to interview people with life histories similar to those of our patients but who were not patients themselves. Since we did not to need to treat the oral historians and they had no expectations of us as healers, the clinical process did not interfere with the telling of their stories.[4]

The oral history interviews of the Cambodian women were approximately two-and-a-half-hour-long sessions, separated by six-week intermissions, totaling more than twelve hours. They occurred in the storytellers' homes, workplaces, or religious institutions, such as Buddhist temples. The pleasant sanctuaries of their homes usually revealed little evidence of their past traumas and invisible wounds, except for the presence of old photographs of relatives, many of whom had disappeared or died untimely deaths.

When we started conducting the interviews, our initial realization was that it is easy to become preoccupied with the tragic events in a story, but to do so is like looking directly into a blinding sun: you cannot see anything else, as these events take up the entire sky of a person's life. Yet the most brutal events are often not the most damaging in a person's life. One Cambodian woman from a middle-class background, Phal Let, explained that the most traumatic thing in her life was not the Pol Pot period, but the fact that her parents had not allowed her to learn how to read and write Cambodian. There was a fear common among parents of her generation that if their daughters were literate, they would be able to send letters to their boyfriends. This woman felt that her parents had denied her the skills to successfully survive the Khmer Rouge regime. More important, she did not have the necessary skills to cope with life in America.

The oral history method, in which we asked the women to begin their life stories with their births, taught us to look away from the "blinding sun" of the most overt traumatic events and to pay attention to other significant events in their life. Oral histories can include any personal accounting of a life, everything from cooking to immigration to the experience of war. Listening to the women recount the small details of everyday life, it became clear that sufferers do not suffer all the time. For all of the Cambodian women, telling us about their marriage ceremonies was an enjoyable part of recounting their life histories. All had marriages arranged by their parents, some never having seen their future husbands until a few days before their wedding. They shared the nuances of their ceremonies, in some cases three days of celebrations and a parade of elephants, and of their wedding nights, when some hid for days after seeing a naked man for the first time. The wedding stories, like many aspects of their life histories, were not infected by the gruesome details of rape, murder, and torture that they would eventually encounter under Pol Pot. No one's life is all bad; no one with cancer is always sick; and no one in a bad marriage is always being abused or mistreated. The oral histories of these Cambodian women remind us to appreciate the full range of human experience that exists alongside tragic events.

Out of the study of these and many other oral histories from traumatized persons in different cultures and places, a stunning and surprising reality emerged. The storytellers revealed an internal logic and essential structure in their trauma stories when they were allowed to speak with few interruptions and little interference.

THE FACTUAL ACCOUNTING OF THE EVENTS

The primary element of the story is the *factual* accounting of events, or what actually happened to the storyteller. These are usually unembellished presentations of the individual's traumatic life experiences. When such facts are collected from even a few persons, they can provide historical documentation of the concrete behavior of perpetrators of crimes against humanity, revealing the intentional, well-orchestrated methods of the perpetrators. Since few perpetrators tell their side of the story, the goals of their violent acts seem to remain vague and elusive. Yet the trauma survivor can clearly state from personal experience the motivation of perpetrators. For this reason a small number of storytellers can describe in exquisite detail the general practices of Pol Pot, the apartheid government in South Africa, or Pinochet's reign in Chile.

In almost every trauma story, the storyteller knows the exact date and sometimes even the very hour when the violence began, creating a radical disruption in his or her life. In each of the oral histories of the Cambodian women, for example, the brutality experienced under Pol Pot was made explicit. The following passage from one of our interviewees, Somaly, who was raised in a middle-class family as a royal dancer, reveals the brutalizing violence all Cambodians systematically experienced under the Khmer Rouge.

> From that time on, three or four months in the Khmer Rouge work camps, my littlest daughter started to get very, very sick. She had diarrhea. I was lucky that I had a soldier who had a crush on me. He would come often to visit me. I begged him; I would do anything just to get the medicine for my children. At that time he did give me penicillin. I did not think it would heal my daughter but it was better than nothing. So I gave it to her, but her condition continued to get weaker and weaker. Our food was getting lower and lower, so I was getting weaker and weaker. To watch my daughter, it starts to...She misses her home, she misses her toys, she misses her food, and she starts to complain and talk day and night all the time.

I have heard thousands of similar starvation stories that occurred under the Pol Pot regime. The first death comes to symbolically herald a cascade of deaths, with no ability to prevent the outcome. For Somaly, her daughter's death changed her entire family.

She's gone. That night I held on to my daughter's body. Our whole family was very quiet. Nobody wanted to say anything. She was the first to die in the family. It started from her. I saw my father start to change his attitude; instead of always being playful, he lost his sense of humor.

Every violent event has a victim, whose reactions are embedded in the reporting of the facts. These intense personal and emotional responses form the invisible wounds caused by violence.

The Cultural Meaning of Trauma

In addition to recounting the facts, each trauma story reveals the survivor's sociocultural history in miniature, depicting the traditions, customs, and values in which their story is embedded. Although men and women in every society perceive violence as deeply injurious and socially degrading, responses differ by culture. Societies may stigmatize the victim to a greater or lesser degree. Trauma stories provide unique insights, both good and bad, within the narrator's cultural framework.

Somaly tells a story that reveals how the Khmer Rouge systematically attempted to degrade and annihilate traditional Khmer culture:

It is horrible. I buried my parents with my own hands. Like I said, you used to put the body in beautiful clothes, the favorite clothes that the person used to like before they died. Okay. You would give them a bath, right? And you would put them in beautiful clothes. You put on them a little bit of makeup. And if the body is a mother, and the mother died and the baby is still alive, sometimes you would put a...watermelon with the body to pretend it was a baby.

Luckily when my mother died I could wrap her in beautiful clothes. A horrible thing happened to her two or three days after I buried her. Somebody told me, this is still a nightmare for me, that a wolf was able to go through her grave because they did not bury her deep enough. How would you feel if you were me? She was the favorite person in my life. She died, and you thought she was in peace. Even the body cannot stay in peace.

In Somaly's case, the sanctity of death and the proper Buddhist funerary ritual was forbidden to her and her family. The perpetrators, who well knew the cultural, traditional, and religious beliefs of their victims, sought the maximum degree of humiliation by depriving them of a sacred burial that would bring the dead person's soul to rest, allowing it to be reincarnated in a new life. This degradation of the funeral ceremony by the Khmer Rouge was a common practice and led, for many survivors, to a lifetime of anguish believing that their relatives could not find peace in the afterlife. Many Cambodians are plagued at night by the spirit visits of deceased relatives seeking peace through a proper Buddhist burial. If and when they are able, the majority of survivors eventually conduct such ceremonies.

LOOKING BEHIND THE CURTAIN

The Quaker scholar, spiritual writer, and guide Douglas V. Steere likens the Trappist monk Thomas Merton's concept of prayer to the experience of "looking behind the curtain" on a stage.[5] In other words, prayer can allow one to see what is really happening spiritually in one's life. But as Merton suggests, this peek behind the curtain is not just benign; the special insight of contemplative prayer can be painful and upsetting:

> The dread and dereliction of the spiritual man is then a kind of hell, but it is, in the words of Isaac of Stella (a twelfth-century Cistercian), a "hell of mercy and not of wrath": "*In Inferno sumus sed misericordiae, non irae; in*

caelo erimus." To be in a "hell of mercy" is to fully experience one's nothingness, but in a spirit of repentance and surrender to God with desire to accept and do his will, not in a spirit of diffuse hatred, disgust and rebellion even though these may be *felt* at times on the superficial level of emotion.[6]

There is a similarity between Merton's description of a "hell of mercy" and the traumatized person's capacity, gained through his or her own personal hell, to achieve an enlightened view of the world divorced from ugly and distressful emotions. Looking behind the curtain, the survivor reaches deep insights when reflecting upon his or her situation. The survivor may have previously supported the social beliefs and attitudes that say he or she is "bad" for having been involved in a tragic event. But now, with the experience of violence, these conventional beliefs seem false and harmful. Out of their pain, they reject these old ways of thinking and look behind the curtain of their previous ordinary lives to find something new.

Traumatized women throughout the world are especially challenged by society's harsh treatment, especially if they have been subjected to sexual violence. Women who have been sexually abused are often treated by their families and communities as if they have committed a crime. In spite of their innocence and painful victimization, they may be beaten, stigmatized, ostracized, and in some cases killed. A popular Cambodian fable called "The King Snake" illustrates society's unfair and harmful attitudes toward women who have been sexually exploited:

> One day, Meernup, a poor merchant, leaves his wife, Neang Nee, telling her he is going on a long journey to sell his merchandise. He will be away a long time and his

wife must provide food and protection for herself and their adolescent daughter, Neang Et, until he returns. Meernup also warns Neang Nee not to leave the vicinity of the house to visit neighbors.

Many months go by and Neang Nee and Neang Et run out of food. So they are forced to disobey Meernup and go out into the forest to forage for wild potatoes and bamboo shoots. In their desperate search for food, they find a big bush of bamboo with many bamboo shoots. As they dig up the shoots they lose their blade. They look all around without success. Out of fear for her husband's reactions to the loss of this tool, Neang Nee cries out, "If anyone can find the blade, I will give you anything you wish."

Upon hearing this, the great King Snake crawls out of his hole and asks Neang Nee if her words are true. Neang Nee replies, "My words are the words of truth." The King Snake then says, "If you agree to take me as your husband I will find the blade." Out of fear and desperation to survive, Neang Nee agrees.

Months pass and Neang Nee and her daughter barely survive on food given to them by the King Snake. However, as part of her agreement Neang Nee takes the King Snake to her bed as his wife every night. Eventually she becomes pregnant.

Meernup finally returns home and learns from his daughter of his wife's infidelity. He makes a secret plan to punish Neang Nee and the King Snake. One day he has the daughter trick the King Snake into entering the house. He waits hidden behind a door, jumps out when the King Snake arrives, and cuts him into three pieces. He then puts the head of the King Snake on a tree in the garden and puts the tail on the kitchen ceiling. He cleans up all the blood and makes a stew out of the King Snake's body.

When Neang Nee returns home that day, Meernup offers her a delicious stew for dinner. The family sits down and together eats the dinner. Suddenly, a crow cries out, "Krawlov! Krawlov! The tail is on the ceiling." Hearing the crow's cry, Neang Nee looks up and sees the tail of the King Snake on the ceiling. She immediately starts to cry.

Now Meernup is certain that his wife was seeing the King Snake while he was gone. Meernup asks, "Why are you crying, honey?" "The rice is hot, the soup is hot, and I am missing the children," replies Neang Nee.

After dinner, Meernup asks Neang Nee to join him for a bath in the river. Meernup sees that Neang Nee is enjoying herself in the river, and that she is not crying over the King Snake anymore. He asks her to come to him so that he can wash her back. She comes over and he cuts her belly wide open with a big knife. As she dies thousands of snakes come crawling out of her belly.[7]

This common tale is used in Cambodia to explain how the world was populated with many different kinds of snakes. In many societies today, the fable accurately describes an abused woman's fate, especially one who has been sexually exploited. Rosa, a Vietnamese boat woman I met in our clinic, had been kidnapped and raped by Thai pirates, then managed to escape from her brief incarceration as a sexual concubine. When she arrived in a refugee camp, she learned that her husband and children also resided there, but because of her shame and the shame she believed her sexual abuse would bring upon her family, she declined to be reunited with them. When her family was eventually allowed to seek asylum in Canada, she chose to go to America. They never learned she was still alive.

In contrast, the Cambodian royal dancer Somaly defied her culture. In spite of all the losses in her life, including the death of her spouse, parents, and children, she learned to overcome the rules of traditional Cambodian culture that would have condemned her to isolation as a widow.

> I think being a human being you have to have love in your heart. If you do not have love you are not a human being. Life is created by happiness, sadness, exciting, unexciting, boring; all those things create life. Sometimes when life is becoming upsetting, I figure out that this is my life and I must accept it although I never chose this life, to be reborn and to be in this present situation. I never wanted to be alone. Never. It is a very scary situation to be without someone. But I also do not want to marry and have an unstable marriage, after all I have been through.... But I am looking to love someone again. One person for one person.

In Cambodian society a woman has only one chance at marriage. If her spouse dies, she must remain celibate and never remarry, even if she is still young. Somaly lost her husband and all of her children during the civil war. She was in her thirties and strongly desired a new relationship. Somaly "looked behind the curtain," rejected her widowhood, and sought out a new loving relationship. Incredibly, she ultimately remarried and had children, breaking her culture's taboos against remarriage. Many women from diverse societies in similar situations acquiesce to a life of loneliness; others do not. Somaly's resettlement in and successful adjustment to American society may also have helped her to see her unchallenged traditions as oppressive. Her new perspective was liberating.

THE LISTENER-STORYTELLER RELATIONSHIP

No normal, ordinary people really want to experience, witness, or hear about extreme violence; they want to avoid the subject. The chorus in Sophocles's play *Philoctetes* recognizes this fact when, upon visiting Philoctetes, they immediately sing, "I am a stranger in a strange land."[8] The island Philoctetes inhabits is strange because it is devoid of all human life except for the loud, painful cries of a former hero and countryman. But it is not only the island and its sole occupant that are strange. The mind of Philoctetes is also a bizarre and twisted place, full of anger, hatred, and despair, lacking joy and human satisfaction. Philoctetes's tormented mind is also frightening. Not knowing how to behave, the chorus asks Odysseus, "What must I conceal, Sir, or what speak, when faced with a suspicious man?"[9] The chorus's use of *hypoptes [ὑπόπτης]*, or "stranger shy,"[10] implies a fear-related mistrust of strangers. "Stranger shy" suggests a special and unique fragility and sensitivity that exists in all human beings who have been through trauma. Traumatized persons are not usually emotionally hardened by violence but are, in contrast, delicately attuned to the nuances of human interactions.

Storytellers are also vulnerable to emotional and physical pain when they retell their stories. They may hesitate to relate an event for fear that a fresh wave of suffering will surface. Traumatized people are extremely sensitive not only because of this possibility of being reinjured but also because they may have gained important insights that they realize are barely holding them together. Previously nonreligious people who now find emotional peace in private daily prayer may be ill at ease sharing this openly with others. Almost superstitiously, they may not want to tell others how they are coping, lest doing so will make their strategies fail. Encounters with others also open up the possibility of the unknown: all dialogue has the potential for future relationships, not only friendship and affection but also disappointment. Entering into the trauma story, therefore, the listener must be accepting of the storyteller's shyness.

A listener's patience and sensitivity are crucial to an essential element of the trauma story: the listener-storyteller relationship. The trauma story does not in fact completely exist unless it is told to someone else; the listener must choose to become part of the story. But there is a price to be paid in terms of time, attention, and pain as the storyteller transfers some of her suffering over to the listener. Being close enough to the listener to receive into one's mouth the little bird of the Sassetta painting also requires an appreciation that all traumatic stories are personal as well as historic accounts by ordinary people who want to heal themselves while also teaching others about survival and healing.

In our world today, where the focus is usually on hearing the facts of trauma stories, there is a disconnect between the storyteller and society. The great lessons to be learned from the other elements of the trauma story are squandered because they are rarely discussed in public settings. Under ideal conditions, the storyteller is the teacher and the listener is the student. The obligation of the listeners is to apply the lessons of survival and healing to their personal and professional lives. By understanding that they are part of a historical process, all involved in the sharing of oral histories become personally stronger and more resilient.

A BOSNIAN TRAUMA STORY

The former Yugoslavia consisted of six republics and two autonomous regions. Today, after the violent civil conflict in the 1990s, the rump Yugoslavia of Serbia and Montenegro remains, and Bosnia and Herzogovina, Croatia, Slovenia, and Macedonia are independent nations. Our group entered Bosnia and Herzogovina immediately after the Dayton Peace Accords in 1995. The war there started on April 6, 1992, when the Serbs began a siege of Sarajevo after a referendum for independence in Bosnia, the republic with the largest population of Muslims. The war in Bosnia killed more than 200,000 persons, injured 200,000 more, and displaced 2 million others, all in all, half the total Bosnian population. Serb forces terrorized Sarajevo and the surrounding country over a three-year period. Through three cold winters in Sarajevo, citizens had limited food, electricity, and water, surviving a constant bombardment of rocket mortars and sniper bullets. The average weight loss among adults in Sarajevo was thirty pounds; more than 12,000 residents were killed, 1,500 of them children.

We were invited to Bosnia at the close of the war to provide a countrywide system of mental health care through the remaining primary health care system. Yugoslavia had been the envy of Europe for its excellent primary health care model. In spite of enormous destruction to its medical infrastructure and the loss of Bosnian doctors and nurses through the refugee exodus and murder, the remnants of the primary care institutions and providers still existed.

We provided a comprehensive mental health training to our Bosnian primary health care colleagues so that they could successfully identify and treat tens of thousands of persons psychologically damaged by the war. One of our innovations was to introduce the collection of the trauma story, including all four elements, into their standard medical practice.

As in all conflicts, the dividing line between patients and practitioners was often blurred. Many medical practitioners had been traumatized by the war, sometimes suffering more than their patients. Bosnia and Croatia were the first places I had an opportunity to collect the oral histories of medical professionals.

Dr. Bakir Nakas, a medical doctor in Bosnia, stands out. With a fiery disposition and a true hero's mission, Dr. Nakas ran the state hospital for the citizens of Sarajevo through the Serb siege. Dr. Nakas remained in Sarajevo during the entire conflict and, at great risk to himself and his family, participated in the medical and surgical treatment of thousands of injured citizens. He and his staff worked under extreme conditions, often without electricity or heat, and with limited medical supplies. Today the hospital buildings are pockmarked with bullet holes as a reminder of a time when an enemy tried to destroy a healing institution, its staff, and its patients. Dr. Nakas's oral history revealed a person, a place, and a cultural environment radically different from those of the Cambodian oral historians, but its basic structure is essentially the same.

The Facts

At the beginning of the armed conflict in Sarajevo, Dr. Nakas entered the hospital and rarely left, even to visit his family, until three years later. His wife and two children, who also remained in Sarajevo, supported him in all ways. He became the head of the state hospital almost by chance. At the outset of the war he was a lieutenant colonel in the Yugoslav army and had been stationed in the hospital. In March of 1992, special forces of the army entered the hospital for "security" reasons and established a forbidden zone on the upper floors. After the shooting began on April 6, Dr. Nakas discovered that the Serb security forces were using the hospital as a base from which to shoot citizens in the streets:

> Later on I was informed that they were shooting people
> from the windows of the hospital. Because of this rumor
> I climbed up to the tenth floor. I saw shells being directed
> at the hills of the suburbs where my mother lived. At that

moment I made a decision to leave the Yugoslav National
Army.

A few weeks before, on March 2, as the killings began in Sarajevo, Dr. Nakas's father had left home and never returned after suffering a fatal heart attack. Dr. Nakas's wife eventually found his
father in the morgue of a Sarajevo hospital. Dr. Nakas believes that
the violent events of that day killed his father because they foreshad-
owed an ethnic conflict between Muslims, Croats, and Serbs that he
found too painful, as a Yugoslav, to bear. As is the case with many
other survivors, Dr. Nakas's trauma story begins with a precise date:
March 2, the day his father died.

For Dr. Nakas, the sniping from the hospital was a betrayal to
his patients and his medical integrity. He gave an account of going
to his military superior and informing him that he was immediately
quitting the army:

> "My military career is over. I want to go out of the hospi-
> tal. I want to be demobilized. Whatever you need, I will
> sign." The general asked me to stay because we had been
> military colleagues for many years. I told him, "Please, I
> am really fed up with everything I have seen. They are
> shooting from the hospital that part of the city where my
> mother lives. I need to be with the family—not to be here
> with military men who are 'protecting' the hospital from
> the ordinary citizens with weapons." And he allowed me
> to go at the end of the day. It was half past five.

As a medical man he could not bear that the hospital now terrified the people of Sarajevo and that no patient would go there for
help. At a risk to his own life, he quit the military.

> I let everything disappear. I went to my home—to my
> flat. I was together with my wife. She was really afraid

because there were some rumors that people who left the military were on a list to be killed. A lot of friends of mine invited me to go outside the country, but I did not accept this.

While telling the facts, many crossroads like this are revealed by the storyteller. At this point, Dr. Nakas had no idea of the great opportunity he would be given to serve his fellow citizens — an opportunity he would have missed had he fled the country.

After quitting the military, Dr. Nakas was unemployed for one month and two days. Then something unpredictable happened: the Serb forces abandoned the hospital. On May 10, he went back to see if he could help.

> I entered the hospital gate where I now see people in different uniforms who belong to the Bosnian territory defense and the Sarajevo police. They ask me who I am; I explain that I am a former military personnel and a medical doctor. I was invited by hospital staff because out of 660 medical staff, only 50 are left. And they allowed me to enter the hospital for another 192 days. I spent all these days in the hospital trying to organize hospital activities since I was promoted to be head manager of the hospital.

Incredibly, it was Dr. Nakas's destiny that because of his tough-minded character he would stay in Sarajevo and eventually return to the hospital. After this life-changing decision, he was elected hospital director and set out on a three-year course of incredible achievements. The traumatic events that he experienced personally were secondary to the sufferings of his medical institutions, patients, and staff. Under his direction, the hospital became a living and breathing personality that he felt must survive at all costs.

> Just three days after I entered the hospital they began to shoot the hospital, first with grenades and then shells.

First they hit the central hospital wards and then they hit the emergency rooms. Soon the hospital was without water, electricity, and food supplies. Worse, the citizens of Sarajevo did not accept the hospital as being safe because of the initial Serb occupation. Really, the people avoided coming to the hospital until the big killings appeared on Markale Market.

Dr. Nakas and the hospital staff coped with the situation and continued to be medically effective by literally grabbing patients from other overcrowded medical facilities and returning them to the state hospital, to reestablish trust in the institution. To avoid snipers and mortar shells, patients and surgical suites were constantly moved to different locations. Rain was collected for water by converting beer cisterns into a collecting system on the hospital roof. It was recognized that electricity was not needed for twenty-four hours a day; it was only necessary for specific machines, especially during surgery. Small generators were only sparingly used at certain times for specific vital activities. Other innovations helped utilize medications, blood, and oxygen to save many lives at this hospital during the war.

Dr. Nakas's accounting of his experiences also included stories of the patients themselves. Personal accounts of trauma often focus on family members and fellow survivors. Dr. Nakas's love and devotion for his patients are an important part of his traumatic biography.

> I would make tours of the hospital every day, two or three times. And I visit patients, and I would look…many of them are still in mind, but I cannot remember their names but I can remember their faces, painful and with happiness. I can remember them really like a film.

In particular, he remembers two patients, both prominent Sarajevans, who lost their legs from mortar shells. One, a bank president, had a great will to live and today manages to carry on without his legs. The other was a famous actor who lost his legs in a café explosion; after being wounded he wanted only to die. The actor felt his life was useless because without legs he believed there were no longer any suitable roles for him. The actor later told Dr. Nakas how an experience at the hospital gave him the desire to live again. Dr. Nakas recalls:

> I tried to arrange public events at the hospital. I even brought in the national philharmonic orchestra. On the first anniversary of the hospital surviving I organized a ceremony. I brought this famous actor against his wishes. At the end of the ceremony I asked the actor to address the audience. It was a surprise. He was afraid and said to me, "Why are you doing this to me?" I told him, "I am only a doctor—you are an actor and this is your stage." He started to speak a monologue from an old Bosnian play. Everyone started to cry. He later told me that if it was not for this event, he would never have acted on the stage again.

In times of violence, doctors are called upon to play many roles they have not been trained to perform. But so it is for everyone who experiences violence.

Dr. Nakas's trauma story is loaded with examples of injustice, cruelty, and human betrayal. The siege of Sarajevo set a new level for barbarism. But the facts of this trauma story reveal not only the brutality but also the unique transformation of traumatized persons into new roles and vocations. Traumatic events can be associated with positive changes in an individual's personality and behavior. This story of Dr. Nakas, representing the first history of how the hospital survived during the siege of Sarajevo, was a worthy exercise, especially as modern conflicts continue to target healing institutions, staff, and patients. Perpetrators believe that if they destroy their victims' healing capacity, they destroy their capacity for survival and recovery.

THE CULTURAL MEANING OF TRAUMA

Traumatic life events are not only personal, they are also cultural and historical. Dr. Nakas explained the cultural expectations associated with torture in the former Yugoslavia:

> When Tito's party made a decision to divorce itself from Stalin, everyone who liked Stalin was accused and punished. Also, many Yugoslavs had been tortured in German prisons or spent time in prisons during World War II. All of these people, however, kept quiet about their situation. They did not want to attract negative attention to themselves or their families.

Dr. Nakas explained that this is why he probably did not hear about torture from his patients during the war, although he saw on television the atrocities that many had suffered.

> I heard some words about these stories but people were afraid to speak about torture and violence. People were ashamed to speak about this. They were ashamed; they never want to enter deeper into this or give more information. This means that in our culture people do not like to talk about violence because it will cause the audience to be suspicious. The audience will conclude you deserved it. What you asked for, you got. And you are ready to explain that the reason why somebody was tortured was because they deserved it. If somebody was on the side of Stalin they deserved to be punished.

During the conflict, the Serbian forces elevated rape and sexual violation of Bosnian Muslim women as an instrument of terror to levels not seen in Europe since the Nazi concentration camps. When asked about the reasons for this degree of sexual violence, Dr. Nakas stated:

> I really cannot imagine in my own mind those cases of rape where one woman is raped fifteen times during the night by fifteen persons.

Dr. Nakas speculated that rape was used as a method of terror so that unprotected civilians throughout the region would live in fear that their women and children would be sexually abused if caught by Serb paramilitary forces. Dr. Nakas also speculated about well-known historical forces driving this behavior: that the Serbs were taking revenge on Muslim women because of the custom of First Night under the Ottoman Empire's centuries-long occupation of Serbia. Under the arrangements of *jus primae noctis* ("right to the first night"), Ottoman administrators in charge of Serb villages had the right to the virginity of all brides among Serbs and other serfs. This history is widely known and discussed today in the Balkans. The sexual retaliation of Serb forces on innocent Muslim women centuries later, leading to an estimated twenty thousand to fifty thousand rapes in Bosnia, has already been incorporated into new folk legends about First Night.

LOOKING BEHIND THE CURTAIN

While telling the story of his and others' suffering, Dr. Nakas revealed deep personal and spiritual insights that had positively transformed his life. In his personal narrative, he gives us glimpses of the curtains he had to pull aside in order to see in a new way:

> Maybe when I think about this I cannot imagine how many lessons I have learned because these lessons have become part of my inherent behavior. I cannot imagine that I had learned this; I just had the feeling that I know

this forever. I learned how to become a truly involved doctor, citizen, and family member.

This process of arriving at new truths is an essential dimension of learning for all who have suffered a tragedy. Old ideas are rejected, new priorities set. Cultural norms for acceptable behaviors and responses to violent events are pushed aside, such as the stigma, shame, and ostracism associated with torture and sexual abuse. Most important, as Dr. Nakas reveals, some of these truths can be shared with others.

> But what I really learned was how to be *healthy*. There is nothing more important than health. There is no wealth without health. You need to be healthy—and if you are healthy you can gain everything back again.

In his role as healer, during the war Dr. Nakas came to fully witness the central importance of health in a human life. All Sarajevans fought to recover from their injuries and illnesses, even though they might soon be killed by their enemies. Dr. Nakas asserts the value of health over material things.

> Also I recognized that everything that is material is not valid for me—house, TV, car, or anything else except the pieces of my body—my fingers, arms, and everything else. If I have no damage to my brain or my physical body, I can do and repeat everything.

Having treated hundreds of patients with missing limbs and eyes, Dr. Nakas is acutely aware of the importance of being physically intact. Maybe this is why the two patients who had lost their legs stand out in his mind. If he is stripped of everything but still maintains his health, he feels he can rebuild a new social life. Dr. Nakas no longer needs the wealth and status given by society to most physicians; he has a philosophical devotion to health, above all else.

> I realized that the comfort in which we are living is some-
> thing we have created for ourselves. We just put up these
> material standards and they get higher and higher for
> each generation. But during this war we survived on very
> bad conditions. Which means one liter of water per day,
> no electricity for three years; there was no TV, no ma-
> chines to clean the house, no refrigerators, and no vac-
> uum cleaners. I realized that without all these things we
> can survive—and maybe even better.

Dr. Nakas's concluding lesson on survival is that this truth has always been within him and, by implication, lies unawakened in many of us:

> Somewhere in the recesses of my memory everything has
> already been written. One moment I recognized that
> everything is lost and it can be rebuilt again. That means
> that if there is a human being, if there is a wish, if there is
> friendship, if there is brotherhood, there is the chance to
> survive.

This is a physician's prescription for healing, taught not in a professional school but on the front lines of a battlefield.

THE LISTENER-STORYTELLER RELATIONSHIP

Dr. Nakas has much to teach as a doctor and as a human being. Listening to his story was bearable because he was able to shift his emphasis away from the intense emotions associated with the facts, especially the death of his father and the depression of the injured actor, to the lessons he wanted to teach about survival and healing. Dr. Nakas did not want his listener to get caught up in his grief and suffering. As with most survivors, he carefully shared with his listener only a fraction of his pain.

Dr. Nakas knew he was speaking to history. "No one can imagine beforehand what it means to be a part of history." He was proud of his leadership during the war:

> No one can tell any story about this hospital without remembering me. Some were born and died without any involvement in society. Somebody discovered dynamite; somebody discovered TV; somebody discovered the telephone and they are recognized by this. I did not discover anything but I am part of history. I am part of the history of this town. I am part of the history of Bosnia and this region.

One can feel the real pride in Dr. Nakas's words. Unfortunately, too many survivors do not give themselves credit for the contributions they made to their families and communities. Some physicians in Bosnia say they feel they wasted years of their professional lives during the war with nothing concrete to show for it. Dr. Nakas sets a good example through his positive perceptions of survival.

> This really gives me a proud feeling because I feel that if I was not here that things could have been worse. I really do not know. That with my being here and my presence, maybe something went in a different way than it would have gone if I was not here. Because of this I am happy. Otherwise I would feel hopeless.

Dr. Nakas also takes up the subject of the listener-storyteller relationship from the storyteller's perspective. He strongly believes, as most survivors do, that telling the story is helpful.

> Whenever you tell a story you feel better. I will give you an example of the Bosnian people from the Muslim religion. They do not cry too much. The females go to the funerals and they speak a lot. They repeat and repeat the story. I have had a chance to listen to this several times in several tragic stories on many occasions. The stories are

like a tape with the same words and sentences. And each
time before they finish, the storyteller is much happier
than before, and the listener becomes wealthier from receiving new knowledge.

As Dr. Nakas explains, the repetition of the story makes the
storyteller more comfortable. In effect, having a listener is part of
the therapeutic process. Dr. Nakas captures another important benefit of the trauma story: by listening, we become wealthier from receiving new knowledge. Of what is this new knowledge comprised?
Just as the pain of the trauma sufferer is transferred to us, so is the
truth of their experienced reality. The listener becomes wiser knowing what the storyteller has accomplished. In particular, the trauma
story, in each of its four elements and as a whole, offers an incredible amount of new information on survival and healing. Dr. Nakas
and the Cambodian women oral historians shared their wisdom, in
part hoping that the listeners will have the motivation and strength
to fight for recovery once tragedy, which is inevitable, has entered
into their lives.

Listeners need to remember that the inherent purpose of trauma
stories is healing and survival. Survivors must be allowed to tell their
stories in their own way. We must not burden them with theories,
interpretations, or opinions, especially if we have little knowledge
of their cultural and political background. We must never be intrusive, but remain enthusiastic and sensitive listeners, and the trauma
story will flow without any outside influence. If the storytellers sense
that we already know what they have to say, they may refuse to speak
or only say what we want to hear. Carefully attending to the four elements of the trauma story lets the storyteller share secret knowledge,
in order that we all might heal from and survive human tragedies.

The trauma story can be told in groups with other people facing similar problems.[11] Examining the cultural meaning of trauma

is especially helpful with life events that are associated with high social stigma and shame. For example, Lynn Franklin, a birth mother and author of *May the Circle Be Unbroken: An Intimate Journey into the Heart of Adoption,* uses this approach effectively in workshops with other women who have given their children up for adoption.[12] Many of the birth mothers were young when they became pregnant and were forced by their families to give up their child for adoption in order to avoid social scorn and embarrassment. The years passed, and they continued to grieve, often secretly, in silence, not knowing anything about their child's whereabouts or general well-being. As the birth mothers systematically reviewed their trauma stories they were able to "look behind the curtain," and realize that their adoption decisions were based primarily on conservative social conventions that had little understanding or regard for the long-term impact of separation and secrecy on the adopted person and his or her birth mother. The workshops began a process of healing that allowed many to relieve their pain by accepting their decisions and/or finding their lost children.

This new approach to understanding the trauma story gives everyone a way to tell and interpret their own stories, not only those of others. We can all look at events in our lives and systematically review each of the four elements. Just telling others about our suffering will help the pain retreat. Chronic asthma and arthritis patients have significant relief in breathing and arthritis pain, respectively, after keeping a daily journal of upsetting situations in their lives.[13] Diaries that record the trauma story associated with other chronic medical illnesses need to be evaluated as a means of lessening suffering. Appreciation of the trauma story's scope and depth allows it to have a significant personal and social role in recovery from violence's humiliating and disturbing goals.

Chapter 3

HUMILIATION

O N APRIL 6, 1994, rebels shot down an airplane carrying
the presidents of Rwanda and Burundi, killing both. Then
on April 7, an unprecedented wave of genocidal killing
began. By July more than 800,000 Tutsi and moderate Hutu were
dead at the hands of organized bands of Hutu militias, more than
three million persons were left homeless, and the country was
thrown into chaos.

In 1996 our clinic conducted a survey of the mental health impact of the 1994 genocide in Rwanda.[1] The survey confirmed the
impression that the perpetrators were trying to annihilate an entire
society. Although the focus of killing was on the Tutsi people, no
one was spared. All Rwandans experienced the entire range of individual traumas, as well as the collective impact of mass violence on
their families and communities. Their experiences ranged from material damage, such as the destruction of homes, farms, and villages;
to physical damage, such as bodily injury, maiming, and death; to
cultural damage, such as the destruction of churches and schools; to

psychological damage, such as the constant fear of being killed or seeing friends and relatives killed and the loss of trust in neighbors.

In 1999 the small Pacific island of East Timor voted for independence from Indonesia, leading to an outbreak of violence with the Indonesian authorities. The following year I was invited to assist in setting up a mental health clinic in East Timor. Although few East Timorese had been killed in the conflict, most of their property and possessions had been destroyed, leaving the local population without even their small fishing boats. Living beside a sea of plenty, the East Timorese were left starving. Not only were their homes and villages destroyed, but their entire way of life was threatened with extinction. It was clear that cultural annihilation was the perpetrators' goal.

In studying these and countless other trauma stories, I've come to recognize humiliation as an emotional state caused by violence that had been ignored by psychology and medicine for more than 100 years. Humiliation is closely associated with the feelings of shame, embarrassment, disgrace, and depreciation that are common reactions to violent actions. Because it exists alongside of anger and despair, humiliation is often hidden by these other intense emotions. Its role in causing mental damage is often difficult to see in situations such as marital abuse and domestic and sexual violence. But in cases of extreme violence, the true nature and damaging impact of humiliation can readily be observed.

The emergence of humiliation after violent acts helps us to understand that mass violence, torture, and terrorism do not appear to be random acts of cruelty. They are planned, purposeful events, aimed at the annihilation not just of individuals but also societies and nations. They are designed by their perpetrators to end, or least radically transform, an entire culture.

CULTURAL ANNIHILATION

The cultural annihilation of a people occurs through a combination of material, physical, social, and psychological damage. Cultural annihilation extends far beyond the destruction of factories and bridges to the death and maiming of soldiers and civilians. Not enough resources exist in the world today to repair the global damage caused by war and ethnic conflict. There is no way to replace all the farmers, teachers, engineers, and public administrators that have been lost. In Cambodia, after the reign of terror of the Khmer Rouge from 1975 to 1979, fewer than 100 doctors remained alive out of more than 2,000. Almost every Buddhist temple had been destroyed, and statues of Buddha were desecrated by being dismembered and thrown into lakes and rice fields. In recent conflicts in the Balkans and Afghanistan, perpetrators have focused their attention on civilian targets, including the wholesale massacre of women and children and the destruction of religious institutions and hospitals. During the war in the Balkans in the early 1990s, the university and the hospitals in Sarajevo were targeted by the Serb forces for elimination. Radovan Karadzic, former professor at the University of Sarajevo psychiatry clinic, ordered rockets aimed at his former clinic to annihilate his professional colleagues and patients. In Afghanistan, the Taliban enslaved its women and children within a barbaric medieval society. In 2001, the Taliban demolished two enormous Buddhas that had been carved into the cliffs of Bamiyan—one of them dating back to the third century. The Taliban considered the displayed images of a deity sacrilegious, even if from another faith. In truth, they used a few sticks of dynamite to destroy a world heritage site as an expression of contempt for other religions, revealing religious intolerance in its most extreme form.

Over the past quarter-century a shift has taken place in the patterns of mass violence, so that now cultural and psychological damage are becoming as important as material and physical damage. Modern conflicts in all corners of the world have moved away from the physical imprisonment of a conquered people to the complete obliteration of their way of life. The systematic murder of doctors and patients, a violent disregard for the role of the International Red Cross, the kidnapping and murder of journalists, and the use of the Internet to display gruesome killings of captured civilians are some of the methods that herald a new era of psychological and cultural terror. The Nazi ideology of annihilating "life unworthy of life" has been recast globally as a sociocultural annihilation of "unworthy" human beings. Perpetrators aim at destroying an enemy's society in lieu of murdering its citizens.

Cultural annihilation begins with the debasement or obliteration of daily activities and personal relationships, whether educational, civic, or religious. A Bosnian farmer who participated in one of our projects described the Serbs' attack on his village during the recent war:

> Most of us ran into shelters to save ourselves as the Chetniks [Serbs] destroyed our cattle and farms. I took my family into a safe refuge, but all of a sudden something happened to me. I told my wife I was going back to see if anything else was left.... The Chetniks were setting everything on fire and the cattle were being burned alive in the cowsheds.

Bosnian farmers feel a deep connection to their land and their villages, as an expression of historical continuity with their ancestors within a small area. The destruction of this man's farm and cattle had extinguished his entire way of life and hence his source of identity. Years after the event he still woke up in a sweat, dreaming of the roars of the burning cattle.

SEXUAL VIOLENCE

In the late 1980s my colleagues and I conducted a worldwide survey of more than ninety clinics caring for torture survivors, which revealed that rape and other forms of sexual abuse are the primary methods of torture inflicted upon women in all geopolitical settings.[2] This finding, along with the shocking revelations of Balkan psychologists that soldiers and paramilitary fighters in Croatia and Bosnia were routinely raping as many villagers as possible, including children, led the United Nations finally to proclaim that rape is not just a violent criminal act but a politically motivated instrument of ethnic cleansing and a crime against humanity.

Cultural annihilation proceeds most effectively not through physical destruction but through sexual violence. Such violence radically transforms social relationships at all levels of community for an entire generation. During the civil war in Rwanda, many of the country's Tutsi women were raped or sexually violated by the Hutu perpetrators. In situations involving mass rape—whether perpetrated on Vietnamese women by Thai pirates in the Gulf of Thailand; in Cambodian refugee camps; in the Great Lakes region of Africa; in Sudan, Argentina, Chile, and Guatemala; or in the ethnic cleansing campaigns of Bosnia—the results include not only the spread of HIV/AIDS and unwanted pregnancies, but the horrendous personal rejection of the women by their families and communities.

A Vietnamese proverb epitomizes the new social reality for raped women throughout the world: "The bowl was clean and someone ate out of it, leaving it dirty." Modern perpetrators know that it takes a victim a lifetime to clean off the defilement of a single act of rape, and that the spouse and community will never again fully accept her, causing irreparable damage to all persons involved. In the Darfur region of Sudan, where rape has been used extensively as an act of terror, scores of babies have been born from the rapes of girls and women by the Arab militiamen called *janjaweed,* meaning "devils on horseback." The prospects for these children and their mothers within the traditional society are grim. As one sheik of a village stated about an infant a few days old: "We will treat her like our own. But we will watch carefully when she grows up, to see if she behaves like a *janjaweed.* If she behaves like a *janjaweed,* she cannot stay among us."[3]

DESTRUCTION OF ORDINARY REALITY

Another goal of the perpetrators in inflicting psychosocial damage is to create the loss of belief in normal, everyday reality. During the siege of Sarajevo, a Serbian kindergarten teacher took to the surrounding mountains to become a sniper, killing her former Bosnian Muslim students. Pregnant women, small children, and the elderly became the prime targets of such snipers. Bizarre and unbelievable social actions became commonplace events even as ordinary citizens in Sarajevo found it hard to believe that these horrors were occurring.

A ten-year-old orphan boy who survived the Hutu massacres in Rwanda described the new social reality he had been forced to experience:

> After they burned my house, I hid. I saw them. I saw everything. They shot my mother and cut off her arm with a sickle. They killed her and other people. The children were told to drink the blood. Then they were killed too.

This boy lost his home and his mother, and was forced to give up all sense of human decency by witnessing a barbaric act. Such forms of violence create a distorted world for survivors, in which they are no longer able to interpret reality. Perpetrators intentionally drive victims to a place where all the values and features of "normal" existence are destroyed. Well-accepted beliefs, which inform the complex web of life, are ripped to pieces and replaced by new rules and new languages. Some traumatized people resist, fighting with the strength of personal and/or religious beliefs, and are never taken over by the perpetrators' belief system. Such people manage to keep their view of life intact and perhaps even strengthened in response to the perpetrators' grotesque world. Many of these survivors focus on aiding others less fortunate than themselves. Unfortunately, other victims see their worldviews crumble, and they come to view the beliefs of their former lives as artificial creations without value. No one is prepared for this disintegration of meaning.

DUMMY PERSONALITY

Many traumatized people suffer a divide in their conscious minds—what Freudians would call "splitting of the ego." The mind struggles to maintain its sanity by cracking in two, one half holding on to all it has previously believed in, and the other half turning toward the chaos and darkness of annihilation. The victim suffers the excruciating pain of trying to survive with both minds intact, the mind of "hope" struggling to avoid dominance by the mind of "despair." This struggle continues long after the trauma has subsided.

Phang, a Cambodian man called a Khmer Krom because he was born and raised in Vietnam, struggled with his own split mind for ten years after leaving Vietnam and arriving in America. As a Vietnamese citizen, Phang was forced to dig deep pits with hidden spikes along the Vietnam-Cambodia border. Cambodian travelers, many from his own village, were considered by the local Vietnamese authorities to be spies for the hostile Cambodian government. Year after year, he watched many of his friends fall unsuspecting into these pits to be impaled by the spikes. Although he hated his Vietnamese bosses, he readily succumbed to their will; otherwise he would have been tortured. As a Vietnamese citizen, he was required to protect his country; as an ethnic Cambodian, he was destroying his own people. Phang has carried this conflict of identities to America, where he can live in neither the local Vietnamese nor the Cambodian refugee communities. He is also estranged from his children, who primarily have Vietnamese friends. His psychological struggles climaxed when he sent his five-year-old son back to Vietnam to visit his relatives. The little boy begged and pleaded not to go; his father still sent him on the trip. After two weeks in Vietnam, the boy died tragically of dengue fever and was buried there. The father collapsed in grief. Vietnam had cruelly taken away his greatest love because he had remained trapped in his split mind. He felt as if his torturers had reached all the way to America to destroy him. Perpetrators count on creating this vulnerability in victims in order to insert their worldview into the minds of the nonbelievers. This process leaves the injured feeling that they deserved their punishment, that they are unclean parts of a whole that needs to be wiped clean, and that they perhaps even stand in the way of the creation of a better world.

It appears commonplace in these environments for communication to be used to create new semantic and linguistic meanings by destroying the subtleties and nuances of everyday interactions. Language becomes monolithic, stereotyped, and ritualistic, repeating at all levels violence's major message: "You are nothing. You are worthless."

Our Cambodian patients and colleagues experienced language stripped of its normal meanings. Many of them developed what they call the "dummy" personality or *"ting muong"* personality. Under the Khmer Rouge, they withdrew into themselves so that they "saw nothing, heard nothing, and spoke nothing." They behaved like wooden dummies, having no reaction to what was occurring around them.

Thang, a Vietnamese prisoner of war, was incarcerated in a Communist reeducation camp for ten years. During one very bad period, he was shackled in a small dark room for three months, but he never showed any emotion. He said, "I kept my mouth smiling. I pretended I was living a beautiful life." He never reacted to his cruel and inhuman treatment because he knew any sign of anger would result in execution. Thang also never gave in to his despair. In his mind, he would translate his experiences into something familiar, something he could control. For example, when he was covered by mosquitoes and worms in the dark room, he would imagine that he was being attacked by enemy helicopters and tanks, but was able with his battalion of fellow prisoners to successfully hold off their advance. He was able to survive by becoming a "great pretender." He could even successfully imagine that the barbed wire of his prison was a beautiful vine of roses.

When social environments are oppressive, human beings will detach their emotions from their physical presence and become great pretenders. Violence disrupts the traumatized person's worldview, turning it upside down. For this reason, telling the trauma story is extremely difficult, as the very foundations of reality are challenged.

Many traumatized persons feel that through violence they enter into a dream in which they are completely controlled by someone else's reality, with no way of returning to their known world. When they ask to leave the dream the perpetrator states, "You cannot go. I am only hurting you for your own good." Similarly, at the social level, governments will deny that violence is occurring. Perpetrators intentionally try to get the tellers of the trauma story to doubt their own sanity. Because of this, survivors in turn doubt a listener's ability to believe in the truthfulness of their experience.

Cultural annihilation occurs commonly in lives that have been exposed to more conventional violence. For example, in domestic violence and partner abuse, violent perpetrators intentionally cause injury while usually denying it. There can be destruction of the home environment, a negative impact on the financial welfare of all family members, and the degradation of a person's gender and ethnic background. Every characteristic of the abused person becomes bad or wrong. It is common in abuse situations for victims to question their own reality. Like the Cambodian survivor, they develop a dummy personality or a hard shell so that they can emotionally resist all that is happening to them. African Americans used this technique during slavery and the Jim Crow era, and many women and children cope with domestic violence in a similar fashion. Victims cannot even tell their parents, friends, or neighbors that they are being abused. Because of the chronicity and low-grade violence of these everyday abuses, it is difficult for society to realize the real intentions of perpetrators.

A patient once came into the emergency room where I was working because her husband had abused her again by forcing her to commit degrading and unspeakable sexual acts. After hearing her tragic story, I offered to have the police arrest her husband. She refused, feeling sorry for him and saying that she loved him. In the ER, for a brief moment she had left his violent reality and was horrified and terrified by her situation. But slowly she began to doubt this assessment and by the end of our clinical meeting denied that she needed help. She had reentered her husband's reality, which meant that the violent sexual abuse was a normal aspect of his love for her. In the end, she accepted her husband's view of their marriage: "I am only hurting you because I love you."

HUMILIATION: THE EMOTION OF VIOLENCE

The goal of violent acts, regardless of intensity, is the same—to create the emotional state of humiliation. In everyday occurrences, small humiliations are common. For example, a husband states, "You humiliated me in front of our guests," meaning that the wife may have done something embarrassing or incompetent or that she is trying to make him look small or stupid. These small humiliations reveal something missing—usually affection, consideration, or love—between the two people. When people say, "I humiliated myself," they are also implying some lack of self-love or self-respect.

But the humiliation involved in violence is in another league entirely. Perpetrators try to introduce into the minds of their victims their fundamental worthlessness. During acts of violence there is a complete absence of love, affection, and empathy. In trauma stories of extreme violence, the feeling of humiliation is fully revealed, allowing us to achieve a complete appreciation of all its dimensions. Humiliation is a very complex human emotion because it is primarily linked to how people believe the world is viewing them. It is not a clear-cut emotion like fear, but rather a state of being, characterized by feelings of physical and mental inferiority, of uncleanliness and shame, of spiritual worthlessness and guilt, and of moral repulsiveness to others, including a god or higher being.

During a lecture I gave in California to a refugee group, I met a Laotian leader named Souvanna. He was an extremely expressive and confident person who had resettled in America in the 1980s. Souvanna was able to confirm the ephemeral nature of humiliation when he said: "Humiliation is a hard feeling to identify. But humiliation is a good word. I think that to me after twenty-seven years since I was imprisoned, it is still a big one." In exquisite detail Souvanna described the events that characterized his humiliation by the Laotian Communists.

> Until my imprisonment I had never stayed in line for food; I never kneeled down before anyone, especially to someone younger than myself. I never begged for anything. When they put me in a prison, I had to do all of these things. This is to make me an ordinary person. Suppose that I was a general, a major, or even a king. Can you imagine the impact of these acts on a person with pride, dignity—on any human being? That is big. That is big.

This viewpoint reveals the universal nature of humiliation, regardless of social status or position in the world; it cuts across culture, gender, race, and ethnicity.

Sometimes humiliation is inflicted by impersonal acts and routine practices. In the Khmer Rouge concentration camps, women experienced a sense of shame and uncleanliness when they were forced to conduct their personal hygiene in public. Some survivors' experiences are more personally directed. Nora, a Chilean survivor, told how Pinochet's soldiers had tortured her by placing a live rat deep into her vagina. She found it impossible to describe the feelings of worthlessness caused by this act. In some cases, humiliation is caused by pubic degradation of one population by another. The Rwandan Radio Television Libre des Mille Collines urged its Hutu listeners to "fill the half-empty graves with the bodies of Tutsi cock-roaches," equating fellow neighbors with filthy insects.

Knowing that feelings of diminishment, degradation, and shame can develop in environments without love, affection, and basic sensitivity can help us identify when humiliating acts are occurring. During extreme violence such as torture, the humiliating actions are obvious. In terrorist situations, the feelings of humiliation may be obscured by more powerful emotions such as fear and anxiety. The violent attacks of al-Qaeda on America on September 11, 2001, clearly had humiliating America as one of the goals. For many family members of those who died on that day, Ground Zero in New York City represents a place where all human love and compassion have been eliminated. It is a place where feelings of humiliation can take over. Similarly, within all acts of violence where basic respect and appreciation for others has been replaced by evil, the feeling of humiliation can take hold and flourish.

Enigmatically, the state of humiliation seems relatively easy to create despite the victim's loathing for the perpetrator or rejection of the perpetrator's goals and values. Why human beings are easily susceptible to humiliation is unclear, but whatever the reasons, this inherent tendency toward fragility and emotional vulnerability makes the job of the perpetrator much easier. The ability to humiliate varies with the traumatic event. Some situations, such as forced nudity or genital violence, have a far greater potential for creating humiliation than others, such as yelling obscenities. Humiliation often begins with the shame being made public, either before a crowd or a small number of observers, and is most powerful when it occurs in front of a spouse, children, relatives, or neighbors. One would not expect this, since our loved ones and friends feel compassion for us. Unfortunately, though, we are most susceptible to being humiliated in front of people we know. We believe, usually incorrectly, that our closest family members and friends will view our vulnerability, weakness, and feelings of shame in a negative way, leading to rejection.

In one extreme situation, an African woman seeking asylum in the United States described an experience when police officers began looting her home and removing her possessions. In front of her younger sister and her children, she was pushed to the floor, stripped of her clothes, and raped. Two officers pushed her legs apart while a third raped her. In this physical struggle, her arms were pulled and twisted, resulting in permanent injury. In recounting this event, the woman was chiefly concerned about her children witnessing the scene. She thought what a horrible thing it was for a child to see a mother being raped, and wondered how her children could respect a mother who allowed this to happen to her.

The closer the relationship between aggressor and victim, the easier it is to humiliate the victim. Perpetrators can use their empathic skills to hurt others. In all ethnic conflicts, the abuse of intimacy and trust, pitting one neighbor against another, contributes to such a deep state of humiliation that peaceful reconciliation may be impossible to achieve.

DAMNATION OF THE MEMORY

Humiliation has occurred on a grand scale in history. In Roman times, the process of erasing a person's memory from all of society was called *damnatio memoriae,* or damnation of the memory. Every public trace of a person was annihilated through the destruction of their statues, writings, and legal documents. In effect, the person never existed. For the erased person and his or her living relatives, this was the ultimate form of humiliation.

Damnatio memoriae was used against Roman emperors, very high officials, and citizens. In modern times, a similar process has been used to "disappear" ordinary people during violent conflicts. Victims, including children, are captured by police, guerillas, terrorist groups, and other violent organizations and are never seen again—their bodies are destroyed without any evidence that they were even held in captivity. Suddenly, they no longer exist, and no one claims to have any information about what happened to them. Throughout the world, tens of thousands of graves are filled with nameless executed and tortured persons. The word *disappeared* or *desaparecido* has entered Argentine and Chilean vocabulary as a personal noun. The breaking apart of African American slave families and the transfer of indigenous peoples in Australia and America to mainstream homes or schools, with the original family often kept a secret, are forms of damnation of the memory. Perpetrators have learned that it is almost impossible for anyone to psychologically cope with the disappearance of a loved one. Whether listening to the widows of Srebrenica who lost eight thousand men in two days, the family members of the September 11 tragedy, or the countless accounts from Chile, Peru, Argentina, Cambodia, Bosnia, and elsewhere, the imagined suffering of the disappeared person is unbearable. Each day, a mother in New York painfully and repeatedly relives the last moments of her son, who disappeared in the conflagration of the Twin Towers. A mother in northern Uganda agonizes about the future of her adolescent daughters, stolen by the Lord's Resistance Army. These thoughts become fantastic and frightening because they have no realistic boundaries; if uncontrolled, they eliminate everything else in the mind.

Stories of the disappeared, regardless of cultural context, produce a strong compulsion in the listener and the storyteller to communicate with the lost one. The "disappeared" are spoken to as if they were physically present and could respond to what is being said. Personal business has been left unfinished, conversations left incomplete. Unlike those who have died and been mourned, the disappeared remain alive in a way.

Imagine one day coming home and finding that your son, spouse, or parent has vanished, never to be seen again. I have shared the excruciating pain of this scenario with many patients over the years. The National Museum of Rome houses one of the few sculptures of Geta, who underwent *damnatio memoriae* after his death had been arranged by his brother, Marcus Aurelius Antonius Caracalla (188–217 A.D.), who wanted to be sole emperor after their father's death. In viewing this statue, I had a brief reverie, one of the *momenti,* imagining the ghost of Geta witnessing his complete extinction in Roman society. Can the pain of personal annihilation extend into death?

The disappeared must be completely incorporated into the healing process; they cannot be ignored or forgotten. This view was confirmed by a disturbing photograph in a book from Srebrenica, where from July 10 to July 19, 1995, Serb forces murdered thousands of Bosnian men and boys and hid their bodies in mass graves. In this photograph, a single shoe, stained with mud and blood, sits on an International Red Cross table, in a bizarre catalog of the only physical remnants of the corpses excavated from the graves. Underneath the shoe there is a caption:

> Mother, Sister, can you recognize my shoes: can you tell this shoe embraced the foot of your lost husband and father? I am with Granddad and our three boys. We have no name. My whole identity delicately clings to this shoe. This is all I am now. Do you remember, a month before the enemy entered our town, we believed we were safe. Our entire family walked happily down our town's main street praising the power of our international benefactors.

In this moment of joy we stopped in at our friend the shoemaker's. He was still holding on to my new shoes from a year ago when the war started. Wasn't it fun as our three boys tried on Daddy's new shoes? How much they envied those shoes, since their own were almost totally worn out with a sliver of sole and a few toes sticking out. It was really fun to try out these shoes, wasn't it?

Please remember I want you and my sister to look closely at this shoe and say, that is HIS shoe. Granddad and the boys are also waiting. You can come and reclaim what is left of us. I love you. Please do not let us fade away in that nameless grave with all the others who have no pieces of themselves left behind as the lucky ones do.

This beautiful vignette illustrates the need of the living to have the disappeared continue to exist in the minds of family members and the community. In many cultures, the disappeared are seen as souls trapped in a shadow world between the living and the dead, endlessly searching for a peaceful death. Until they are found, they cannot escape their anguish and pain. They also cannot join the other deceased relatives that are the foundation of a human being's life. "Please do not let us fade away in that nameless grave" touches on the central importance of ancestry for survivors and the bringing of some mystical peace to the deceased. Damnation of memory is not just a historical phenomenon; for many, it is a personal reality. For those whose family members have disappeared, violence has created a loss so intense that it consumes most of the individual's mental space, thereby challenging the person's very capacity to survive.

THE TWO POLES OF HUMILIATION

Despite the common occurrence of humiliation in traumatized persons, the study of its destructive force has been almost totally neglected by modern psychology. One reason for this lack of attention may be that the initial state of humiliation rapidly transforms itself into emotions such as anger, grief, and despair.

Souvanna, the Laotian leader, describes feelings associated with prison:

> When you feel humiliated you have low self-esteem, you feel shame. You feel your pride has been taken away from you. Humiliation can turn into revenge and depression. I would say both. It's like someone is taking your bravery away and replacing it with something to make you smaller, afraid, and worthless. When I was young, I was taught that human beings are equal and I was proud of the equality. When they take you away, they make you feel worthless. You feel afraid, worthless. You have fear.

Twenty-seven years later, Souvanna's humiliation is still strong. Once the state of humiliation is generated, it has a force and momentum independent of its original cause. As Souvanna reveals, the distress created by humiliation occurs at opposite poles of the emotional spectrum:

> The humiliated person will want revenge. If you have your way and someone has humiliated you, you have nowhere to go, you will fight back. The animal will bite.

At the same time, Souvanna describes his feelings of depression:

> You feel sad because you are a victim, because you are no longer like others. You are not a normal person anymore. You are a second-class citizen. And then of course as a human being nobody wants to be in that position.

Sometimes traumatized people oscillate between the two poles. The Vietnamese POW, Thang, describes the intense emotions that raged inside him as he suffered ten years of degradation in Communist concentration camps:

> When we face humiliation we are very unhappy. We are
> also very angry. Sometimes we want to kill ourselves — or
> kill the one who is humiliating us. One of us must die.

If the prisoner could not control his feelings, he might do something rash and as a consequence be executed by the prison guards.

> But there is no alternative when we want to kill ourselves
> or when we want to kill others who humiliate us. Death
> is the only way to calm our anger.

Many of his fellow prisoners could not calm their anger and ended up being killed. Thang also spoke of a psychological death within one's own mind. He relates how on many nights he and his fellow prisoners would pray to God, be it the Buddha or Jesus, to take them away in their sleep so that they would not awaken to suffer another day. He would murmur in French the last paragraph of a poem by the French poet Alfred de Vigny (1797–1863), *La Mort du Loup (Death of the Wolf)*, which he was taught as a young student in Vietnam.

> *To whine, cry, or entreat, is equally cowardly.*
> *Accomplish energetically your long and hard work*
> *in the road that Fate has called you to walk.*
> *Then, afterwards, like me, suffer and die without speaking.*[4]

Thang recited the poem as a prayer throughout his imprisonment in order to gain energy and strength and to overcome the difficulties of life. In the poem, the wild wolf is the POW's spiritual teacher. Although the wolf is brutally shot by hunters, he shows his killers how to die a dignified death. Thang chose to accept his fate in the concentration camp and die, if necessary, without fear. This was the ultimate way he succeeded in calming his anger. In this survivor's life, only silence was great. For him, reacting to the anger of humiliation would have been a defeat and an act of cowardice. He called the reality he created for himself "the dignity of unhappiness."

The emotional responses at each pole of humiliation are maintained and even strengthened by the social sanctions of the family and the community. In most conflict-ridden societies today, revenge and hatred are encouraged over reconciliation. The breakdown of trust and the sense of betrayal among neighbors in the Middle East, the Balkans, and Rwanda create almost impossible conditions for reconciliation. Revenge seems to be the only answer. In other traumatized societies, hopelessness and despair are the prevailing social attitudes of traumatized persons. In the Cambodian community in America, depression is slowly destroying the fabric of everyday life. One Cambodian community center found that many clients scored positive for depression. Yet the director of the agency explained that these high levels of depression were "normal" in his community; there was nothing his agency could do except ignore it.

Worldwide, there appears to be no acceptable, socially sanctioned middle ground that can serve as a therapeutic alternative to depression or revenge. Quite possibly the status quo is productive for societies that want to manipulate the despair or anger of populations for political and nationalist purposes. It is also possible that the general public simply avoids survivors, fearing that their feelings will come out in self-destructive or socially violent acts. A true process for the collective recovery from humiliation demands new social approaches, focused on the power of self-healing.

MOTIVATION OF VIOLENCE: UTOPIA

Trauma stories can reveal not only the criminal actions committed, but also the justifications given for those actions. Trying to understand the motivations of perpetrators can be risky, because such efforts can seem like a rationalization or even an acceptance of the aggressor's brutality. But the attempt at understanding is essential to the healing process because the bodies and minds of traumatized people are imprinted by the belief systems of their victimizers. Long after the perpetrators have vanished, their ideologies continue to prey on the minds of survivors.

Perpetrators believe they are killing and injuring their enemies because of a just cause, and often justify their violent acts by partial truths and humanitarian dreams of creating a utopia or heaven on earth. This purpose is often revealed in the facts given in the trauma story. This quest for utopia can also be found in documents outlining the perpetrators' mission.

In some cases these mission statements use and distort the principles of eighteenth-century Enlightenment philosophy. French philosopher Jean-Jacques Rousseau (1712–1778), one of the founders of the modern democratic tradition, wrote in the *Social Contract* (1762) that *"L'homme est né libre; et partout il est dan les fers."* (Man is born free; and everywhere he is in chains.)[5] According to Rousseau, human civilization has corrupted the "noble savage" or early primitive man, who was isolated, self-sufficient, and self-governing in his original state. This theme that human civilization is corrupt and needs to be replaced influenced his country's evolution to democracy, but Rousseau's philosophy has also informed many violent movements, such as the Khmer Rouge. Pol Pot and his lieutenants, who trained in Paris in the 1950s, were heavily indebted to Rousseau's revolutionary philosophy that an ideal civil order could be established through the "general will" of the people, ensuring the possibility of human social perfection. During one of his few public speeches after taking power, Pol Pot stated, "We all know the Angkor of past times. Angkor was built during the slave period. It was our slaves who built it under the yoke of the supporting classes of that time, for the enjoyment of the king. If our people were capable of building Angkor, they can do anything."[6] Unfortunately, Pol Pot also believed, as with the Jacobin Reign of Terror following the French Revolution, that all those who resisted the new social order must be forced to leave it or be eliminated. He believed that the new society had to be cleansed of all persons and social institutions that interfered with the creation of a new and perfect world.

While the radical social transformations that occurred under the Khmer Rouge are well known, including the transformation of a country's entire population into a primitive totalitarian society, the utopian dimensions of other situations of mass violence are not as familiar. For example, the missionary zeal of al-Qaeda to restore a world based upon Islamic rule is just emerging out of Osama bin Laden's public statements and discovered videos. His desire to strike out and avenge himself and his fellow Muslims can be seen in a poem he recited at his son's wedding in January 2001, nine months before the events of September 11. In this poem he is celebrating the attack on the American destroyer, the USS *Cole*.

> *She sails into the waves flanked by arrogance, haughtiness and*
> *   false power.*
> *To her doom she moves slowly,*
> *A dinghy awaits her,*
> *Riding the waves,*
> *Your brothers in the East readied their mounts,*
> *and the battle camels are prepared to go.*
> *The destroyer was moving towards its altar of death,*
> *with its false sense of invincibility!*[7]

This poem does not tell us why bin Laden has such a fierce hatred of America, but in a videotape found in Kandahar, Afghanistan, he reads this poem to a group of his supporters:

> *I witness that against the sharp blade*
> *That always faced difficulties and stood together*
> *When the darkness comes upon us and we are bit by a sharp*
>   *tooth, I say…*

> *"Our homes are flooded with blood and the tyrant*
> *Is freely wandering in our homes"*
> *And from the battlefield vanished*
> *The brightness of swords and the horses…*
> *And over weeping sounds now*
> *We hear the beats of drums and rhythm…*
> *They are storming his forts*
> *And shouting: "We will not stop our raids*
> *Until you free our lands."*[8]

Here he is clearly stating that the West, in particular the United States, is destroying the Muslim people. He portrays himself as a liberator of the Muslim people and the Middle East from Western and American dominance. In 2002 bin Laden published a "Letter to America" that articulated his utopian vision of creating an Islamic state because it is the true religion and because, unlike Western culture, it believes in "equality between all people without regarding their color, sex, or language." This letter lists, in Rousseau-like fashion, all the evils that exist in Western civilization and American society ("the worst civilization witnessed by the history of mankind"), including sexual immorality, usury, extensive abuse of drugs and alcohol, separation of religion from politics, gambling, commercial use of women in entertainment, the sex industry and tourism, global spread of HIV/AIDS, environmental pollution, laws privileging the rich and wealthy, failure to sign the Kyoto treaty and other international human rights laws, and the protection of freedom and democracy only for the white race.

Bin Laden's solution is the Islamic Nation. In his letter to America, he concludes that: "You are well aware that the Islamic Nation, from the very core of its soul, despises your haughtiness and arrogance." Finally, in the spirit of all utopian dreamers since Rousseau, he states that it is permissible to kill the enemy in order to achieve a perfect world.[9] In a February 2003 Aljazeera broadcast, bin Laden stated, "It is permissible [speaking of the United States and Israel] to spill their blood and take their property." And to fight all of the American-supported regimes in the Middle East, "To establish the rule of God on earth."[10] The ultimate paradox—the perfection of man means the just and permissible killing of other human beings.

Terrorism and torture intentionally strive to destroy the social and cultural institutions and peoples they despise. An understanding of the linkage between violent tendencies and political belief systems needs clarification by scholars and policy makers so that a program of prevention and recovery can be developed. David Trimble, the Protestant leader in Northern Ireland who was instrumental in forging a historic peace agreement, articulated in his acceptance speech of the 1998 Nobel Peace Prize his interpretation of the violent utopian agenda by citing the words of the distinguished Israeli writer, Amos Oz:

> A political fanatic is not someone who wants to perfect himself. No, he wants to perfect you. He wants to perfect you personally, to perfect you politically, to perfect you

religiously, or racially, or geographically. He wants you to
change your mind, your government, your borders. He
may not be able to change your race, so he will eliminate
you from the perfect equation in his mind by eliminating
you from the earth.[11]

Eliminating the old culture and values of their enemies explains
the perpetrators' emphasis on the cultural annihilation of the individual, family, and community. Using humiliation as an instrument
of violence is essential to degrade and exact revenge on those believed to have been corrupt, exploitative, and "evil" within the previous social arrangements. In almost all of the modern utopian
quests for power, ordinary people are not considered innocent.
They are, in fact, the very foundation of a corrupt society. As a consequence, the new society can only be built upon their punishment.
Large masses of ordinary citizens must be "cleaned" out of the new
society to make it "pure." Pol Pot stated he would kill as many Cambodians from the old society as necessary in order to produce a new
society of pure Khmer, and proceeded to kill millions.

In Cambodia and the terrorist attacks of September 11, survivors have borne the full assault of utopian dreamers. Awareness of
the existence of this utopian vision is essential not only for understanding the powerful incentive it provides for perpetrating acts
of unspeakable cruelty, but also for grasping its ultimate impact on
the healing process. The utopian dreamers try to confuse and block
the healing process by asserting that they were doing a great thing
by hurting others, that the damage they caused should not be repaired, and that the injured should be allowed to die or live a life
debilitated by their injuries.

It can now be clearly stated that humiliation is associated with all
aspects of violence, and it can no longer be ignored or neglected in

the healing response to traumatized persons. Potent and sophisticated rationalizations for damaging others can be counteracted with an appropriate therapeutic process. Although it might seem obvious that acts of savagery, such as September 11 or Srebrenica, would be readily condemned by the outside world, this is not the case. For many, including victims, the utopian visions of the perpetrators make sense. At some basic level, Rousseau's ideas for the perfectibility of human society still positively influence our democratic traditions that strive to eliminate unfairness, oppression, and social inequalities. Utopian goals usurped by perpetrators justify inhumane acts of violence by exploiting real situations, creating confusion and doubt as to the role of violence in serving a "just" cause. The healing and recovery process must consciously strive to overcome these distortions. The healing response must be clear that violence is wrong, no matter the rationale, and that the injury of others will lead to new cycles of violent revenge. Beginning counseling with a clear statement of absolution is very effective: "You are not in any way responsible for the violence that has occurred to you. There are no reasons or excuses that can justify these actions."

For healing to move forward, it is important to identify the feeling of humiliation and its associated emotions. As Thang poignantly stated, "Humiliation takes away a person's power. Its goal is to turn you into a powerless person who cannot perform, who cannot work or take care of his family and friends." Here he was not speaking about the effects of physical torture, but of the humiliation he felt being spat upon every day by his prison guards. Every traumatized person, sometimes with the help of a friend or therapist, needs to find that solid ground of original sanity—unblemished by the lies of aggressors—where their personal power still exists and upon which the healing process can grow.

Chapter 4

THE POWER
OF SELF-HEALING

W ITH THE COLLAPSE of the Khmer Rouge regime in
1979 and 1980, hundreds of thousands of malnour-
ished Khmer tried to flee into Thailand. Initially they
were denied access by the Thai government, resulting in thousands
of deaths at the border. After protests by the international community, the Thais allowed the United Nations to take responsibility for
them. The first waves were given official refugee status by international law, until they could be gradually resettled in America,
Europe, Canada, and Australia.

The Thais later refused the designation of refugee status to ar-
rivals, labeling hundreds of thousands of Cambodian refugees "displaced persons." As such, they were not allowed the protection of
international law, nor could they be resettled in a third country.
More than 350,000 Khmer lived as displaced persons in camps along
the Thai-Cambodian border after 1982. They were cared for by a
special UN agency, the United Nations Border Relief Operations
(UNBRO), with the assistance of the World Food Programme

(WFP), the International Committee of the Red Cross (ICRC), the American Refugee Committee (ARC), and more than a dozen other humanitarian relief agencies. These organizations provided direct services, including health care and social services. UNBRO provided camp residents all food and water.

The host government to these displaced persons, however, remained Thailand, and its supreme military command had ultimate authority over all camp residents and activities. The military was responsible for policing the camps, inside and outside, and establishing all the rules and regulations it deemed necessary for protecting Thailand's national sovereignty and interests. Thailand especially feared the Vietnamese army, which had occupied and controlled Cambodia after driving out the Khmer Rouge and was now ranked along its border. Each Thai-Cambodian border camp soon became a civilian satellite to a secret Cambodian guerilla camp, sponsored by the international community, including the United States and Thailand, dedicated to driving Vietnam out of Cambodia.

The largest of the Thai border camps, called Site 2, was a community of more than 150,000 people, each identified only by a number. Site 2 had a long oval perimeter surrounded by a barbed wire fence. Families of six lived in bamboo structures twelve by eighteen feet in size. Sixteen families shared a common latrine. The camp had no light or electricity. Water was trucked in daily, as Site 2 had no natural water supply. For more than a decade the residents were fed the same daily diet of rice and canned fish.

In the early days of the Boston clinic I heard about Site 2 over and over again from scores of Cambodian refugee patients. The UN presented these camps to the world as safe havens for fleeing Cambodians. But the patients described a different reality: for many, the camps were places of rape, murder, and human cruelty.

One day a Cambodian refugee family at the clinic showed us a photograph of their relatives' thatched hut in Site 2, which had been struck by lightning and burned to the ground. Everyone inside was killed. As we looked at the charred debris, the patients asked if someone could go to Site 2 to help their surviving relatives. We were taken aback by this request, because none of the American clinicians had ever been to a refugee camp, or even to Southeast Asia. It seemed like an extraordinary thing for patients to ask of their caregivers, yet we decided to do our best for them.

A few months later, in October 1988, after receiving a small grant from the Episcopal Church of Boston, I headed to Thailand. Traveling with me was Russell Jalbert, a retired American policy maker who had been responsible for resettling Cambodian refugees on the eastern seaboard of the United States. Our mission was to evaluate the conditions in Site 2 and their impact on the psychological well-being of the refugees who lived there.[1]

During the eight-hour taxi ride from Bangkok to the Thai-Cambodian border, reality gradually sank in. The huge expanse of vibrant green rice paddies and water buffalo, familiar from images of the Vietnam War on television, made us worry that we had entered into a dangerous environment similar to that in which many American GIs had died. As a medical doctor on a humanitarian mission, I believed we would be safe, until we heard rocket explosions in the distance as we arrived at our headquarters in a village close to the refugee camps. At this frontier between Thailand and Cambodia, a war was still raging between the Vietnamese army occupying Cambodia and the Cambodian guerilla fighters hidden along the border. Our initial determination to feel safe gradually eroded once we became aware that the Thai government had placed nearly a half-million Cambodian civilians in eight camps along the border as a human shield or buffer zone in order to protect Thailand. I never became accustomed to the daily noise of exploding rocket and mortar shells.

On our first day the UN authorities took us to Site 2. Sprawled out before us, on huge fields of dry brown earth, were tens of thousands of thatched bamboo huts crowded with people. In spite of the dense foliage and bright red and pink flowers blossoming near the area, there was nothing green in the camp itself, not even a single blade of grass. The most vibrant forms of life at Site 2 were the dusty, naked children running in droves among the bamboo huts. We looked for some sign of normal civilian Cambodian life, some organized activity as evidence that the people were trying to move on with their lives, but could not find a single store, playground, or Buddhist temple.

The camp looked exactly like the Cambodian patients' photos, only now the distant sounds of rocket blasts and exploding mortar shells brought those images to life. The overcrowded huts, looking like individual prison cells, occupied a vast wasteland where people were unable to listen to radios, newspapers were nonexistent, and residents were forbidden to write letters even to family members in the same camp. The Khmer people were confined under the threat of severe punishment and even death if they tried to escape. Many Site 2 residents were shot to death by Thai guards as they desperately sought firewood outside the camp's perimeter. The rapes and beatings of refugees by bandits and Cambodian and Thai security agents were a daily feature of camp life.

Overwhelmed by the poverty we saw around us, we began asking the many UN authorities and international relief workers about the nature of Site 2, whether it was a ghetto, an immigration prison, or a concentration camp. We could not make any recommendations to camp authorities on improving the psychological and humanitarian conditions of the camps until we could find the proper terms to describe its residents. Yet the UN and Thai authorities would not clarify whether these refugees were prisoners (as they seemed to be), were being punished (though no laws had been broken), or were in need of medical and psychiatric assistance for their genocide experience (medical care was limited and psychiatric care was nonexistent). The painful reality of the camps as violent places of confinement never matched the rhetoric of the authorities, who represented them as places of protection, safety, and humanitarian aid. This contradiction between our perceptions and those of camp authorities created a bizarre world where nothing was as it was supposed to be.

The hundreds of refugees we interviewed spoke loudly and clearly of their pain. "On April 17, 1975, the Khmer Rouge came into my village and started killing," a story would begin. They told tales of loss and horror in Cambodia and of despair in Site 2. In contrast, the camp authorities, including the doctors and nurses, actively denied the pain and suffering of the refugees they were assisting. Even my medical colleagues seemed to speak a foreign language, although we had all trained in the same scientific tradition. They said things such as, "Almost all of the residents in Site 2 have gotten over the Pol Pot genocide." "Past trauma no longer bothers them." "They have adapted well to the harsh conditions imposed upon them by the Thais in Site 2." "You get used to the daily rockets, which sometimes fall into the camp and kill people." "Why are you here? The Khmer have no mental health problems."

One evening, after a full and exhausting day of disturbing interviews, I relaxed in a small bamboo hut surrounded by beautiful palm and banana trees. As I closed my eyes to relieve the stress, images from the trauma stories I had heard that day flooded my mind. I could not free myself from the cries of anguish and despair that grew louder and louder as the refugees poured out their stories to me. There was no way I could help them. Not only had they suffered unspeakable violence, but they continued to suffer in the very place they had naively hoped would be a refuge. As I lay with my eyes closed, I imagined myself climbing out the window onto the branch of a palm tree and looking out over Site 2. I felt myself slip and saw myself fall out of the tree and down to my death, engulfed by despair. I thought I was losing my mind. It came to me then that I, as a doctor, could not cure the pain and suffering. There were too many people with too many traumatic life experiences living in too terrible poverty and confinement.

Then I became aware of the music I had been playing to help me relax—Neapolitan folk songs given me by a friend. These simple songs—of love, of food, of mother, and of homeland—sung since the Italian renaissance, and helping generations of poor people to survive oppression, poverty, and violence, brought me safely down to earth because they traced my own family's history and love of culture. The music activated my inner vitality and belief that, as a person and as a doctor, I could effect some good in the world, and that my skills were especially needed in a place as bizarre and depressing as Site 2. What I couldn't see then but would soon discover was that my contribution would not be as difficult to effect as I imagined, for there is a healing force hidden in all of us, even if depleted by violence, that is always striving for survival. The same powerful healing force that had turned my ear toward the music and pulled me out of the palm tree and away from death was already at work within the residents of Site 2.

SELF-HEALING

This force, called self-healing, is one of the human organism's natural responses to psychological illness and injury. The elaborate process of self-repair is clearly seen in the way physical wounds heal. At the moment of injury, blood vessels contract to stanch bleeding. Chemical messengers pour into the tissue, signaling a multitude of specialized cells to begin the inflammation process. White blood cells migrate into the wound within twenty-four hours, killing bacteria and triggering a process of cleansing and tissue repair. A matrix of connective tissue collagen is then laid down, knitting together the ragged edges of the wound in a repair that may not be perfect but is highly functional. How well the damage heals depends on whether or not the process has been aided by treatment.

The healing of the emotional wounds inflicted on mind and spirit by severe violence is also a natural process. Mind and body are powerfully linked, from the molecular level up to the thoughts and social behaviors of a person. Mind and body are similarly interrelated in their potent curative influence. After violence occurs, a self-healing process is immediately activated, transforming, through physical and mental responses, the damage that has occurred to the psychological and social self. For example, the resiliency of persons in torture prisons, such as Vietnam War POWs, or of the besieged citizens in Sarajevo is well known, as few had mental breakdowns and most were resistant to infections and physical collapse caused by malnutrition, lack of shelter, or untreated injuries. Dr. Nakas observed this phenomenon in his patients at the hospital in Sarajevo, who did not develop the postoperative infections that had been expected due to lack of antibiotics and unfavorable operating conditions. As he observed, "Maybe when we are pushed back into a situation of survival, our resistances become unusual to meet the increased pressure on our bodies and minds—a response that current medical science still has not fully recognized."

There is evidence of self-healing at the biological or physical level in individuals following all forms of violence.[2] Studies reveal that there is not a separate biology of response for ordinary persons and for trauma survivors. The human body, including the brain, is prepared under normal conditions to respond to any threat to survival. This includes the stress response, commonly called "fight or flight," in which a sudden and immediate release of hormones such as cortisol activates the body to immediately remove it from danger. Cortisol serves to mobilize the body's energy, increasing arousal, attention, memory, and learning. But some traumatic events are so disturbing that the stress response does not shut itself off. Sustained release of cortisol sometimes occurs in traumatized persons, leading to the metabolic syndrome, which includes, hypertension, heart disease, and insulin resistance. The dampening of the stress response therefore is critical to prevent these and other serious physical illnesses from developing.

It is now being discovered how other self-healing reactions can ameliorate an overzealous stress response. Dihydroepiandrosterone (DHEA), another adrenal steroid hormone, has been shown to counteract the deleterious effects of cortisol and have positive effects on emotions when activated in individuals resilient to stress. Beta-endorphins, which have opiatelike effects, are also released immediately after trauma and act to lessen physical and emotional pain.[3] The role of other neurotransmitters and hormones in the self-healing response, such as corticotropin-releasing hormone (CRH), dopamine, neuropeptide X, galanin, serotonin, testosterone, and estrogen, is just starting to be determined.

The science describing the neural routes underlying the formation of traumatic memories has made enormous advances.[4] Neuroscientists offer important insights into the encoding of traumatic memories in the brain, the relationship of these memories to emotions and to traumatic dreams and nightmares, their role in healing through the expression of the trauma story, and the possibility of identifying memories that are destructive to the body and mind. It is essential to understand how memories are formed since they are critical to learning, adaptation to life experiences, and personality development. At the core of each human being are the memories of experience that comprise their life history, including their memory of traumatic and tragic life events.

There appear to be two pathways in the brain for the laying down of traumatic memories. One pathway is cortical, emanating from the cortex, the brain structure associated with human consciousness. This pathway establishes *declarative memory,* which stores new facts and events and is associated with the conscious review of earlier learning and remembering. The locus of declarative memory is the hippocampus, part of the midbrain. In traumatic and dangerous situations, especially events that evoke fear, a different kind of memory is established, known as *emotional memory.* This form of memory has its seat in the amygdala, an almond-shaped structure adjacent to the hippocampus in the midbrain. Emotional memory encodes unconscious emotional associations and experiences that impact on conscious behavior. The amygdala is the fear-response command center of the brain, and it does not wait around for the conscious mind, located in the cortex, to decide if a threat is real or not. The amygdala can activate an emergency response throughout the body within milliseconds by calling the stress-response system into play.

While the declarative memory system has stored the details of the traumatic event as facts, the intense emotions associated with the event are laid down as emotional memories. For example, one patient I treated was injured in a burglary in which the attacker knocked aggressively on the door and repeatedly rang the doorbell to gain entry into the apartment. The patient's declarative memory causes her to remember her attacker's face, the time of day of the attack, the objects that were stolen, and the reactions of her children to the event. Her emotional memory causes her to automatically become tense and frightened, with a rapid pulse and sweating, whenever anyone rings the doorbell or knocks on the door. These two memory systems combine facts and emotions to create a situation in which the patient is a terrified prisoner within her own apartment.[5]

Unfortunately, traumatic events can create emotional memories in the amygdala that keep on replaying and are difficult to extinguish over time. People do not seem to have direct conscious control over emotional memories. This is why traumatic emotions associated with flashbacks and environmental cues of the original trauma may strongly affect the survivor. A proper clinical approach to emotional memory avoids triggering the emotions stored in the amygdala and enables the cortex to assert conscious control over the recollection of traumatic events. A proper telling of the trauma story can bring the declarative memory pathway into play by eliciting rational thoughts about the traumatic situation while simultaneously sidestepping the stimulation of strong emotions. This approach can lead to the reduction or elimination of emotional memories that have outlived their adaptive value.

Self-healing also occurs at the psychological level when the mind is able to construct new meaning out of violence. At that point, behaviors are implemented that help the traumatized person cope with their emotions of humiliation, anger, and despair. Feelings and actions do not spring out of us spontaneously but are based upon learned beliefs and values, which are bound together into a single system, like a galaxy of stars. To philosophers the concept of the "life-world" describes a person's natural and commonsense concept of the world, consisting of all the possible experiences that can occur to them. Although persons from different cultures or occupations, such as farmers and professional musicians, may pursue different activities in their lives, their life-worlds are very similar if they believe in a fair, just, and rational life. Then when violence strikes, this world is thrown into shock since something is happening outside their range of expectations. They think, "How can this terrible thing happen to me!" Perpetrators count on this reaction of bewilderment. They count on intense humiliation flooding into the person's world and eliminating all other emotions, especially hope and joy. In some cases of violence, this effect may be relatively minor and easily repaired; in other cases, especially those of extreme violence, everything the person believes in is destroyed. Psychological self-healing is activated, leading to either the restoration of the old life-world or, more commonly, the creation of a new one.

At the core of the psychological dimension of self-healing is the will to survive and recover. The individual makes a decision to do whatever needs to be done, not to "cave in" to the violent acts. I witnessed this aspect of self-healing in Site 2 with a young boy of sixteen named Chiemrouen who had lost everything: his family, his home, his fellow soldiers, and his eyesight. When I first entered his small hospital room, he was walking with his hand on the nurse's arm. Large bandages covered his damaged eyes. This disturbing sight made me wonder what a doctor could possibly say to him or what medicine could help. Fortunately, at that moment he came up to me and whispered, "Don't worry, Doctor, I'm going to be all right." After explaining that Pol Pot had killed his family and that his military commanders had taken him into their new family, only to reject him once he was injured, he spoke about the new world he was creating. By focusing on education, which could begin in the clinic, he had hopes of living a productive life, even if blind. His motivation for learning came from his drive for self-healing. This young man saw a future that could not even be imagined by others until he verbalized it. His optimism drew the entire staff into assisting him with his educational goals.

In traumatized persons a struggle often occurs between their destructive thoughts and emotions generated by the violence and their constructive reformulation of the meaning of that violent experience. For example, Truong, a former soldier in the Vietnamese army who had been a prisoner of war under the Vietnamese Communist government for more than ten years, illustrates this battle in the quivering smile that he often has on his face. He knows no English and speaks Vietnamese almost in a whisper, slowly and respectfully. A delicate and sensitive man of seventy, who had been "reeducated" by the Communists, he now lives alone and states that he has not felt affection for more than ten years. He claims that the goal of his "teachers" was to spoil his life, and they succeeded. Because he was taken away from his immediate family members for so long, they abandoned him. Upon his release, other relatives brought him to America, but now his only contact with others is at his Catholic church. He prays at home every day and attends mass twice a week.

When Truong speaks about his current life, the tension between his feelings of despair and his faith in his god is palpable. His depiction of himself as a young Vietnamese soldier, proudly marching along in a military parade in Saigon as a member of the color guard, contrasts with the image he paints of merciless beating and degradation in a Communist torture cell. All his precious honor and dignity were lost until he found them again by kneeling to pray in his church.

Truong is struggling with depression; he feels that if he were to let go of his faith, he would die. His ability to balance, however tentatively, his depression with a belief in his own "sacredness" keeps him from committing suicide, although he acknowledges that every day he contemplates ending his life. While many doctors would view the depressive symptoms of this man as urgently in need of psychiatric care, he is surviving through his own agency by prayer. In this form of self-healing, he actively and aggressively keeps himself alive, by shifting his identity from a "spoiled" human being to someone worthy of existence in the eyes of God.

Self-healing involves a social dimension as well as a psychological dimension. Human beings choose to do all sorts of social activities in order to repair their damaged life after violence has occurred, despite the fear, stigma, and isolation that make it difficult for survivors to engage in any social relations. Positive social behaviors such as altruism, work, and spirituality enhance neurobiological processes that promote health and reduce the negative consequences of stress. These behaviors and others, such as the use of humor, social support, and physical exercise, help the individual recover psychologically.[6]

Just as torture and other forms of violence can have a negative effect on the organ systems, compensatory social actions can have an equally powerful positive impact on the body and mind. The social dimension of self-healing emerged starkly in Site 2, where in spite of the human misery, camp residents struggled for survival. As the Venerable Monychenda, a young Buddhist monk who lived in the camp, exclaimed, "No matter how terrible the conditions in Site

2, because of the life-affirming actions of the Khmer people, Site 2 is a 'Camp of Hope.'"

The refugees lived in Site 2 for almost a decade. It was a violent, impoverished place, where inmates were forbidden to work, go to school, or practice their religion. In the midst of this forced dependency, the residents were almost universally considered by camp authorities and aid workers to be lazy, unappreciative, and unmotivated. The officials thought the refugees had recovered from the Pol Pot genocide and were now doing little to help themselves.

How wrong these officials were was shown when we visited the camp to interview residents, and could find no one home. Little by little the existence emerged of a secret society of illegal endeavors, as often happens in POW camps. Residents were out doing anything and everything to survive, from buying and selling chickens to engaging in prostitution, babysitting, taxiing aid workers on bicycles, and sneaking outside the camp to forage for firewood. There were many activities going on, never noticed by the authorities. Instead of succumbing to the situation, the residents engaged in work, altruistic acts, and covert spiritual practices—all social activities that contributed to their overall health and well-being.

Residents living in already overcrowded houses readily took in and "adopted" homeless and orphaned children. Every child in Site 2 "belonged" to someone. Buddhist prayer and the enactment of Buddhist rituals and holidays occurred secretly in almost every household, although families, if caught, were seriously punished by beatings and the withholding of rations.

Another revelation of self-healing came when people living in Site 2 were asked whether they took care of their basic hygiene. They all laughed at this question. In spite of the fact that each resident was given few clothes, little soap, and only one bucket of water for cleansing every two weeks, not a single resident, no matter how poor, went without caring for their hygienic needs and those of their children. They all washed their hair and brushed their teeth, and the women were meticulous about feminine hygiene. Self-healing among these camp residents occurred daily in many ways, both overtly and covertly.

ASSISTING NATURE'S HEALING

In the days before modern medicine, self-healing was the major therapeutic force in the care of sick human beings.[7] Ancient physicians were well aware of nature's healing power, which they described in the Latin saying *vis medicatrix naturae,* or the healing power of nature. They knew that their role was not to infuse patients with drugs or to impose their therapies upon them, but to work with the natural healing forces that begin after an illness or injury. They developed ways to support and strengthen these forces in order to cure physical and emotional distress, or at least to lessen their disabling effects and delay death. Because ancient doctors understood how illnesses would unfold, they could recommend medications, diet, and changes in lifestyle that they knew were most likely to bring about a cure or the relief of suffering. They also remained close to the patient; since the treatment process was almost always a public event, doctors had considerable incentive to produce a good result and thereby maintain a good reputation.

This type of practice is still around today for people who do not have access to modern medicine, including the medically disenfranchised communities in America and Europe. Patients who have no access to modern doctors and institutions primarily use local folk healers to treat their illnesses. Traditional medicine, similarly to ancient methods, relies on herbs, diet, and especially the empathic relationship of the folk healer with the patient and family. Unfortunately modern doctors sometimes criticize folk healers, saying that they use placebos (harmless inactive substances), instead of recognizing the power of such practitioners to activate and effectively use the self-healing response. This criticism also ignores the historically and scientifically established positive effects of empathic communication between healer and patient.[8]

It took more than two decades of work with the survivors of mass violence and torture for me to discover their natural processes of self-healing. My experience in Site 2 of being pulled back from the edge of despair by music made me look for this capacity in survivors, which turned out to be a difficult task. Asking refugees directly how they were doing, hoping to get a glimpse into the self-healing process, resulted only in vague reports. But asking a specific question—"How healthy do you feel? Poor, fair, good, or excellent?"—almost always yielded a clear answer. Refugees are especially in touch with their physical and mental well-being, but few will declare outright: "Doctor, this is how I am repairing my life." Even in relatively safe environments, traumatized persons often do not take a conscious inventory of their self-healing efforts. Fostering self-healing cannot be done until the traumatized person understands its role in recovery. It took many years for me to go from the simple question "How healthy do you feel?" to "What can we do together to make you healthy again?" This question acknowledges that self-healing is a real process that needs to be consciously and actively supported. As in ancient medicine, the groundwork for encouraging this natural process must be laid with the patient.

Unfortunately, there are many potential barriers to the development of the self-healing process. Foremost among them is the understanding by the perpetrators of mass violence that the local healing system is important to the individuals they are trying to destroy. So they try to annihilate hospitals, medical practitioners, traditional healers, clergy, and family elders. In every violent situation, from the torture cells of prisoners of war in Vietnam to the villages under attack in Bosnia, the survivor almost always ends up relying exclusively on self-healing for survival and recovery. Paradoxically, the stripping away of the conventional healing structures lays bare the miraculous power of self-healing.

Another barrier to self-healing is its neglect by modern society. The individual's emotional suffering gets lost in the sociopolitical and media reactions to a catastrophic event. On a daily basis we receive news reports of violent acts in the Congo, Iraq, or Palestine/Israel, citing the numbers of dead and injured. Rarely is it reported how many of the injured are suffering in the hospital or at home, how they will survive without their eyesight or a limb, or what will happen to the family members of those who were killed. The news never provides such information as "Today, Mr. ___ lost his legs in ___, and he is now coping with his situation by ___." Because of the worldwide focus on the brutal facts of traumatic events, emotional healing in the aftermath of violence goes unaided.

The medical profession itself can also be a barrier to self-healing. While it may be assumed that practitioners would be able to recognize, appreciate, and encourage the survivor's innate healing process, this is often not the case. Doctors are taught to listen to all patients, especially those who are extremely ill and distressed, with a rational, scientific, objectifying mind. This approach is part of a long tradition in modern medicine. In 1912, the Canadian physician Sir William Osler explicitly stated that doctors must remain detached from the patient's emotional state—and must feel nothing in response to the patient's suffering—in order to "see into" and "study" the patient's "inner life."[9] Actually, rather than helping to understand the patient's inner life, this detachment creates a blind spot. The physician ends up missing not only important clinical information, but also opportunities to foster the self-healing process.

Medical school teaches young doctors to look for illness, base their diagnoses on established clinical criteria, and follow up those diagnoses by prescribing medications or physical treatments. Rarely does the medical practitioner inquire about the patient's own capacity for self-healing. Doctors being trained to interview refugees and other survivors of extreme violence often object to asking about trauma, because they do not want to open up a Pandora's box. They also avoid the hard questions because they don't know how to cope medically with the answers. This ignores the fact that the patient's natural healing responses can guide doctors in their medical care.

Doctors fail to see the patient's innate healing process because they are interested only in the healing generated by their own medical interventions. The patient's efforts become a sideshow to the enormous medical apparatus that the doctor brings to bear. According to the profession, a brief visit with a doctor is the single most important step in the patient's healing process. Yet a twenty-minute medical visit every six weeks is minuscule compared to the time patients spend at home healing themselves. Because medical practitioners rarely step out of their offices to discover what patients are doing in their everyday lives, the patients' intrinsic healing processes are trivialized or ignored.

THE RECOVERY SETTING
Although it flows out of our bodies and minds, self-healing still needs a physical presence in society. While the creation of self-healing

centers for traumatized people along the lines of domestic violence shelters seems unlikely at this point, the medical settings for assisting traumatized people need to be transformed. A first step would be developing attractive environments for the treatment of violence-related problems. Low-status psychiatric patients in America and elsewhere are almost exclusively treated in dilapidated, shabby clinic spaces, even in elite academic institutions. These facilities, which tell the patients and staff that they are not worthy of better conditions, are not proper healing environments. Refugee patients, who generally come from the poorest and lowest rungs of society, are further relegated by their poverty, traumatic life experiences, and non-English speaking background to the lowest status among the mentally ill. Attention must be given to creating beautiful environments that show respect to all traumatized patients regardless of their social class and level of poverty.

The warmth and attractiveness of a clinic help to restore pride and respect in patients who feel humiliated and degraded. At the Indochinese Psychiatry Clinic in Boston, the patients brought in their own traditional artworks for display. Eventually the clinic became a folk art museum, every surface covered with an original piece, including hand-sewn tapestries by Burmese refugees, shadow puppets from Cambodia, silk needlepoint of Vietnamese dragons, paintings of family scenes in reeducation camps by Vietnamese prisoners of war, and brightly woven "trees of life" overflowing with animals and people by the Hmong people of Laos. The beauty of the clinic was a major reason that patients were willing to engage in treatment, especially to communicate their trauma stories. In part because of the beautiful clinic they had helped create for themselves, few patients dropped out of treatment. This stands in contrast to the usual 50 percent drop-out rate among poor patients in American institutions.

After rebuilding a clinic in the town of Siem Reap, Cambodia, that had been gutted and burnt to the ground by the Khmer Rouge, our local team planted a garden of flowers outside. The patients and their families, some of the poorest people in the province, flocked to the clinic, in part to sit peacefully within this healing space—the only calm, respectful environment they had experienced in years. They also assisted the staff in maintaining its soothing presence.

Because the creation of beauty is a part of self-healing, the arts became an important aspect of our clinical and community work. Artistic activity can aid the healing process even when therapy based on talking and medications fails. Along with patients and community members, our clinic created a photographic exhibit based on extensive oral histories of the Cambodian women and developed a comic book for young people who had lost their parents.

Our group also learned how to use puppets to communicate health concepts and provide counseling to children and adults. Puppets have the ability to say wild and wonderful things, often disrespectful of authority, whether as part of the *commedia dell'arte* in Italy or of the shadow puppet tradition in Indonesia and Cambodia. Because of the social power of traditional puppets to communicate complicated ideas, while we were in Site 2, we asked the monk Venerable Pin Sem to revive the Cambodian folk puppets for our therapeutic use. These wonderful puppets reached out to survivors and entered into their very souls, bringing out smiles and laughter and stimulating the audience through their vitality and energy. The humorous antics of the puppets lifted up everyone's spirits. The despair of survivors can be deadly, but so can the despair of therapists. The puppets magically helped both survivors and therapists overcome that despair.

When we revived the traditional Cambodian folk puppet theater in Boston, survivors who had been through unspeakable horror smiled for the first time when the shadow puppets appeared on the screen. Strange and wonderful characters such as the hermit monk and the queen snake were able to penetrate the private world of even the most depressed and traumatized patients. The puppets alone opened up a pathway for the survivors to express elements of their trauma story and to describe the new life they hoped to create.

There is hope that through current scientific efforts, self-healing will come to be recognized as playing a major role in the recovery of traumatized persons. All evidence suggests what ancient physicians already knew: that the biological, psychological, and social processes of self-healing are powerful mediators of recovery and that those processes need to be supported by modern medical institutions and society. It is exciting to realize that as far as the human body is concerned there are no special classes of traumatized people but only ordinary people who have unfortunately experienced the tragic dimensions of life. It would be counterproductive to tell the medical establishment, "Get out of the way, and let traumatized people and their communities help themselves!" If acknowledging the power of self-healing led to this conclusion, it would be a cynical result, because healing and social institutions are integral parts of every human being's life. As the traumatized life transitions from its ordinary, conventional reality to a new, more resilient outlook, it needs strong relations with family, friends, neighbors, doctors, and other social agents.

One of the first steps in a traumatized person's recovery, whether child or adult, is to break his or her social isolation by acknowledging that the forces of self-healing are at work and will ultimately lead to a good outcome, including the return to a normal life. Self-healing drives all human beings away from illness toward health and well-being. In this regard, helpers are essential because they can use their empathic skills to reinforce this therapeutic optimism in survivors.

Chapter 5

STORYTELLING
AS A HEALING ART

I N HIS MEMOIR *Survival in Auschwitz*, the late Primo Levi describes a recurrent dream he had while in the death camp. In it he has returned home and is telling his story to his friends and family:

> It is an intense pleasure, physical, inexpressible to be at home, among friendly people and to have so many things to recount: but I cannot help noticing that my listeners do not follow me. In fact, they are completely indifferent: they speak confusedly of other things among themselves as if I was not there. My sister looks at me, gets up and goes away without a word....A desolating grief is now born in me.[1]

For traumatized persons who leave a world like Auschwitz, the ultimate fear is being unable to ever reconnect with the normal world. They dread that those closest to them will turn away in neglect or indifference when they try to share their most intimate experiences. A listener's detachment only reinforces the survivors' humiliated feelings, instilled by their aggressors, that they are worthless and their stories meaningless. Levi's dream, in its premonition of his relatives' failure to acknowledge his suffering, symbolizes the universal crisis of connection between the traumatized person and the normal world.

But the dream may also have guided Levi to a solution. Perhaps at some level it helped him understand why his sister could not tolerate the emotional distress associated with listening to his story. Although trauma survivors must share their experiences with others in order to heal, they must also try to do so in a sensitive way, so as not to overwhelm the listener. Levi came to see that people like his sister could be reached only if properly addressed. Before traumatized persons can engage effectively in telling their stories, they must assess the capacity of others to hear them.

The medical doctors, social workers, community activists, and many others who are in contact with traumatized persons can serve as "storyteller" coaches. Grasping the full therapeutic potential of the trauma story means successfully working with traumatized persons on their storytelling skills. And this does not just include those who have experienced extreme violence. The abused housewife, the victim of domestic violence, those suffering from serious medical illnesses, and troubled adolescents and children can all benefit from the effective sharing of their stories with others. Adolescents and the elderly need special help at this, because each group feels disenfranchised and marginalized, believing that no one cares about their interests.

POOR STORYTELLING

A Chilean's story illustrates the failure of the traumatized person to share her experiences of torture under Pinochet's regime in such a way as to invite in a listener:

I have been interrogated five times, and every single time
I was completely naked; they ordered me to take off
all my clothes. Yes, I was completely naked. During each
of the five interrogations I started menstruating even
though it wasn't the right time for it; maybe it was due to
nerves. Anyway it resulted in me always being covered
with blood. There were always at least five torturers present, and they forced me to take off my clothes at the same
time, always making me look at them in their eyes. They
then humiliated me verbally in all possible manners, saying that they would rape me while they mauled me all
over my body; it was extremely sexually humiliating…
and they kept on making me look them in their eyes.
They then lined themselves up in a row making me walk
in front of them as if it was a fashion show, still making
me look them in their eyes. It keeps on coming back to
me that I had to keep on looking them in their eyes because it felt so incredibly humiliating.[2]

This story does not allow us to consider anything but the event
itself: the sexual humiliation of a Roman Catholic woman that maximized her shame and degradation. As we visualize and experience
the torture scene in our minds, our emotions overwhelm us. The
Chilean woman, whom I will call Maria, is forced to participate in
a perverse fashion show, where all aspects of feminine beauty are
mocked and ridiculed by her tormentors. Her own body is forced to
betray her as a very private female experience is made public. We
want the perpetrators punished, but the story paralyzes our empathic response. While the courage of this woman is implied, since
she had the strength to endure, the story reveals little of her resiliency and survival skills. It teaches us little, in fact, about coping
with and surviving adversity. If this woman had been encouraged to
tell her full trauma story, that is, the cultural origins of her experiences and examples of her resiliency and insights following the

trauma, she would have contributed significantly to a listener's understanding of the healing response to violent sexual abuse in a Latin American country. Instead, she chose to emphasize the brutal details of the experience.

In contrast, a middle-aged Cambodian man named Dara used his story to repulse and emotionally wound his listeners. Dara, who had resettled in Boston, encountered a man in his new community who he believed had killed his family members, including his previous wife and children, under the Pol Pot regime. Although in America Dara had tried to put the past behind him by remarrying a Cambodian woman and having two more children, this brief encounter threw him into a homicidal rage. He found himself reliving the massacre and losing control over his life. No one could calm him down. Eventually he painted a four-foot-square canvas, depicting in more than ten cartoonlike scenes his family members being disemboweled and roasted alive over a fire by the Khmer Rouge. After completing the painting, he folded it and placed it in a canvas bag, which he wore attached to his belt. Every night in his sparsely furnished home, he hung the painting over his bed for his wife and children to see. Eventually, because of his intense despair, he was brought to the clinic by the local Cambodian community.

Dara took his caregivers to the brink of empathic collapse, for it was impossible to look at his painting, the primary representation of this man's trauma, for more than a few seconds without feeling nauseated. It revealed a life frozen in time at the moment of the massacre, with no potential for transformation or healing. The rage it expressed was at the highest level I had ever witnessed. Yet we could not enter into his suffering with him because the images were too repulsive. Their emphasis solely on the facts excluded any regard for other elements of the trauma story. In order to cope with his emotions, Dara had chosen a living death of homicidal rage and rank depression. Listening to his story meant you had to allow yourself to be psychologically brutalized as well. After even a brief encounter with Dara's canvas, your head would ache and you would struggle to remove the images from your mind.

Dara's recovery began with his acknowledgment of the intended toxicity of his painting toward all those who were forced to witness it, especially his new wife, children, and therapists. Culturally the painting also revealed that his entire family, having been slaughtered more cruelly than animals and buried in a mass grave without benefit of a proper Buddhist ceremony, was destined to suffer until their souls could be brought to rest by proper religious actions. The symbolism of the painting further revealed that his slaughtered family would remain alive as long as the painting existed. Hanging on to his deceased family in this way prevented him from engaging with his new life and family.

After recognizing and discussing these issues, Dara achieved a germ of self-healing by reaching out to his new children. Little by little, over many years, he was gradually able to fulfill his roles as parent and husband. As this slow transformation occurred, the power of the painting subsided. Eventually a Cambodian staff member told him that he had to put the painting away. At first Dara flew into a rage, all his grief for his lost loved ones again bursting out, but then he was able to put the painting away in a closet. He now could shift from an emphasis on the facts as represented in his painting into more subtle discussions of his grief for his dead relatives and his fears of never being able to function as a normal human being, especially with his new wife and children. Once Dara recognized his destructive style, he slowly began to heal.

A BIOLOGICAL MIRACLE

The foundation of storytelling is the capacity of human beings to empathically listen to the suffering of others, an act that is therapeutic for the storyteller and beneficial to the listener.[3] Not only can storytelling establish a human connection with others, abolishing the isolation caused by violence, it can also enhance the biological extinction of traumatic memories and hasten the psychological recovery of a traumatized person. These positive outcomes emerge from the biological miracle of empathy.[4]

Empathy is defined as the "power of identifying oneself mentally with (and so fully comprehending) a person or object of contemplation." In modern psychology the term describes the process by which the therapist puts him- or herself in the shoes of the other person in order to experience fully that person's feelings and emotions. But by emphasizing the survivor's emotions, these modern concepts of empathy may fail to acknowledge a more valuable aspect of the experience.

More than a hundred years ago the German psychologist Robert Vischer coined the term *einfühlung,* or "empathy" within the context of art. Theodor Lipps, another German psychologist, later adopted the term for use in psychology, using it to explain the process by which art, as the object of our perceptions, generates emotions within us and prompts us to respond by exploring its meaning. He and other early psychologists were aware that art is capable of generating in us emotions and thoughts that mirror those within the artwork itself. Human beings are able to attribute human qualities to nonhuman objects, such as paintings, thereby rendering the process of making meaning in art a thoroughly human endeavor. The concept of *einfühlung* gradually transformed into the current concept of empathy, as used in counseling and other human interactions.

If empathy is an act of perception that emerges out of an aesthetic attitude, then the empathic listener to a trauma story does considerably more than merely project himself into the survivor's emotions. The empathic observer must first become aware of the mental image of the survivor's traumatic world that is being illuminated in the observer's mind. Through the act of empathy, the observer can then "look" at these mental images and experience the physical sensations, emotions, and thoughts associated with them. If the observer thinks of the traumatic mental images as a painting, he or she will naturally explore them in detail, with keen interest and curiosity. This exploration can result in a deeper, more meaningful understanding of the survivor's world. Viewing the trauma story as a work of art allows for a slightly detached but more careful kind of listening, which, paradoxically, can be more healing to the storyteller and more informative to the listener.

Storytelling is a powerful process because of the listener's ability to form pictures of what the teller is saying. For years, I formed in my mind vibrant and colorful images of my patients' stories but did not consider such images relevant to the therapeutic process. One Cambodian survivor, Sokham, experienced the physical sensation and mental panic of drowning each time he washed his face. He reported that when he had been a prisoner in a slave labor camp under the Khmer Rouge, he was used like an ox to pull a plow through the flooded rice fields. Often Sokham slipped under the heavy weight of the yoke and fell into the muddy water. With the wooden yoke pushing him face down, he would slip deeper and deeper into the water and begin to drown. Eventually fellow slave workers would pull his head out of the water so that he could breathe again and continue to pull the plow. While caring for Sokham I had a difficult time coping with this image. It never left my thoughts; indeed, sometimes while washing my face, I experienced an intense feeling of water closing in over my eyes and mouth and a panic that I was drowning. This sensory congruence between my experience of the water and Sokham's experience of torture threatened to shut down my capacity for empathy.

Over time, as I worked more closely with my patients, the pictures became clearer and more intense, as if a movie were running simultaneously inside my head. Ultimately I reached a breakthrough in acknowledging that patients were placing these images in my mind and that, despite our cultural differences, I could actually experience their reality visually. This realization came when Marina, a Cambodian Buddhist nun in her sixties, participated in the Cambodian women's oral history project. From all outside appearances, Marina seemed cheerful and undamaged from the Khmer Rouge experience. Dressed in white and with a shaved head, she had a round face that looked like a bright and shiny apple. Her smile radiated joy.

Yet as a child, Marina had suffered from severe poverty in a small rural village in Cambodia. In order to give her a better life, her father arranged a marriage with a man twenty-eight years her senior. This joyless marriage resulted in many miscarriages until she conceived one child, a son, who made her extremely happy. She devoted herself to him. But as with most Cambodians, the Khmer Rouge revolution swept away all of her family except for herself and her son, who was then twenty years old. The two tried to rebuild their lives, but then in 1980 Vietnamese soldiers occupied their village, looking for Cambodian men, especially young boys, to join their military operations against the Cambodian resistance on the Thai-Cambodian border. Marina and her son hid in their makeshift home, but the soldiers found them and, as his mother screamed for his release, forced the boy at gunpoint to join the army.

At this point in Marina's story, she offered the explanation that she had lost her son not because of the Vietnamese soldiers but because she had played with a bird irresponsibly as a small child:

> I think in my mind that, perhaps, in my previous life, or in this life, I don't really know, I may have tampered with a young bird. The Cambodians believe that we have Karma if we tamper with a baby bird, and we will be separated from our own loved ones. We have Karma when we make the birds lose their feathers, or if we take the young birds and play with them. I would say that maybe I did this in the previous life or in this life, and that is why I am separated from my husband and my child. This is what I tell people. This is the reason I try my best to do good deeds so I don't have Karma. Because, in this life, when I was young, I played with Tradiev Dey's young in their burrows [a kind of large swallow that lives in holes in the ground]. I put my hand inside their burrow and I took out its young and played with it. When I had enough, I put it back in. I don't know how many days I played with it, or even how many months before I stopped doing it. At the time I was young and I was still running around and playing and was still wearing a pair of shorts, without any blouse, and my upper part was bare.

The beautiful scene of a little girl playing with a small bird replaced the more immediate reality. Marina's life experience appears as a vivid landscape painting. Her impoverished but relatively peaceful childhood was transformed by the actions of violent perpetrators. Marina tried to find a "why" for her daily suffering, not knowing the fate of her son, through her story of the bird. The world of Marina can be made whole again as pieces of it that have been destroyed or damaged are repaired or replaced. The self-healing process creates a new natural world. When a listener allows the powerful images from these worlds-in-transition to be visualized, it contributes to the recognition and support of the storyteller's healing process.

BRIDGING CULTURES

Empathic understanding of trauma storytellers is often blocked by social and cultural biases. If the listener is prejudiced against the storyteller, the empathic process will not develop; it is easy to become deaf to people we do not like, respect, or trust. However, bridges can be made between cultures in order to understand and empathize with each other's traumatic life experiences. This reality became apparent among survivors of an earthquake in Kobe, Japan.[5] At 5:46 A.M. on January 17, 1995, an earthquake struck the Japanese mainland, causing massive physical and emotional trauma. The earthquake lasted for twenty seconds, with its epicenter about twenty kilometers off the shore of the city of Kobe. Approximately 5,500 persons were killed, 34,500 injured, and more than 320,000 left homeless. More than 80,000 homes were demolished, and 100,000 homes were partially destroyed. Our team of mental health professionals from the Indochinese Psychiatry Clinic, along with a Japanese anthropologist, went into the ruins of Kobe ten days after this disaster.

One of our major goals was to determine the psychological status of the earthquake survivors in order to assist Japan's humanitarian relief efforts. We interviewed hundreds of people made homeless by the disaster. Although it is widely believed that Japanese citizens do not openly express emotional distress, especially to outsiders, this conventional wisdom proved invalid. The earthquake survivors engaged readily in warm and friendly conversations, sharing intimate details of their trauma experiences and making it easy to cross the linguistic and cultural divide.

Our interview with Kyoko, a delicate elderly woman, was typical. She was sitting on a mat the size of a small rug, surrounded by her few remaining possessions in the school shelter where she was now living. The tatami mat was her home in a sea of thousands of other mat homes. The shelter was very cold, and during the interview she noticed my discomfort. In spite of having no food, she prepared hot green tea for me. Though my impulse was to refuse because of the scarcity of her resources, I understood and accepted her cultural need to be hospitable in this way.

Although Kyoko had lost nearly everything, when asked to describe her traumatic experiences, she focused entirely on her lack of privacy and the humiliation of living passively with strangers in an evacuation shelter. It bothered her that she was asked to do absolutely nothing to help herself or others. She described one incident of waiting in line for hours to meet the shelter doctor. When her turn came, she told him that she was feeling depressed, that she could not sleep, and that she was afraid in the shelter. In a loud voice, in front of many waiting patients, the doctor screamed that she was selfish, self-centered, and weak for making a ridiculous personal request for help. He said that she was wasting his time and his other patients', who really needed medical care. After publicly degrading her, he angrily chased her away, revealing a complete failure in empathy. As we drank our tea after she concluded her story, tears streamed from her eyes.

This strong feeling of mutual connection between a Japanese citizen, especially an elderly woman, and an American was thought at the time to be impossible to achieve. Fifty years earlier on the very day of our meeting, American bombers had attacked Kobe, leaving the city in ruins and rendering Kyoko homeless and destitute. She said she could never have imagined that fifty years later an American doctor would be sharing tea with her and listening to her traumatic life experiences. Empathic perception had bridged our cultural and linguistic divide. The emotions we felt are expressed beautifully in the *tanka* poem written by a fellow earthquake survivor, Sumako Harada:

Our true faces
Are said to reveal
Their true faces
When we lose clothes, food and houses
At the limits of existence.[6]

THE TRAUMA STORY AS OBJECT OF ART

The human capacity for empathic listening does not guarantee that others will listen to traumatic life histories. Often listeners have to fight off their own reactions to the tragic events by telling themselves, "I've heard enough," or, "This story is too upsetting, like all the others I've heard." When repetition is combined with empathic overload, people withdraw and refuse to listen. In fact, empathic listening is a double-edged sword because the sensitive and compassionate listener is not only better able to connect to the trauma storyteller, but can also easily be overcome by the emotions and traumatic pictures the storyteller has experienced. Storytellers must understand how to give "just enough" and not to overwhelm the listener. The storyteller needs to work with the listener's empathic capacity using an engaging storytelling approach.

Storytellers should understand the method for good storytelling. For example, they must know how to work with the symbols that are unique to their own experiences. Trauma stories are filled with symbols of the storyteller's personal biography and cultural background. Powerful images are used to represent life experiences, emotional reactions, and behaviors; they convey things that we have no words for or cannot speak about directly. A Rwandan journalist symbolized his experience of the genocide in his country by speaking of coming across a man cooking his meal over a fire of human bones, a simple image with a complex meaning. The symbolic process takes all of the pieces of the traumatic world and fits them together to make a coherent whole. When survivors come in for their appointments and begin to tell their stories, they are struggling to create something whole from the physical and psychological destruction that has happened to them.

In the doctor-patient relationship, medication can symbolize the self-healing process. Tran, a middle-aged Vietnamese patient who had been a prisoner of war, said he would die if his medication was taken away from him because of state budget cuts, although his medication was not crucial to his survival and he did not have a life-threatening illness. For him, medication was a potent symbol of the life-giving force of the new society after decades of torture in Vietnam, and he religiously took it to control his chronic medical and psychiatric problems. Other storytellers refer to themselves as little birds or as other small, vulnerable animals.

Expressing emotions is a powerful aspect of storytelling. How can the storyteller do this without overwhelming the listener? Many traumatized persons are plagued by the two poles of humiliation—sadness and despair on one side, and anger and revenge on the other. Some traumatized people swing between each of these poles, while others fixate on hatred and revenge. Some who are sad due to traumatic loss also experience hope, joy, and humor. Another common feeling is fear. Survivors may be afraid to leave the house by themselves, fearing that something bad will happen to them and their family members. Fear restricts what they do, whom they see, and where they go, to the point where they can become prisoners of fear. Storytellers must be aware that a sensitive listener will experience their emotions at comparable levels of intensity.

When the trauma story is viewed aesthetically, like a work of art, it possesses stylistic as well as symbolic and emotional characteristics. The style in which a survivor presents his or her experiences is significant. Some styles of communication are easier to connect with and understand than others. Some survivors are aloof and reserved, while others are dramatic and outgoing. Some can be delightful and charming; others are morbid and depressing. Outsiders are not prepared for the black humor that characterizes so many tales told of the war by Bosnian citizens. A popular joke in Bosnia tells of a Muslim boy who, having lost his arms and legs from a land mine, was said to be throwing all of his artificial limbs out of a school window because he was "trying to escape his life in pieces." The style is the rhythm by which the survivor moves through the world. The story contains the unique "signature" of the artist, in this case the trauma survivor.

A well-crafted and communicated story fosters the biological, psychological, and social processes of self-healing. Traumatized persons have so much to gain in their interactions with listeners if they share the full trauma story. But communicating the details of the trauma story is not enough. The story must be told in a manner that can be readily received by the other person without causing the listener to be overwhelmed and to withdraw. With coaching, in which a concerned therapist, relative, or friend positively supports the storytelling process, storytellers can learn to successfully share their experiences with others.

Coaching can help the storyteller to modulate the intense emotions associated with violent experiences and how they are expressed. Strong emotions need to be contained so that they do not dominate the story. In our society, many forces act to carelessly and even intentionally elicit toxic emotions associated with trauma — debriefing sessions, media reporting of violence, films, and public ceremonies that emphasize the most sensational aspects of a community's violence. Once survivors realize the importance of expressing their feelings in a way that does not overwhelm the listener, they can usually bring their emotions under control and share them in an appropriate way.

Coaching can also help by encouraging the use of imagination and creativity to communicate the full trauma story. Traumatized persons need to deliberately consider how metaphors and symbols can express their feelings and ideas, and how the style in which they tell the story can enhance their message. It is rare that interesting details and insights are lacking, but the storyteller might need encouragement to effectively incorporate them into their story. Sometimes reviewing the story in written or tape-recorded form can assist this process. An empathic listener acting as a coach can be helpful when the process evokes too much upset to be undertaken in isolation. It is also important to recognize that that trauma story can be told in brief segments rather than all at once. In our clinic we have a saying to describe this: "A little bit, a lot over a long period of time."

The confidence of the storyteller to reach out to others may also need to be reestablished. Suffering caused by human aggression often diminishes a person's capacity for a creative and open exchange unencumbered by fears of humiliation and future violence. Traumatized persons should be helped to realize that they have something to offer that everyone in society needs and desires. Everyone wants to learn how to deal with losses, tragedies, bullies, and hurtful families or communities. The great classics of literature are based upon our human craving for this kind of knowledge. Survivors of violence have been pushed out onto the stage by fate and given the opportunity to teach us about coping with tragedy and human violence. The survivor need not pretend to have a falsely positive attitude, but should be aware that the healing process has the potential for insight, hopefulness, and even joy. Most traumatized persons are interested in the idea that their stories can help others.

The best way of helping survivors tell their stories is to have them take on the role of teacher. This approach recognizes that everyone has something to learn from those who have experienced violence. It also deemphasizes the therapeutic aspects of telling the story for the traumatized person and stresses the benefits to the larger social group. This underscores the altruistic nature of storytelling. As we will see, altruism is one of the most powerful social means to foster self-healing.

GOOD STORYTELLING

FINDING THE RIGHT BALANCE

In 1999 the Harvard Program in Refugee Trauma introduced a new course into two of Bosnia's three medical schools, the department of social work at the University of Sarajevo, and the Franciscan Theological Seminary. In a radical departure, the curriculum formally turned the trauma survivor into the "teacher" and the healing professional in training into the "student." The new course was greeted enthusiastically by patients as they became good storytellers and by health professionals as they became good listeners.

In one such case Majda, a young educated woman from a middle-class Muslim family in Bosnia, was the "teacher," and a medical doctor at the University of Sarajevo medical school was her "student." Majda told us that she had never trusted men because her father drank too much and her older sister's marriage had failed. Because she was also raising her nephew, she did not want to get too involved with a man. "I refused every relationship that would exclude my nephew. I could not find the right balance where someone would respect me and where I would respect the man." When she met Franjo, though, "It was love at first sight." As she explained, "All of my life I dreamed of meeting a person like Franjo. For the first time, I found myself in a relationship I did not want to break too soon." The fact that Franjo was a Croat and Roman Catholic had no influence over her. She immediately realized that he was exceptional:

> I was attracted to him because he was intelligent, good, generous, open with a sense of humor, sociable and gentle. He treated me with respect. The only thing I did not like was that he would drink sometimes and he would openly say things others would not dare to say. In a way, he was in conflict, because of what was happening in Bosnia and to its people. One day he came to our house and warned us, "Muslims are fasting and praying, and they do not see what is waiting for them."

When the war broke out, Majda briefly joined Franjo at his family's house in Fojnica, but worried for the safety of her own family, she returned home. As the conflict intensified and Franjo was called away to help out with the war effort, their contact diminished and they lost touch. Majda feared their relationship would not last:

> It was New Year's when my friend called. I was hoping she was going to wish me a happy New Year. But she said, "Did you hear what happened to Franjo? He was killed." As if that did not reach my brain, I continued talking to her. Then she interrupted me and said, "He was killed in an ugly way. It seems they slaughtered him." I went to the bathroom and started to cry. I kept saying that it was not possible. Even now it seems like a bad dream.

Later she found out that he had been killed by extremists from his own people. Because he was a devout Catholic, they killed him on Christmas Day. But she maintained her beliefs:

> I still believe in the goodness of mankind, in humanity, honor in Bosnia, and all the good things Franjo tried to

preserve. He gave his life against darkness and primitivism. He was a symbol of an educated man who loved his country. Some tell me that with his death they killed Bosnia as well—and that hurt me.

They tried to kill love among the people, and everything that was good in human relations. We never had religious hatred here. We celebrated in Bosnia all religious traditions equally. This was an attempt to destroy our traditions. People who only carried evil in themselves, and who had deranged values, did this. They do not love people and are only after their selfish interests.

As for her own goals:

I am still looking for his characteristics in other people. I learned that real value exists, it is just difficult to find it in people. I am glad that I loved the right man. I learned that only a small number of people are spiritually rich. With time, I have learned he is gone forever. I am going to stay the way I was when I met him.

This story illustrates good storytelling. Unlike Maria and Dara, Majda was given the opportunity to teach her medical doctor something about healing through telling her traumatic life history. She took her teaching task seriously. She told her story directly and in her own words, without coaching, censorship, or the need to meet anyone else's expectations. While the facts were presented, Majda did not tell them in a direct and violent way. As part of her self-healing, she spared us the details of her lover's slaughter. Through her gentle description of Franjo's death, she avoided the risk of turning her listeners away from her story. Symbolically, her fight against evil was clear. She did not succumb to ethnic hatred, because she continued to celebrate all religious traditions as well as her love for a Croatian man. She remained undeterred and continued to believe in human goodness.

Majda's story illustrates the many elements of the trauma story. She was forced to look behind the curtain after Franjo's death and discover the real value that exists in the world. She was able to get past the political rhetoric to see that the conflict in Bosnia was not a religious war but one promoted by primitive people with selfish interests, who were attempting to destroy Bosnian culture and civilization through religious and ethnic intolerance. One can imagine her now being a force for reconciliation within her family and community.

Through Franjo's death, Majda came to a sense of her own dedication: "I am going to stay the way I was when I met him." She did not allow the brutality of Franjo's killing to corrupt her own values. Though she told us she was depressed after his death, her love of her job, her responsibility to her family and nephew, and her memory of Franjo's goodness brought her out of her social withdrawal and helped her cope with everyday life. The student doctor shared her sad and painful emotions, but also her love and affection for Franjo. She was able to activate our empathy so that we could in turn participate in the healing process. The violence in her life had transformed her into a vital healing force in spite of the social chaos and fear that exist all around her in Bosnian society today.

As a teacher, Majda never withdrew her attention from her student doctor. When he asked her what kind of relationship she wanted with her primary care physician, she stated, "I expect a relationship full of warmth, trust, and honesty. It is important for the doctor and patient to have a sense of openness, trust, and respect." These were the very characteristics that she valued in her relationship with Franjo; she had finally found the right balance in herself. Her ultimate challenge was to teach this balance to her society so that all of its citizens could achieve a collective good.

MAKING A MARK ON THE WORLD

In June 2002 ABC News *Nightline* aired a program that focused on the Harvard Program in Refugee Trauma's work with refugees around the world. The next day I received a telephone call from Liz and Steve Alderman, whose son Peter had been killed in the September 11 attacks, saying they wanted to contribute to our activities. A partnership was launched between the Alderman family and our group that led to the Peter C. Alderman Masterclass. The mission of this project is to provide scientific training and professional support to health-care professionals from around the world who work with persons damaged by extreme violence. Medical doctors, psychiatrists and other mental health professionals, and policy makers from countries that have experienced violent conflicts—such as Afghanistan, Iraq, Cambodia, Rwanda, Uganda, Peru, Bosnia, and Chile—are brought together with faculty from Italy, the United States, and England. During the annual gathering, held in Orvieto, Italy, participants have opportunities for learning new clinical skills and practices as well as for self-care. Liz Alderman and her husband Steve, who is a medical doctor, participate fully in each Masterclass, contributing in a direct and meaningful way out of their own traumatic life experience. As with Majda in the class of student doctors, Liz Alderman transformed herself in this setting from a housewife into a teacher and a colleague of the group.

Liz illustrates all the characteristics of a good storyteller. She is sincere, direct, and strives to be honest when presenting her life experience, avoiding theorizing and rationalizations. As did Majda, she speaks from the heart. The symbol that characterizes her life experience since September 11 is the Peter C. Alderman Foundation, created in honor of her son. In spite of her tragic loss, Liz is rarely angry. She never offends or emotionally overwhelms the listener. Yet there is always an undercurrent of grief, and in hearing her story one feels close to that grief. As she says, "What happened is your worst nightmare coming true. We lost our child in a brutal and totally unexpected way. This is something I have learned that you can never recover from."

The youngest of the Aldermans' three children, Peter was twenty-five years old when he died. At the time Liz was in France with her husband and realized that Peter might have been attending a conference in the World Trade Center when the planes struck. As Liz describes that day:

> The bottom fell out. I was on the other side of the world and I did not know where my son was...it was just this hopeless frantic feeling. I took all of the dishes out of the dishwasher and washed them by hand.

Later, she realized that her son had died in the building: "I knew Peter was dead but I did not really know what being dead meant. I did not really know the 'foreverness' of it. And that took a long time to set in." As time passed, she had to decide how to continue on with her life:

> I had two options when he died. I could either kill myself...I do not mean literally putting a gun to my head, but getting into bed and never getting out. Or, just put one foot in front of the other.... You tend to grieve and mourn the same way you live.

Four years after the loss of her son, Liz's heartache is as great as it was at the moment she realized he had died.

> I do not know who I am anymore. I always felt that I knew who I was and what I was about. My parents gave me a strong ego and I marched to my own drummer.

Now I do not have the slightest idea who I am. I do not
know how I will act from day to day and from minute to
minute....I have not given myself permission to enjoy
life. My grief as awful as it is for me cannot compare to
Peter's loss. Peter lost his future. He will never have the
opportunity to have a wife, children, and the joys life will
bring you....I have not given myself permission to enjoy
things. I used to love to hear opera, I cannot listen to that
music because it makes me cry. I cannot look at a nice sky
that is beautiful because Peter cannot see it. I do not like
beautiful days because Peter cannot experience it....I
have not given myself permission to go back to the things
I enjoy. It is difficult for me. Maybe it is my image as a
mother. How can I enjoy my life in this world if Peter has
no life?

In spite of her pain Liz is making important contributions
through her family's new foundation. She says, "Maybe I am
screaming inside and do not know it. But I do think if this were so
I would not be able to function. But I am functioning at a very high
level." Liz, her husband, and her children have worked to transform
their tragedy into a constructive effort to create health and well-
being in the lives of people damaged by war. Her radical drive to
produce good in the world is even a surprise to Liz.

I never cared about leaving a mark in the world. My mark
was my children. But Peter was too young when he died
to leave a mark so the foundation was set up to make up
for this.

I would teach others out of my experience the following
things I have learned. The pain has not gone away and it
is not any less than four years ago when Peter died. I will
never recover and will never be the same person and I
have to accept this. But Peter is always there. I feel good
at the Masterclass and I feel good that I am really making

a mark in the world in Peter's name. I have started a foundation, which is like running a small business. I've gotten good on the computer. Although Peter will never know these things, I know he would be thrilled to see what I am doing.

Liz and her husband, Steve, began their altruistic efforts eight months after their son's death. She was wrapped in Peter's blanket on his bed when the *Nightline* program came on. There she saw three children orphaned by the war in Afghanistan. She felt an urge to gather these children in her arms and bring them into her home, take care of them, and make life good for them. And as she continued to watch the program she realized that perhaps she could do more than just help these three children. She had an overwhelming feeling that she had the need to do something positive.

Liz still suffers from the tragic death of her son. She is always sad, although her sadness cannot be readily seen on her face or in her behavior. She declares, "I am not a basket case," and "I am trying to bring pleasure back into my life." Most important, she feels she is accomplishing tremendous things to benefit others. Liz tells us that she believes she makes some people very uncomfortable. She thinks people do not want to hear about the work of the foundation because they are doing little to help others. But she also feels that they stay away from her because she has become so direct and honest that she cannot tolerate everyday lies and deceptions.

Liz readily shares her inspiring story at the Masterclass. Many listen to her words, learn about the difficulty of recovering from the loss of a child, and are energized by her spirit and altruism. As with Majda, Liz's story allows the listener to share her painful emotions but also to share her love for her son Peter. She activates our empathy so that we can believe in and participate in her dream to heal the suffering and pain of others damaged by violence. She has been able to transform her suffering into a powerful healing force for others, for her family, and for herself.

Strong emotions comprise the traumatic memories that are imprinted in the survivor's brain. One of the mind's key tasks after trauma is to take these strong emotions and gradually reduce them over time through good storytelling. A poor storyteller tells a toxic trauma story, unhealthy to mind and body with its focus on facts and high expressed emotions.[7] In our society situations that demonstrate this type of storytelling are common, including superficial, sensational media reporting of tragedies and debriefing therapy by misguided mental health workers. In contrast, a good storyteller is able to express tragic emotions with the artfulness of a musician playing an instrument, engaging the listener's interest and involvement.

The trauma story is one of the survivor's greatest tools for healing. For the listener, a well-told story takes advantage of its cultural and revelatory wisdom to teach the storyteller's profound lessons about human survival and recovery. The mutual sharing and emotional solidarity between listener and storyteller occur, becoming a source of vitality and creativity for each of them.

Chapter 6

GOOD DREAMS
AND BAD DREAMS

THE TRAUMA STORY is only one self-healing pathway that has not been fully acknowledged. Another psychological process that has been long neglected and considered relatively useless is the dream. Dreams are now slowly being appreciated as major self-healing responses in traumatized persons.

Daytime memories and nighttime dreams, forming a continuous state of awareness of the world in which we live, are the building blocks of our personal biographies and personalities. Awake, human beings consciously process their memories and form new ones. Asleep, this process continues just as intensely, but outside our awareness unless we awaken and remember our dreams. Traumatized people especially seem to live in a world of an endless flow of memories, with a seamless connection between the memories of the day and the night. For some victims of mass violence, dreams—and even their frightening relatives called nightmares—can add insight to the trauma story and aid the healing process. For other victims, dreams and nightmares prolong the suffering. When harnessed for healing, they are important adjuncts to the trauma story.

Sigmund Freud awakened modern interest in dreams with the publication in 1900 of *The Interpretation of Dreams*.[1] He proposed that dreams were the *via regis,* or "royal road" to the unconscious, because they revealed in distorted symbols the true and often disturbing desires of the dreamer. More than a half-century later scientists began to psychologically characterize dreams as meaningless brain phenomena or as normal cleansing filters discarding unwanted memories of the day. My experience with the dreams and nightmares of survivors over the past two decades fits neither of these models.

In the Indochinese Psychiatry Clinic most of the Southeast Asian refugee patients had nightmares. This phenomenon is not surprising, as all of them were severely traumatized, but their dreams and nightmares played critical roles in their current lives. A conversation with Sipo, a Cambodian teenage girl hospitalized for attempted suicide in the early 1980s, led to the realization that the dreams and nightmares of traumatized persons can shed light on their trauma stories. Sipo was being treated in the intensive care unit for self-inflicted poisoning. The medical staff was bewildered, because she not only denied that anything was wrong but also denied that she had tried to hurt herself. She responded to the question "Is there anything upsetting you?" by stating in English, "No." Again, "Are you upset about anything?" "No." "Can you tell me why you tried to kill yourself?" She said firmly, "I have no idea." But when asked if she had dreams or nightmares, she revealed that she had the same nightmare every night: "I am holding my father in my arms. He is very sick from starvation. He looks at me, then suddenly he dies." She began to weep.

Though Sipo had not connected her recurrent nightmare to her waking mental state, the dream revealed the young woman's guilt. She had been unable to save her father in the Pol Pot concentration

camp and also felt that she had contributed to his death by not sharing enough of her small rations with him. Her loss of her father and
her feeling of responsibility for his death, revealed in her nightmare,
led to her suicide attempt.

This interview—one of my *momenti,* or clinical revelations—
taught the importance of traveling along the road of the dream state
with the teller of the trauma story. The way dreams and nightmares
relive and reprocess the trauma story is an essential aspect of self-
healing and human survival. The victim's mind seems to be saying,
"I remember to survive, and I dream to heal the harm caused to me
by others."

POSITIVE ROLES OF DREAMS

Modern findings on the biology of memory and dreams confirm the
intuitive sense that traumatic memories and dreams aid in healing
and survival. The physiology of dreaming was first described in
1953 when researchers discovered that a night's sleep is punctuated
by periods during which the brain's electrical activity (called brain
waves, as measured by an electroencephalogram or EEG) is similar
to that observed when people are awake. These periods, called rapid
eye movement or REM sleep, are the only times when dreaming
occurs. Although it is still not definitively proven, scientists believe
that because the eye movements during sleep seem to conform to
the actions in our dreams, we are literally watching our dreams as
they occur.

The memory biologist Jonathan Winson has proposed that
dreams emerge from a neural process whereby information gathered during the day that is essential to the survival of the species is
reprocessed during sleep.[2] This hypothesis is based upon the discovery in 1954 of theta rhythms in the brains of normal rabbits, tree

shrews, moles, rats, and cats in their wakened state. Theta rhythms are associated with waking behaviors pivotal to the survival of the animals, such as seeking prey and exploring for food; they were also found in the animals' REM sleep stage. Winson demonstrated the linkage of theta rhythms to the formation of memory by making lesions in the brains of rats, thereby eliminating the theta rhythms and hence the rats' learned survival skills. Although theta rhythms have not been found in humans or primates, Winson concluded that they provide a clue to the origin of dreaming in humans. "Dreams may reflect a memory-processing mechanism from lower species, in which information important for survival is reprocessed during REM sleep."[3]

In the dangerous landscape of our ancestral past, it is easy to visualize early humans sharing experiences that threatened their existence, including violent episodes related to hunting, cultivation of the land, weather, and most important, animal and human predators. Animals and most likely humans continuously replay traumatic events in their dreams in order to learn how to survive future dangers. All the brain information brought to bear on problem solving during sleep may in fact be the core of the unconscious. Dream content is clearly derived from all knowledge and information accessible to the brain, of which little is available to the conscious mind. The dream represents the nexus of this information, available to aid us in our daily lives.

This biological view of the importance of dreams to survival helps in understanding the dreams and nightmares reported by traumatized persons. Winson and others have reported that the meaning of dreams and nightmares in traumatized persons is not disguised by distortions and repression but is readily retrievable.[4] Although dream content is often sketchy and the way the brain assembles it is unknown, it can shed important light on the trauma story. In therapeutic settings, traumatized persons can be asked about their perception of the content and meaning of their dreams. From a biological and evolutionary point of view, dreams seem to be great internal problem solvers and teachers of survival mechanisms.

Good dreams teach about survival and contribute to physical and mental healing from within. Bad dreams generate strong emotions that result in little insight and can lead to an impoverished life condition for the person. In the latter case, the biological processing of memory linked to the dream state is in overdrive, betraying the survivor in a way similar to an autoimmune disease; that is, the mind attacks itself. Physiologic responses associated with dream content, such as the stress response, can injure the body. Replaying the negative events of the trauma story without resolution or relief can foster hopelessness and despair in the waking state.

Focusing on the critical problem-solving role of dreams allows the emergence of new therapeutic approaches. All memory phenomena, including daytime memories and dreams, are essential dimensions of the survivor's self-healing process. Healers must listen to the trauma story within the dream and sort out, if possible, what the dream is teaching. The healer is no longer passive or neglectful of the patient's dreams but a student learning from and being guided by them.

In establishing the therapeutic power of dreams, culture is an important factor. Phalla, a middle-aged Cambodian woman, had a brother who had recently died in Cambodia at only thirty-five years of age. She sent money to Cambodia for a traditional funeral ceremony at the temple, but her relatives stole the money. This became the context for a recurrent nightmare in which her dead brother appeared, emaciated. Phalla wanted to go to him, but an old man warned her to leave him alone because he was a ghost and could invade her body, making her sick. She rejected the warning, picked her brother up, and began to carry him on her back over a bridge. At this point the woman usually awoke.

When asked if her brother's soul was at rest, she explained in tears her belief that her brother would never be at peace until the monks conducted a ceremony for him. Plans were made with the patient to hold such a ceremony at the local temple as soon as possible. The next time Phalla arrived for therapy, her nightmares were gone and her depression had receded—an improvement she attributed to the ceremony.

For some victims, communication in dreams with lost and deceased relatives can be healing. In 2004 an elderly Bosnian woman in Srebrenica named Ermina lived in a house surrounded by the physical ruins and memories of three families of relatives who had been murdered, including her own husband and son. When asked how she could still live there, she said that sometimes she felt she might lose her mind from grief. But she continued, "My husband comes often in my dreams and tells me it is good I returned home to reclaim our land." These nocturnal visits from her husband, and sometimes her son, kept up her spirit and helped her to live an ordinary, mentally healthy life on a small piece of land desecrated by death.

NEGATIVE ROLES OF DREAMS

Survivors of violence vary in their natural abilities to cope with their memories and dreams. In our large-scale study of Bosnian refugees, which recorded over time their memories of more than sixty possible war-related trauma and torture events, we found that the natural course for the majority was to stop thinking about many of the events that had occurred to them. Over the three-year period between our interviews, most reported a decrease in the original number of traumatic events they had experienced, apparently by placing their traumatic memories "out of their minds."[5] Their problem-solving dream narratives may have contributed positively to this result.

Two groups in this study, however, stood out from all the other participants. The first included those who spoke during the first interview of witnessing or experiencing sexual abuse, including rape. Sexual violence during the war in Bosnia was extremely common, aimed at both men and women. However, three years later, not a single individual admitted to having had or witnessed this experience. These results suggest the powerful role of cultural factors, such as stigma, on memory recall. In this case the stigma associated with sexual abuse may have caused the affected individuals to completely lose their memories—a phenomenon possibly necessary for their survival within their families and communities.

The second group who stood out in the study included those who described having more trauma memories and related nightmares three years later. All of these individuals, small in number, had posttraumatic stress disorder (PTSD), a psychiatric illness resulting from a life-threatening traumatic event and characterized by recurrent memories and nightmares of the event; avoidance of thoughts, places, or persons that evoke the trauma; feelings of detachment and withdrawal from people; and ease of being startled or physiologically excited.[6] These refugees, in contrast to their equally traumatized counterparts, may have become obsessed with their violent experiences because of the failure of their self-healing mechanisms.

The proportion of traumatized persons whose dreams and nightmares are therapeutic to those whose are seriously disturbing and illness-causing is unknown. As a result, the healing professions have no consensus on whether traumatic memories and dreams should be clinically encouraged or suppressed because of their possible detrimental effects. Dreams are especially feared if they develop into nightmares. When nightmares are frequent, the psychiatric diagnosis of PTSD is perhaps too often used. Traumatic dreams and nightmares are so common in traumatized populations that they may not indicate an illness or disease but may actually manifest a problem-solving and self-healing process. It is likely that in only a small minority of survivors does the traumatic memory process fail its therapeutic purpose, leading to negative health and social outcomes. The diagnosis of PTSD should therefore be applied cautiously.

If the memories of disturbing experiences could be eliminated just by wishing it so, the problem of traumatic memories and dreams would vanish. But thought suppression is not easily accomplished, as shown in a study by Daniel M. Wegner and his colleagues. Two college groups were instructed to think aloud about a white bear. One group was then asked to suppress thoughts of the bear. This group subsequently reported a higher number of white bear thoughts than the other group, which had not been asked to suppress their thoughts of the bear.[7]

Many experiments have now consistently revealed that attempts at the suppression of unwanted thoughts are paradoxically responsible for the return of unwanted thoughts, often stronger than before. Because the attempted suppression of memories is generally not effective, many neuroscientists are striving to develop medications that can extinguish traumatic memories. To date, however, no medications are capable of eliminating or preventing unwanted memories.

Recent neuroimaging studies, however, have demonstrated that conscious activity in the cortex of the brain can suppress unwanted memories in the areas of the midbrain that are believed to regulate traumatic memories. Although consciously eliminating traumatic memories, especially emotional ones, is difficult, these neuroimaging studies show that there is a natural tendency for the intrusive remembering of traumatic memories but that the intensity of the associated emotional response diminishes over time.[8] The exact conditions under which individuals can suppress the unwanted awareness of past experiences is still unknown. The full range of cognitive strategies used by survivors to cope with traumatic memories and dreams is not fully understood. Strategies such as good trauma storytelling that can support, stimulate, and enhance the natural problem-solving and healing powers of memories, dreams, and nightmares must be developed, taking precedence over the pharmacologic extinction of memory.

FAILED MEMORIES

Some trauma victims nevertheless undergo vicious cycles of memories and dreams, in which unsuccessful attempts to suppress them are followed by their recurrence even stronger than before, with disturbing consequences. Those who keep their sexual abuse a secret may also quietly suffer from internal obsessions with their traumatic past. For these people, the natural healing forces of their dreams and nightmares have lost their efficacy.

This problem of "failed memories," or repetitive, harmful dreams and nightmares that do not resolve themselves over time, is illustrated by the story of the successful Laotian community leader who resettled in California with his family after escaping from Laos in 1979. Thereafter Souvanna suffered from the same nightmares for almost three decades. He linked his dreams to two major traumas in his life, which he kept relatively private, although they were not a secret from his family or fellow Laotian survivors.

The first event occurred during his imprisonment by the Laotian Communists:

> I worked for the Americans in Laos right after I graduated college. When the Communists took over Laos and the Americans left, I decided to stay inside my country. On March 18, 1977, at 3:00 P.M. I was arrested by the Communists. I was taken away in shackles and transported to a prison camp on the north Lao-Chinese border. The prison camp was hell. They took everything away from me. I was in very bad shape the first six months. I was forced to live in a small space like a pigpen with twenty-two other prisoners. They would call your name and you would have to kneel down. They wanted to punish us because we were the bad people, the enemy of the government.
>
> A lot of my fellow prisoners died. When people tried to escape they would catch them, kill them, and bring their mutilated bodies back to the prison for all of us to see. I became a walking body without a spirit.
>
> One day, twenty-one prisoners escaped. After this escape they came to take me away. I was brought to the top of the mountain where some escaped prisoners had been crucified. I saw them and they were still alive. For some reason, after my interrogation they did not kill or torture me. They brought me back to the camp.

The second trauma occurred after Souvanna was released from prison in 1979 and escaped into Thailand across the Mekong River with one of his three daughters. Shortly afterward his wife followed with the other two children. They were escaping on a small boat, which broke apart mid-river. The two children were washed away by the river's current, and their bodies were never found. During this escape attempt his wife was captured and arrested but released shortly afterward to join her husband. He describes the loss of his two daughters as a "deep scar in my heart."

Thinking about these two events, especially the prison experience, triggers this man's nightmares. When he is awake, he contemplates the events of his past without any clear focus. At night, he repetitively experiences two main dreams. In one a snake, buffalo, or elephant is attacking him in a jungle. The snake, usually a python or cobra, is big and powerful. He is very afraid of it and always tries to kill it. In the other dream, he is being chased by Communists who are shooting at him, and he just runs away.

The trauma story embedded in these dreams is readily retrievable. They are not in fact the random neurobiological firings of the brain, the so-called cleaning of the garbage of mental life. Nor do these nightmares need free association, the interpretation of hidden desires, or the suppression of shameful behaviors to clarify their meanings. And while snakes are important symbolic images in Laotian folk tales and culture, representing positive forces in nature, Souvanna does not feel the need to interpret the dream symbolically. The emotional reality of these repetitive dreams is more gripping: He is in mortal fear that somebody is trying to kill him, and he worries that through the dreams they will actually succeed.

Souvanna's waking memories combine with his nightmares into a continuous and disturbing reality. But as with many survivors, his nightmares are less frequent than when they began more than twenty-seven years ago. In the beginning they occurred every day. Now they occur weekly, sometimes even monthly.

I have noticed that these memories and dreams are less frequent. I cannot tell you how often they come because they can come at any time. They just come when they come. They are associated with strong emotions. You do not want to interact: you just want to stay inside yourself because you feel sadness. Inside you, yes, inside you the emotions easily pop up even if you are a brave man and you try to cope with them by sealing them off and not letting them out. You want to say to these emotions, just forget it. Goodbye. It is not easy.

The dreams have taken on a life of their own, living independently within the mind of this survivor and causing him emotional distress. They cannot be controlled, suppressed, or extinguished. It gives Souvanna hope that they are not as frequent or intense as before, yet when they come, they do so at a terrible price. He is afraid that the dreams, by generating such intense emotions, will actually kill him:

I have high cholesterol and I'm afraid that I will have a dream like that and I will die. When I have a dream like that, I have to wake up, walk around, or watch TV. After five or ten minutes I can go back to sleep. My wife knows I have these dreams, and sometimes she comforts me after they occur.

When Souvanna wakes from the dreams, his heart is beating fast and he is sweating. This stress response of increased blood pressure, increased heart rate, and other involuntary nervous system signs of heightened fear have for almost three decades been placing his body and mind on frequent "boil." Souvanna's nightmares do not contribute to his overall well-being. Indeed, for many refugee and other traumatized communities, the chronic distress of traumatic nightmares contributes to high levels of hypertension, cardiovascular disease, and stroke.

When I attempted to obtain some indication from Souvanna of the problem-solving or survival lessons of his dreams, nothing emerged:

> I have no clue what these dreams are teaching me. I cannot think of anything I have learned from these dreams. I do not have the answer to your question; I wish these memories and dreams will disappear. They are scary. I do not believe they are spirit dreams, as older people in my culture believe. I have tried everything without success to get rid of them. My life would be much better without these dreams.

With no salutary and healing benefits, these dreams compromise Souvanna's life and threaten his health. Neurobiology has no answer as to why these dreams are attacking the mind of the dreamer. It is unclear why this particular Laotian has developed a failed memory state, whereas many other Laotians with similar histories are able to put their traumatic images out of their minds. For him, the actual traumas and his nightmares are emotionally equivalent, each culminating in intense fear. Souvanna's mind may have generated these dreams to remind him, "You have experienced unbelievable trauma, and you have survived," but unfortunately he fears this important lesson may be simultaneously destroying his physical health. Souvanna no longer wants the dreams; he wants release from them. These are indeed failed memories that need to be extinguished.

Hope exists for Souvanna and others who suffer from traumatic dreams and nightmares. The first case studies using imagery techniques in the treatment of nightmares date back to the 1930s. Sophisticated clinical trials that use randomized control groups have demonstrated more recently that the failed repetitive nightmares of survivors can be removed and replaced with more beneficial dream content. The therapeutic approach involves sufferers learning to master their nightmares during their waking state. In effect, the nightmares are cognitively "dissected" from the survivor's mind and successfully replaced by new dreams with positive content.

In a study conducted at the University of New Mexico of rape victims who had chronic and severe nightmares for almost twenty years, the number of nightmares was dramatically reduced from approximately six to slightly more than two per week, with associated improvement in sleep. Therapists achieved these remarkable results in three sessions by teaching the rape survivors that their nightmares had become "bad" habits, causing unnecessary emotional distress and sleep loss. The survivors were coached to write down their nightmares, change the content to more beneficial images, rehearse the new dream for ten to fifteen minutes each day, and then monitor the disappearance of their nightmares over time.[9] Souvanna is an excellent candidate for this approach as he is ready to gain mastery over his dreams.

Unfortunately at this time the therapeutic approach of the New Mexico study is largely ignored by therapists caring for the survivors of mass violence. Consequently, failed memories are not systematically identified and treated. Nightmares are usually dumped into the PTSD basket and treated with psychotropic drugs that are largely ineffective against them. The nightmare remains a powerful symptom that is difficult to extinguish by current conventional approaches.

COLLECTIVE SHARING OF DREAMS

Dreams and nightmares go beyond the individual to become a social phenomenon. Investigations by W. Gordon Lawrence of the Tavistock Institute in London have revealed that dreams are extremely sensitive to their social and cultural context; that is, they are in dialogue with their social environment.[10] Dream content is related to everyday experiences. As a consequence, they can provide critical information about social functioning and cohesiveness. Unfortunately, this social mining of the dream state rarely happens. The dream in the modern world no longer has the prophetic and spiritual voice it had in ancient times and in the lives of so-called primitive peoples. The trauma story, along with its related dreams and nightmares, has no assigned social role. Just as trauma stories should be shared with society for the sake of survival and healing, so should the dreams and nightmares induced by trauma stories.

Historical recollection of traumatic events that comes to be believed by most members of a society and officially sanctioned by the government is often not based on the cumulative experiences of those who actually lived through the events. Such collective memories are usually created by the winners in order to affirm the righteousness of their cause. The Bosnians today, having recently engaged in a civil war where three distinct national groups—Croats, Serbs, and Bosnian Muslims—engaged in killing each other, tell a cynical joke about this phenomenon:

> A famous psychiatrist was visiting patients at the mental hospital with his students. He chooses one of the students to interview a patient while all observe the interview. The student asks politely, "Why are you in the hospital?" The patient answers back calmly, "Because of you. Yes, you made a decision that I am mentally ill because you are in the majority. When we, the patients, are in the majority, I will come to this hospital to make visits and ask you the same questions."

Each side of a violent conflict represses or distorts memories that negatively affect the image it wants to project of itself and its society. The group experience of humiliation may also encourage the development of social memories that promote revenge by the winners and despair in the defeated. The memories of victims might not be considered valid by the group in power. In many countries today, such as Sudan and Republika Srpska (Serb Republic), the trauma stories and dreams of affected populations are not listened to and processed in constructive social activities.

The formation of shared social memory, sometimes called collective memory, can be witnessed in Srebrenica today, a decade after the massacre of Muslim men and boys in 1995. The town and region of Srebrenica in Republika Srpska, which was originally 80 percent Bosnian Muslim, is now almost 80 percent Bosnian Serb. Bosnian Muslims, however, having fled for their lives during ethnic cleansing, are slowly returning to their villages. During a visit I took to Srebrenica, local Serb authorities could not or would not discuss with me the atrocities committed against their Bosnian Muslim neighbors. Few local Serb citizens would openly discuss what some of them called "The Crime." Some actually denied the mass killings of local Muslim people, in spite of the identification and uncovering of many mass graves. Some blamed the local Muslim people for causing the atrocities; others justified the killings by claiming the Muslim people were preparing to kill their Serb neighbors. But the majority of Serbs maintained the government's position that the mass killings had never occurred.

In contrast, the returning Muslim refugees in neighboring villages told a different story. On one occasion a few villagers joined my Bosnian Muslim colleague, Dr. Aida Kapetanovic, and me in the middle of their village—which had an unpaved road, remnants of building construction, and destroyed homes everywhere—to tell us about their current travails in trying to re-create their lives in Srebrenica. Soon the entire population of men, women, and children was gathered around, eager to describe their own situation. At the end of this discussion one elderly man pointed to two elderly women and whispered to us, though all could hear, that these women had lost their husbands and male children during the massacre. No one knew what had happened to their men, who were among the disappeared, perhaps in still undiscovered mass graves. Aida and I asked them delicately how they were coping with their losses. Quietly, they stated that they were waiting to die, since they felt nothing was left for them.

In spite of the Serbian authorities' political and public position that no massacre had occurred in Srebrenica, the reality of it emerged in our interviews. Dreams and nightmares began to enter our conversation, such as those reported by Ermina, who told us about visits from her deceased husband and son.

Our experiences in Srebrenica emphasized the need for societies to establish mechanisms — through town meetings, school discussions, and other gatherings — for the public to share the trauma story and related dreams and nightmares. The entire population in Srebrenica is thinking and dreaming of those events, in spite of a self-imposed silence, reinforced by Serb authorities. Now only religious professionals, family members, and human rights workers routinely have access to this important material. The media could play a critical role in supporting reconciliation between Serb and Bosnian by sharing, through in-depth television documentaries and newspaper stories, the traumatic history of its citizens, instead of constantly repeating the emotionally charged accusations and denials of the violent events.

The situation in Srebrenica parallels the untold trauma stories and related dreams of Native American survivors who were ethnically cleansed from their tribal lands in the nineteenth century. Reports by the invader's agents are available:

The newly arrived, impatient, disorganized, aggressive Americans did not know how to live with Indians. They streamed westward, lacerating the earth. George Bent, a half-breed son of trader William Bent, mentions emigrant trains several miles long, the huge freight wagons with white canvas tops resembling ships at sea. Indians who watched these creaking trains approach every season—growing longer and longer—could foresee the results. Cottonwood groves where they had camped for generations began to diminish. Grass in the valleys was eaten down to the ground.

With the 1849 Gold Rush came cholera. The Sioux and Cheyennes, closest to the emigrant road, suffered most, but the epidemic spread northwest to the Blackfoot, southward into Kiowa and Comanche territory. Bent visited empty villages where he saw tepees full of bodies.

In the summer of 1853 a longtime trader and Indian agent, Thomas "Broken Hand" Fitzpatrick, traveled among the Cheyennes, Arapahos, and Sioux. He wrote: "They are in abject want of food half the year, and their reliance for that scanty supply, in the rapid decrease of the buffalo, is fast disappearing...their women are pinched with want and their children constantly crying out for hunger."[11]

Outside of these accounts, few records exist of the traumas as personally experienced by Native American survivors themselves. All traumatized peoples are eventually challenged by this lack of a personal history. Sharing the trauma story is not just about our biological drive to survive the current disaster; it is also about providing our ancestry with a record of coping with and overcoming human-to-human violence. Native Americans, African Americans,

Bosnians, Cambodians, Rwandans, and all other traumatized people need to know the survival history of their own people.

The terrible consequences of not knowing this history are illustrated in the tragic killings by a Native American teenager of his grandfather, his classmates, and himself on the Red Lake reservation in Minnesota in 2005.[12] The elders who still know the old healing ceremonies are in despair because so few of their own generation are available to deal with this tragedy using properly conducted spiritual rituals. The trauma stories and dreams of the Chippewa people, with their important lessons, were lost to the current generation when these conquered people were sent away by the U.S. government to residential schools, where they were forbidden to learn their language, cultural heritage, and history of survival. Knowledge of the cultural resiliency of generations of Chippewa people, which could dramatically aid the community today, is extremely limited.

Traumatic dreams and nightmares need to be an essential part of the social sharing of personal experiences. Societies need to value this material and establish opportunities for public discussion. Most citizens are ready to participate in this experience since the capacity for sharing dreams socially exists not only in adults but also in children. Ron Balamuth, a psychoanalyst who has focused on dream-sharing exercises in children, found that preschool children as young as age five enjoy sharing socially relevant dreams with each other and their teachers when given the opportunity to do so.[13] Adults from every cultural and ethnic background are quick to participate in social dreaming groups once they have overcome the fear that their dreams will be ridiculed or ignored. Those who engage with others in the social sharing of individual dreams and nightmares find it an exciting and stimulating exchange.

The lack of public interest in personal narratives of trauma in a community can be so extreme, as in Srebrenica, that it is difficult to know where to begin to fix the situation. One essential step is to collect and archive the oral histories and dreams in all refugee and traumatized civilian populations. Otherwise, much rich historical material will be lost for the edification of future generations. This archiving of human experiences should not be left to the political will of governments but should be an automatic priority of a United Nations agency, such as the Education, Scientific, and Cultural Organization (UNESCO), or in America, the Smithsonian Institute. For example, just a few days after the catastrophic destruction of New Orleans by Hurricane Katrina in August 2005, local social scientists began to collect the survival stories of hundreds of citizens from all walks of life for archiving in the city's public libraries. New Orleans citizens were asked to provide descriptions of their traumatic experiences while the storm was still fresh in their minds. The destruction wrought by Hurricane Katrina undoubtedly represents one of the most significant catastrophes to affect the United States. The archivists in New Orleans provide a model for others to emulate in other parts of the world afflicted by violence or natural disaster.

Lack of interest in trauma narratives and dreams by medical and mental health practitioners has already led to a loss of historically valuable healing knowledge and skills. In 2004 the sharing of social dreams was introduced in the Peter C. Alderman Masterclass among clinical professionals from Afghanistan, Iraq, Chile, Cambodia, Uganda, Rwanda, Bosnia, Republika Srpska, Spain, Italy, and the United States. The aim of this exercise, led by the Italian psychoanalyst Franco Paparo, was to use the group's dreams to help them form an international network of technical and emotional support. Each day the participants reviewed their dreams and discussed their relevance to the mission of the Masterclass.

The primary dreams to emerge were of the group members' fears of not being supported by and of being alienated from each other, their colleagues, and their patients. One psychiatrist from Madrid, Mar, who at the time was treating people injured in the Madrid terrorist railroad bombings of March 2004, shared a potent dream:

> In the first scene I am with a childhood friend, who I remember with fondness for being very noble. We are walking on a narrow path between a cliff and a mountain filled with trees. We are walking calmly, enjoying each other's company, and we hear someone cutting down the trees (we do not see him). All of a sudden the trunk of one of the trees falls, hits my friend in the head, and she falls off the cliff.
>
> In the next scene I am seated at a table with a phone; I am crying because I have to talk to my friend's family to tell them what has happened, but I am unable to. Then I see Mevludin and Yosef [doctors in the group from Bosnia and Iraq, respectively], who come to me and encourage me to talk to her family. At this moment I wake up.

The group resonated to the issues revealed in this dream. As Mar said, "When someone suffers violence [the childhood friend], it tears them up inside, creates a deep wound. It leaves them without the foundations of life [trees without their roots]." In the second half of the dream, when she is unable to tell her friend's family about the loss of their daughter, she cries because of her inability to communicate her own profound grief for the loss of her friend. The group mentioned the silent tears they too shed when they hear the trauma stories of their patients. They felt that perhaps they could be more effective in sharing and relieving the pain of their patients and families, and that the Masterclass could help them do so.

The dream ends on a hopeful note as two group members, Mevludin and Yosef, come to Mar's aid, comforting her and encouraging her to speak to the family. According to Mar, her dream is saying that the group was taking many risks as it entered into the lives of violated patients, and that its members would have to courageously confront the many threats that make innocent people suffer. Yet the dream is also optimistic, for through the sharing of fears and problems the group can overcome these threats.

CONNECTING THE INNER AND OUTER WORLD

The dream in traumatized people is a significant biological, psychological, and social event. It is not surprising that human beings, who spend so much time asleep, would evolve a seamless process of problem solving between the waking and sleeping states. When dangerous situations occur, the dream appears, ready to help us get out of trouble by limiting physical and mental damage. Enough is now known about the therapeutic value of dreams that they need to be actively employed in healing after trauma. No longer can their content and associated emotions be neglected or discarded.

It has also become apparent that dreams affected by trauma can become dangerous over long periods of time. It is as if an electric heater keeps trying to warm up a house but because the thermostat is broken, the heater does not turn off and eventually breaks down. Similarly good dreams can turn into nightmares that can plague a traumatized person for years with insomnia, fatigue, and other chronic health problems. Bad dreams and especially nightmares need to be extinguished once their therapeutic impact is over. Fortunately simple and inexpensive techniques exist that are effective in eliminating traumatic nightmares without the use of medication. Knowledge and training in the use of these techniques must be widely disseminated to traumatized persons and their helpers. No one who has experienced domestic or sexual violence or any other violent act needs to suffer from bad dreams or nightmares.

The discovery of the social relevance of dreams and their potential contributions to society bridges the inner life of traumatized persons and their social world. If large numbers of people contributed their dream input in public group discussions in places such as Bosnia, the regions of Asia impacted by the tsunami of 2004, and the hurricane-devastated areas of the American South, the positive social impact would be great. This sort of social dreaming experiment has never been attempted on a large scale, although it has been done with hundreds of people in Italy and across western Europe on the topic of European unification. Social dreaming has great relevance for communities traumatized by ethnic and political conflict as well as those affected by criminal acts and economic hardships. The psychological reality of traumatized people manifested by their dreams displays an inner world striving for wholeness, normalcy, and health. Socially beneficial practices such as altruism, work, and spirituality are extensions of the dreaming process to the next level of self-healing, that of active engagement with the social world. Extending outward from the inner world of the dream to the outer world of social activities benefits the mind and body. The inner experiences of a traumatized person and their social behaviors are intimately connected in the phenomenon of self-healing.

Chapter 7

SOCIAL INSTRUMENTS
OF HEALING

HEALING BEGINS WITH A CHOICE. Survivors of extreme violence must decide which reality to live in—their old, broken world or a new one. Day by day and hour by hour, violence challenges people to use their traumatic experiences to build new lives and to focus on the present instead of the past. The French Postimpressionist artist Paul Cezanne captures the importance of the here and now when he advises artists:

> Right now a moment of time is fleeting by! Capture its reality in paint! To do this we must put all else out of our minds. We must become that moment, make ourselves a sensitive recording plate...give the image of what we actually see, forgetting everything that has been before our time.[1]

This quote is also fitting advice for survivors, because the act of healing is a form of artistry. Through their traumatic experiences survivors become, most unwillingly, "sensitive recording plates."

Traumatic moments become engraved in their minds, and these images can overwhelm them. In the depth of their anguish, survivors cannot see that they still have a choice in how to live their lives. They can remain locked in a world of horrendous images and unbearable feelings, or they can create something entirely new in their lives, which will be a source of strength and vitality.

Cezanne's observation does not explain the process by which artists are able to forget "everything that has been before our time." For survivors, this process begins with a decision that takes an exceptional degree of courage. In our modern world, the word *courage* conjures up images of bold, aggressive action in the face of a life-threatening situation. But the courage required to go on living after a horrific past is different: It is a mental attitude, which is usually invisible to others. People who have experienced extreme violence, whether rape, torture, or the murder of a parent or child, often have to decide not only to live in a certain way but also whether to live at all. Ordinary life traumas, although not as severe, can involve this choice as well. It takes courage not to give in to despair. The opposite of despair is hope, and to hope is to imagine and desire again the very things in life that were cherished and destroyed.

Survivors and their therapists often take for granted that this fundamental decision to live is made daily. The choice to go on is needed to begin, as well as continue, the process of healing. Self-healing cannot function and complete its rehabilitation unless there is a continual, active affirmation of life. But health professionals are afraid to discuss this decision openly with the survivor, since many would not know what to do if the patient articulated feelings of hopelessness and the wish to die. Healers need to be wary of absorbing the survivor's pessimism, thereby becoming unsure of their ability to assist the patient.

At a meditation offered by the Vietnamese Buddhist monk Thich Nhat Hanh, who as a young man four decades earlier had resisted the Vietnam War, this Buddhist sutra was read:

> A man dying of thirst is walking along a dusty road and he eventually comes to a crossroads. Miraculously, he notices on the road a few drops of water left by a water buffalo that had just passed by. Seeing the drops, he falls to his knees and puts his lips to the earth in order to suck up the drops. After finishing this act, he tries to determine where the water buffalo came from. Not knowing, he chooses one of the forks in the road to follow.

Imagine this thirsty man kneeling down to put his lips to the road to take in a few drops of water. We do not know if he died of thirst or not, yet at this moment he saw reality clearly, tasted the water, and tried to follow the water buffalo. Certainly those few drops did not quench his thirst, but they represented the hope that a life-giving source was up ahead. All therapists have the privilege of witnessing this act of courage in traumatized persons.

A Rwandan woman who survived the mass killings in her country, in which her parents, husband, and six of her seven children were all murdered, was trying to escape with her small son to a refugee camp when she came across a gang of men who demanded her child. Out of fear for her boy's life, she gave him up, and the gang took him away. As the men were walking off, her boy cried out to her, "Mommy, Mommy, please don't let these bad men take me away with them." After she arrived safely in the refugee camp, she looked for her son but could never find him. Over the next few years the sound of his pleas for help never left her mind. She heard them over and over again, every day. Finally she committed suicide.

Although this woman lost many family members during the initial months of the Rwandan genocide, she still had the hope of saving her little boy. This child was the most precious thing that remained in her life. When she was forced to give him away her heart was finally broken. She felt responsible for committing the act that destroyed her son.

A Macedonian farmer also went into a permanent state of despair after his village was attacked as the conflict in Kosovo spread into Macedonia. The farmer and his twenty-four-year-old son had talked about taking the family away to a safe area protected by the Macedonian army, but the son encouraged the father to take his pregnant wife and his mother to safety, while he stayed behind to join the local militia and protect the family's farmhouse and cattle. Shortly thereafter, Albanian fighters invaded the town and killed the young man. The father, who was living safely with his family in a refugee camp, became overwhelmed with grief upon hearing of his son's death. He became withdrawn and isolated, refusing to participate in the birth of his son's child. Although he was still head of the family, he gave up on life, feeling ashamed and guilty that he had not stayed behind to protect the family property. He had similar feelings to the Rwandan woman: that an act of cowardice on his part had led to the boy's death. Each of these parents felt that they had not chosen to make the supreme sacrifice of giving up their lives in order to save the lives of their children. Both decided that they would not try to overcome their tragic decisions, and would not strive to create a new life.

A Cambodian woman made the opposite decision in order to survive the personal crisis brought on by the murder of her husband by the Khmer Rouge:

> My pains were lessened. When I recite the Dharma, I reflect according to Buddha's principles. There is death. When there is life, there is bound to be separation. When

I reason this way, I try not to be too sorrowful. I do this when I am sorrowful, and my face is very sad. Happiness is the counterpart of sorrow, and laughter is the counterpart of crying. When I think about this precept, I feel better. This way, I think that those who died escaped the sorrow temporarily. Those who are alive always have sorrows.... The old folks would come to me and tell me that my children had no father and I should not make them orphans again by not having a mother. I was reasoning about this for a long time, and I felt better, but in the back of my mind I still had some sorrows. Not all of the sorrows were gone. I thought about my children, about their future. They were born, they saw the sunlight, I would not abandon them. The father had died, so the mother should remain.

The Rwandan woman and the Macedonian man were not able to summon the courage needed to suck up the drops of water and find the water buffalo. They were unable to say yes to life and affirm their own existence. The Cambodian woman, on the other hand, was able to decide to keep living. There is no equation establishing a hierarchy of pain by which it can be concluded that the loss of a child is worse than that of a parent or spouse. There is no formula for predicting who will be able to act courageously in their efforts to recover from violence.

Sometimes self-healing is buried so deep within a person's hopelessness and despair that it is impossible for the trauma sufferer to feel its existence. Yet nothing can eliminate the self-healing force. Another person, such as a family member, friend, therapist, or any caring person, can tap into this intrinsic vitality and direct the person to a rediscovery and embrace of life. The Rwandan woman did not connect with such a person; the Macedonian farmer was surrounded by his family, including his new grandson, but he wasn't able to stimulate his commitment to life. The Cambodian woman responded to the loving attention of the "old folks," who shared with her their wisdom and a rationale for overcoming sorrow.

COOPERATION AND SYMBIOSIS

When survivors find the courage to give the nod to life—to agree to live through another day, to interact with the world—they open themselves up to the power of social relationships. This affirmative act is similar to the spark that ignites an ordinary pile of wood and turns it into a conflagration. In all traumatized persons the power of self-healing is ready to break through its inner biological foundations and expand into the world around it. However, it has taken modern society and modern medicine an extraordinarily long time to acknowledge the healing power of social relationships.

For more than a hundred years Western thought has emphasized social Darwinism, based upon the theory of evolution put forward by Charles Darwin and summed up by Herbert Spencer as "survival of the fittest."[2] This theory highlights the tendency of human beings to compete with each other in order to gain power and thus ensure greater human adaptation, reproduction, and survival. Raymond Dart, a physical anthropologist of the 1950s, described this version of human aggression in a way that anticipates the cannibalistic killings in Uganda, the savage massacres in Rwanda, and the brutal executions in Srebrenica:

> The blood-bespattered, slaughter-gutted archives of human history from the earliest Egyptian and Sumerian records to the most recent atrocities of the Second World War accord with early universal cannibalism, with animal and human sacrificial practices or their substitutes in formalized religions and with the world-wide scalping, head-hunting, body-mutilating and necrophiliac prac-

tices of mankind in proclaiming this common blood lust differentiator, this mark of Cain that separates man dialectically from his anthropoidal relatives and allies him rather with the deadliest of Carnivora.[3]

Momir Nikolic, a former Bosnian Serbian intelligence chief, testified at The Hague in 2003 that for two days after Bosnian Serbs had overrun the Muslim enclave of Srebrenica, most of the captured male civilians were being held by soldiers, police officers, and armed guards in schools, a warehouse, an airplane hangar, and a gym as well as piled into buses and trucks around the town. But on the third night eighty to a hundred prisoners were removed from confinement and shot. The mass executions continued for four days, and the bodies were dumped into secret graves.[4]

From an evolutionary point of view, this kind of human violence can hardly be seen as adaptive. The phrase "survival of the fittest," which is sometimes used to rationalize brutal acts, condemns the victim as the weaker and therefore less valuable side of the human equation, while at the same time ignoring the healing power of social activity.

In recent years evolutionary biology has emphasized a long-neglected element of Darwin's theory, the notion of cooperation and symbiosis. From bacteria to primates, a complex web of interconnectedness ties living organisms together, promoting the survival of *all* species. A wonderful example of interspecies cooperation comes from a colony of South American ants. These ants cut bits of leaves from nearby vegetation and chew them into a pulp, which they then use to fertilize their underground mushroom fungus gardens. In exchange, the fungus produces "fruits," called *gongylidia,* that the ants keenly devour. The ants prepare for any attack on their fungus by another by growing an antibiotic bacteria on their bodies to kill the unwanted fungus. This complex system of interrelationships provides maximum benefit to the ant colony.[5]

Primate studies affirm the importance of society in evolutionary survival. Primatologist Alison Jolly concludes that social relationships are the only evolutionary pressure that can accelerate biological change within a species. Humans reveal the extraordinary capacity to work together in order to produce results that no single individual could produce alone. By cooperating with your friends and allies, you and your genetic line will benefit in the end. Jolly states that the basic principle is: "To profit yourself, think first of others; betray when there is no other alternative."[6] Studies based upon experimental games that simulate real-life situations also reveal the advantages of cooperation in times of adversity. Individual aggression might be more readily rewarded, but the more difficult and less secure route of partnership is necessary to maximize outcomes.

The most telling evidence of the power of social cooperation comes from those who have experienced extreme violence. Despite the material destruction around them and their own physical exhaustion, after a human catastrophe or natural disaster survivors often reach out to help others, as witnessed in the South Asian tsunami disaster of 2004. They do not wait passively for assistance. The outpouring of human caring and cooperation begins to reverse the damage caused by mass violence. This response was also seen after September 11. In their attacks, the terrorists' goal was to cause mass social chaos, but New Yorkers and Americans everywhere pulled together to help one another. Stories of heroism and personal sacrifice, recounted daily in newspapers and on television, made all citizens aware of their interconnectedness.

SOCIAL ASPECTS OF HEALING

Social activities are key instruments of self-healing because they provide methods and tools for mediated recovery from trauma. Three social activities—altruism, work, and spirituality—have been scientifically demonstrated to have a restorative impact on traumatized persons. They act as catalysts in reducing the negative health consequences of an overactive stress response, stimulate biological repair, assist in the construction of positive post-trauma attitudes and beliefs, and shift the survivor from isolation to engagement. These behaviors may also serve as the primary evolutionary social forces enhancing human survival.

ALTRUISM

Principal among these is altruism, the practice of unselfish concern for the welfare of others, which is often associated with the concept of charity. Altruism is a special kind of mutual cooperation in social relationships, since it is active and is not contingent upon the response of the recipient. While it is generally hoped that those who benefit from altruistic acts will appreciate them, this response is not necessary. Altruism as a behavior enhances the healing of traumatized persons, because everyone has someone who needs them and can profit from their help, no matter how difficult their own situation.

But altruism is often misused in the healing process, as relief workers force their help on traumatized persons, creating dependent relationships rather than giving survivors the tools to care for themselves. Some international efforts are well-meaning but superficial and consequently do more damage than good. Jusuf, a young Muslim man working on a cheese-development project in Srebrenica in 2004 for an American company, touched upon this phenomenon:

I try to introduce a modern cheese-production approach in Srebrenica but it is hard. They do not want to give up their traditional cheese-making technology. The problem is that donors and others who try to help the people do not stay here. They come for a short time. They bring compliments, cheap houses, and tools and leave as soon as they can. They hardly can wait to leave.

This story of helpers invading a victimized community and then leaving after a short time resonates in refugee camps and other traumatized populations throughout the world. Helpers sometimes preempt self-healing by foisting their own caregiving and care-receiving requirements on others, often focusing on useful but minor aids to people trying to establish a new life-world out of the ashes of the old one. These helpers usually do not have sufficient knowledge of the natural healing processes of the local community. Because of their alienation from the psychological and cultural forces of the people, they "hardly can wait to leave." The rescue effort in New York City after the September 11 attacks exhibited a similar invasion of relief workers, particularly mental health workers.[7]

Although altruism is rarely viewed through the eyes of the survivor, such reaching out by the victim can aid considerably in self-healing. Even when people have few material possessions to share, many find a way. There are many stories of parents in concentration camps who shared their last morsel of food with other family members, especially grandparents and kids. During an illness of mine, a female Cambodia colleague offered a blessing for me by putting in water a few drops of the perfume her husband had given her just before his execution.

In an environment of extreme violence, where the perpetrators aim to destroy social coherence and trust, the survivors have to reclaim their ability to help others. Traumatized persons sometimes lose confidence in their ability to care for their children, teachers lose confidence in educating their students, and health practitioners lose confidence in caring for their patients. Yet the damaged person in all of these situations still has something positive to give to others; by helping someone else in a nonselfish way, the survivor engages in self-healing. Altruistic behavior is a form of mirroring: I find in you my pain and joy, and you find in me your pain and joy. This is fundamentally an emotional sharing, not only with one another but also with the wider community.

Altruistic actions by refugees and other traumatized persons can form the foundation on which to build their new lives. Almost all survivors have at least one altruistic story that has been forgotten or buried within their tragic life histories. With the rediscovery and public sharing of these lost tales, new lessons emerge. However, since altruism involves risk-taking and sacrifice, such stories are filled with hesitation and fear, dangerous situations, and unforeseen, sometimes bad results.

Sothea, a thirty-year-old refugee in Site 2, was working as a teacher when he joined our mental health training in the spring of 1990. His parents, also teachers, had not survived the Khmer Rouge. Sothea had many altruistic tales to tell, one of which illustrated that altruism has a price to be paid:

> I worked at the military hospital for a year, during which time I witnessed many events that were frightening. I am going to talk about one account which broke my heart. It was a time when some people were taken away to be killed. I had talked to five people before they were taken away to be killed. These people did not say anything at all and just shook their heads. They seemed to have lost their senses. Their faces were dark, their eyes were pale,

and their eyes fixed on us without blinking, as though they wanted to tell us something. I am not able to forget their bodies and their faces, which I see in my mind whenever I cannot sleep.

Sothea risked his own mental health by extending himself to others. In aiding those who were going to be killed, he gave up forever a clear mind and sound sleep. Though he could not save them, he committed an altruistic act, common to survivors, healers, and relief workers, of incorporating their traumatic suffering into his own consciousness and, in the process, remembering and honoring them.

In spite of his good deeds, Sothea seriously questioned whether helping others had brought him any material advantage—or done any good at all. He told us that through his teaching he had saved thousands of children from illiteracy, yet, "I did this for many years, and it didn't seem to help me because I can't even afford a bicycle." Sothea's doubts about the wisdom of aiding children moved quickly into an account of risking his life to save four small children from drowning. "I jumped into the reservoir with my boots and all to save them. The danger was nearly fatal to me." When he pulled the children out, two were unconscious, but eventually all made a full recovery. He realized his own good fortune in performing this dangerous rescue: "I am very lucky, because I was able to save four people at one time. According to Buddha, this action gives one more merit than holding religious ceremonies in a hundred temples."

There exists no sure pathway from altruistic acts to positive personal and material benefits. In fact, every altruistic action holds within itself the possibility of risk; it might take something away, even a life. Although Sothea questions the lack of material benefit from teaching, he cannot refrain from describing his risking death in order to save the drowning kids, which leads him to a revelation: Instead of money and power, his altruistic acts have gained him great spiritual benefit. This is part of his recovery from the damage caused by the Pol Pot regime.

Barnabas, a thirty-two-year-old refugee and teacher's aide at Site 2, revealed a brighter view of altruism. He came from a farm family and had the equivalent of a high school education. While he was trying to escape the Khmer Rouge, Barnabas traveled to the borderland between Thailand and Cambodia, a lawless area overrun by bandits and smugglers of all sorts. While he was there, he met a man whose experiences had made him suicidal:

> Among those smugglers there was a man who borrowed gold and silver from his relatives to make a living like everybody else. Unfortunately for him he was robbed by bandits along the way. After losing all of his belongings, his composure weakened. It seemed as if he was forgetful. He was suspended in time. He was very frightened and shocked. If he were to go back home, he would have nothing to pay his debts. On the other hand, if he continued his journey to the border, he would not have any money to start a trade. He was delirious; he could not think of anything at all. All he saw was a state of blackness as a barrier in front of him.

Barnabas tried to talk sensitively to the man:

> Because I was quite suspicious of him, I then walked toward him and asked him some questions. He related his story to me in a choking manner with a saddened face. At the end he told me he did not want to live. After telling me this, he took leave of me. Seeing the state of being he was in, I felt great compassion for him. I asked him to stay. I talked to him in order to straighten his state of mind, to make it normal as before. I did this by explaining about the sufferings and dangers of each human being.

In spite of the burden, Barnabas invited the man to come with him into Thailand; he was "very happy that he helped save a person from death." Over time they became friends. Barnabas had the natural therapeutic skill of empathic listening, which led him to understand the plight of the suicidal stranger. Though Barnabas's altruistic act appeared easy for him because of his gift for interpersonal relationships, it hid a serious risk taking on his part.

In this story, as in all altruistic tasks, no good can result unless someone is willing to give something important to someone else. This experience reverses the usual feelings of humiliation spawned by violence. The "powerless" and "unworthy" survivor, no matter how deep his or her humiliation, is able to share something, even if it seems small, with another. Through this sharing, the survivor has a powerful, positive impact on someone else's life. According to a legend based upon eyewitness reports, a very old woman mysteriously appeared at St. Paul's Chapel next to Ground Zero and offered to give up her cane to the exhausted rescue and construction workers resting in the aisles. As in Sothea's and Barnabas's stories, the essence of altruism is here: I heal you and, by doing so, heal myself. Those who engage in altruism, whether they realize it or not, are on the road to self-healing.

Work

Work, work, work—this is the single most important goal of traumatized people throughout the world. Since the beginning of time men and women have done many of the same basic tasks: they form unions, have children, and support themselves and their families by farming, trading, fishing, buying, selling, and creating useful and beautiful things. From refugee camps in Thailand and Kenya to detention centers in Australia and Europe, and from the thatched houses of displaced persons in Sudan to the tenements full of refugee newcomers in the South Bronx, there lives the survivor's drive to work and provide for himself, an incredible healing force. A month after a Thai fishing village lost half of its five thousand inhabitants to the tsunami, fishermen returned to sea. The description of their efforts invokes the metaphor of self-healing:

> The groups of fisherman who have banded together here are like the sutures of a slowly healing wound. A fistful of flesh has been ripped out of their community and they are knitting together what remains.[8]

Work is many things to the person emerging from a traumatic experience. At its most basic it is a means of survival, keeping the person alive from day to day. It is also a psychological life raft, assuring the survivor that he or she is not completely helpless, that not all is lost.

When the power of self-healing ignites the survivor, it generates an intense desire to work. An Iraqi refugee who had been an ally of the Americans and participated in the futile rebellion against Saddam Hussein's regime in the first Gulf War was admitted to the United States by the State Department; he wandered homeless from state to state, because he could not get a job due to his "suspicious" immigration status. When he arrived in Maine, he was admitted to the mental hospital by the police, to whom his story sounded delusional. To them, he appeared to be seriously mentally ill. A Maine immigration officer was called to verify his alien status. Upon meeting this officer, the man stated, "Please help me; I need a job." When his tragic history was verified, he was soon provided with employment, and he no longer showed signs of mental illness.

Another story depicts a traumatized person who was able to break out of his own social dependency. A middle-aged Cambodian man whose family survived the Pol Pot regime was living on welfare in a violent American ghetto. Every night he locked himself in his apartment's small bathroom and worked on memorizing an auto repair book cover to cover. After a year of studying the book, he began fixing the cars of friends and neighbors, most of them non-Cambodians. His reputation as a wizard car mechanic grew. The local teens who used to threaten him now sought his advice on car repairs. Eventually he took up a full-time job as a car mechanic in a local gas station and stopped receiving welfare.

The word *work* refers not just to conventional forms of employment but to any activity that enhances the material well-being of a person, family, or community. Fishing, hunting, and tending a garden along with the great variety of domestic tasks, like caring for children or grandchildren, are all forms of work. Little is known about the healing power of work; research is almost nonexistent. In the 1990s, from interviews with thousands of refugees, it became apparent that traumatized people of all ages and cultural backgrounds were extremely resilient when they were involved in work. It did not matter what they did; if the activity helped them with their daily survival, it had tremendous healing power. For people threatened by violence, work becomes the anchor that holds them steady within their old world as a new one is being formed. During the time of healing after violence, work is the compass that shows the survivor the direction he or she must take to get out of a psychological dead end. Work not only gives survivors an opportunity to earn money and be productive, but also a concrete time and place where they must show up, a familiar cast of friends, including the farm animals and industrial machines, and an overall sense of purpose and value. Work provides an environment for camaraderie and friendship. It also allows survivors the opportunity to leave their traumatized thoughts behind them, at least temporarily, as they focus on their jobs. Through work the survivor uses old skills and learns new ones, and in the process repairs a shattered life brick by brick.

Work is a complex factor in the emotional healing of humiliation. It can certainly act as a balm to humiliation by increasing respect within the family and community to all who are earning a living. But humiliation can also increase after the violence has ended through joblessness and enforced dependency. The father who cannot provide for his family and the mother who cannot care for her children are humiliated in the eyes of their children, their neighbors, and themselves. The father can quickly feel castrated and impotent; in turn, his children, especially teens, lose respect for him. Many refugee children report that their fathers are nothing, worthless, because they do not work. Refugee women may be spared this judgment by their kids, but like their children, they also can become enraged at a husband who cannot support the family.

In spite of the many reasons that survivors need to work, the political systems they encounter universally try to force them into dependency and sustained unemployment. It is easier and cheaper to keep people idle and jobless. Survivors know this and do their best to remain self-sufficient. In order to become independent, they often must trick the system that aims to help them. Humanitarian aid workers, for example, are puzzled when the very people they try to help steal from them or show no appreciation for their efforts. When healers and politicians frustrate the survivors' autonomy, the survivors come to believe that the rhetoric and actions of their helpers are dishonest. Survivors then adopt the strategy of publicly playing the helpless role while clandestinely carrying on activities that foster their own economic interests.

While in Bosnia, we visited a small village that was widely known to be desperate. Almost every family had lost someone during the recent war. The factory was idle; there was no employment. The villagers barely survived on their local agriculture, and no future industry was in sight. An important opportunity had been lost by the international development community immediately after the Dayton Peace Accords in 1995, when local citizens were pumped up with energy to construct their new lives. In Somalia, Sudan, Rwanda, East Timor, countries affected by the tsunami, and the hurricane-devastated areas of the American South, traumatized people similarly cannot wait five years for a new job. They need to work now.

At Site 2 during the 1980s, Cambodian survivors of Pol Pot were not allowed to garden, farm, or hold jobs. For more than a decade the UN and international relief community supported this policy, giving Cambodian refugees only food handouts of Japanese rice and fish while depriving them of the real means of recovery such as schools, jobs, and opportunities for religious or social events. The Thais called this policy of keeping people at a minimum level of existence *humane deterrence.* Today many refugee camps in Africa and Asia follow the same principle. Some countries of first asylum routinely treat refugees in an ungenerous and cruel fashion. Asylum seekers in Australia, many of whom have been tortured in their homelands, are incarcerated in remote prison camps under brutal conditions in spite of their trauma and the fact that they have committed no crime, as a warning to others to stay out of Australia.

The European process also denies work to traumatized people seeking asylum. Sweden has one of the most progressive asylum policies in the world, offering asylum seekers extensive financial and social support. In spite of these excellent housing and social benefits, asylum seekers in Sweden cannot seek employment until they are fluent in Swedish. Once they achieve this almost impossible language threshold, few jobs are available. Rates of depression among asylum seekers in Sweden are as high as 40 percent.[9]

In America, the integration process for millions of refugees is an initial period of support followed by a sink-or-swim entry into the job market. Refugees have great potential for economic success as well as considerable opportunity for failure. The medical and welfare systems in the States are big factors in many refugees' failure. For being medically and psychologically disabled from depression and posttraumatic stress disorder, the refugee is put on welfare, less than adequate in most situations. Few refugees return to work once on Supplemental Security Income (SSI), because no job-training opportunities exist and the medical system has no linkage to the job market. In fact, the welfare system encourages refugees to remain disabled; otherwise they will lose their benefits. The social message to the refugee is "Why work? If you can maintain a minimal standard of living on SSI, it is best to stay sick." While most refugees do not buy into this model, for those who are on SSI, transition into the workforce becomes impossible, because they are provided with a negative incentive to work. Globally and in America, one of the most neglected aspects of the response to violence is the urgent need to provide traumatized persons with jobs.

SPIRITUALITY

Alleviating human suffering is at the center of medical and psychiatric healing. Unfortunately no medication can heal the psychological and social damage that occurs to survivors of violence. These victims often experience pain as they never have before. This can happen as readily to a victim of domestic violence as to a torture survivor. The very essence of the *Philoctetes* story is that the wounded hero, having been harmed by the gods, lives in a strange land where terror and suffering become routine parts of life. Therefore traumatized people often seek help from divine authorities.

Survivors from different parts of the world, for example, tell strikingly similar stories of the role played by the sun and stars in their survival. Looking up at the heavens, they saw something that was eternally unaffected by human actions. The stars helped keep them alive while they were being tortured in reeducation camps or prison cells. Every morning the sunrise reminded them that they had survived another day. The constellations, fixed in nature, represented for them the permanence of life itself, a force that could not be dimmed by human cruelty. Following the movement of the stars, survivors could detach themselves, if only briefly, from their harsh reality on Earth.

As survivors look into their own minds, they often find a similar fixed set of beliefs and values. They take comfort in the aid of their god, whether Buddha, Allah, Yahweh, or Christ. Divine beings, including animist spirits, protect and assist survivors during their moments of greatest need. When the traumatized inner self is thrown into chaos by violence, spirituality can prevent a total disintegration of the person. Many survivors find within themselves the supportive spirit of a mother or father; some survive for their children. Others draw strength from their political beliefs and their commitment to social justice. Their own minds provide them with a place that they can enter at will at any time, whether locked in a prison cell or trapped in a refugee camp. Seneca, an ancient philosopher, observed what most survivors know firsthand: "Only within the inner self, not by changing the external world, can true peace be found."[10]

The healing powers of spiritual activities have undergone scientific examination. Both biological research and clinical experience confirm that unhealthy body changes associated with negative life experiences can be brought under control by spiritual and humanistic practices such as prayer, meditation, religious rituals, and groups that focus on self-care.[11] When our morals and values are shattered by violence, strong beliefs can halt our decline into disillusionment, anger, and despair. This phenomenon, well-documented in POWs, torture survivors, and refugees, is epitomized by Nelson Mandela, the first black president of South Africa. After his release from twenty-seven years of abusive imprisonment under the apartheid regime, he sought reconciliation instead of revenge. Under the South African Truth and Reconciliation Commission thousands of victims revealed similar extraordinary levels of resiliency as a result of their strong spiritual and political orientation.[12]

Unfortunately survivors are not often taught how to deal with their overwhelming emotions; as a result, they become lost in a storm of negative feelings. A father whose son, a soldier, has recently been killed in Iraq cannot bear the feelings of pain and grief he experiences when he sees pictures of his son as a small child; a mother, two years after September 11, still cries whenever she mentions her dead son's name; a Cambodian man sits in anguish twenty-five years later when he remembers his failure to bring medicine to his dying child in a neighboring Khmer Rouge camp.

But when self-healing expresses itself through spiritual actions, thoughts and emotions do not run wild. The emotions are contained by concrete rituals and practices, which give survivors a specific time and place where feelings can be expressed and understood. Participation in spiritual practices requires the discipline to control one's feelings and the commitment to make sense out of them.

Spiritual practices can be small private events. Just as the nature of human violence seems incomprehensible, so too does the cure, unless it is broken up into meaningful pieces. As in the Buddhist allegory of the thirsty man who bent over reverently to touch his lips to the drops of water on the earth, small daily rituals, including prayer, meditation, keeping a diary, and cultivating a general appreciation of life itself, can produce powerful therapeutic results over time.

In 2000, when East Timor was struggling for its independence from Indonesia, the departing Indonesian rulers and their local helpers did everything they could to demolish what they left behind, including the nursing school. The home of the dean of the school was a wreck. Yet one night, as his wife and children looked on, the dean held a dinner party for an Australian colleague and me. We were served a modest meal, which was probably the family's only food for the week. The sole piece of furniture in the living room, besides chairs, was a huge wooden armoire containing a statue of the Virgin Mary. When asked why she had not also been destroyed after everyone fled, the East Timorese smiled and looked at each other. The dean's little daughter giggled, as he explained, "When we fled into the hills to survive the massacre, five of us carried the armoire and the Virgin into the woods. The Virgin lived with us in hiding the whole time. She protected us. How could we leave her behind to be defiled by the destroyers? She is our mother." These survivors knew that their well-being depended upon preserving their spiritual world.

Violence can forge new relationships between survivors and their sources of spiritual sustenance, and conventional religious institutions are challenged to adjust to these shifts. Mainstream religious institutions in Bosnia, Cambodia, Rwanda, and East Timor have gone through enormous changes after recent periods of conflict. In Cambodia, in spite of almost total destruction of all religious institutions during the Pol Pot period, country people rebuilt their Buddhist temples even before reestablishing their own homes. Muslim and Catholic religious traditions are once again flourishing, respectively, in Bosnia, a former secular Communist state, and East Timor. Practitioners of animistic and traditional healing in Rwanda and East Timor are modifying their local and ancient customs to adjust to the high levels of violence. In Rwanda, for example, the *gacaca,* or local tribal and village justice, is being used to judge, punish, and reintegrate into the local community those who organized the murder and sexual torture during the genocide. Traditional values of forgiveness in the *gacaca* courts emphasize community service as a punishment in order to foster reconciliation.

In contrast to the value of spirituality at the individual and community level, the therapeutic power of conventional religious institutions in post-conflict societies is questionable. In some countries, such as El Salvador, the Catholic Church protected the people from violence, whereas in others, such as Rwanda, Catholic churches were allegedly places of mass murder, with the clergy participating in the atrocities. Islamist terrorism that may be fulminated by governments and religious institutions is generating considerable criticism as to the violent nature of organized religion. Many religions of all types have been stained by their role in mass violence, either through active participation, tacit consent, or failure to assist in the recovery.

In most societies, institutional religious structures have difficulty helping women who have been sexually violated, both because of theological limits on women's role in the religion and because of conservative views on women's sexuality and sexual purity. For almost two decades Cambodian Buddhist monks at the highest level of the hierarchy have been asked to administer special cleansing rituals to Cambodian women who have been raped or sexually tortured, but this request has not met with success. Within Buddhism, women are traditionally considered unclean. They are not allowed to touch monks. Thus a special purification ceremony would run counter to Buddhist theology.

Similar beliefs about female cleanliness exist in Islam. In Bosnia, however, Derviš Ahmed Nuruddin, a highly regarded ninety-year-old cleric who was a judge in the law of Shariah — the Islamic law based upon the Qur'an and the traditions of the prophet Muhammad — issued a decree that Bosnian Muslim women who had been sexually abused should be given the status of martyrs. In his fatwa he declared that as a human being and as a scholar, he needed to implement the truth and return these women to their rightful place within society:

> Is there anyone who can say these women are guilty and sinful because of what they have been through? Thus they can be guilty for some other reason but for this event — no way. Therefore, no one should talk about them in this manner.

> We Muslims, and especially their closest, should accept them as heroines, as martyrs, and support them both morally and materially.

> We recommend especially to men, husbands of women who have experienced this tragedy, to be sufficiently strong and to embrace their wives, both in literal and figurative sense of the word. Thus they will show that they really sympathize with their wives' pain and they are willing to make it easier for them to endure.

The healing of Bosnian women thus found expression through a wise old cleric. This is not always the case, however. Ordinarily the traumatized person is challenged to establish a more direct line to God without the help of religious institutions or clergy.

The therapeutic power of spirituality is a sensitive topic for modern medical and psychiatric practitioners, who generally do not believe that divine beings enter into the healing process.[13] The medical and psychiatric attitude toward the healing power of spirituality leans more to the side of skepticism and passive neglect. Although the medical profession deals with mortality on a daily basis, many doctors seem unable to address the spiritual issues of patients. In spite of the hard scientific data demonstrating the efficacy of prayer, the average physician would be uneasy at the thought of praying with his dying patient or of offering spiritual support to a rape victim or torture survivor. Because medical science is so enormously powerful and effective, medical practitioners usually do not allow any other healing system, especially one based on faith, to interact with their own. While it is understandable that patients facing death might want to know whether their doctor has a religious or spiritual frame of reference, few ask, "Do you believe or don't you?" Through their mutual silence, the doctor and patient proceed in their relationship to ignore this important instrument of healing.

At Site 2, in contrast, the Cambodian refugees training as mental health practitioners often spoke about the common occurrence of spirit possession among the people they helped. In this culture three types of spirit can enter a person, primarily producing bad results: a relative who has died and whose soul has not found rest; a famous person, such as King Jayavarman VII, who built Angkor Thom and helped introduce Buddhism to Cambodia; or a demon who wants to destroy the person possessed. All three spirits can cause physical symptoms such as convulsions, dizziness, fever, fainting, and chronic insomnia; they will also appear to their hosts in nightmares. The spirits will sometimes speak through the voice of the possessed person without the person's knowledge or understanding. Only the listeners can understand the spirit's communication. If not properly cleansed from the person, the spirits can lead to serious illness and death. Spirits of restless souls can be brought to peace through Buddhist funeral ceremonies, while the chants and herbal medications of folk healers can eliminate the spirits of historic persons and demons.

The highly educated Cambodian trainees all believed in spirit possession and wanted to know where I stood personally and professionally on the issue. Being asked directly if I believed in spirit possession created a crisis for me. How relevant was my medical knowledge in a refugee camp where spirit possession was common in the patients? The response my Khmer students expected from an American physician—namely, that I did not believe in spirit possession but it was fine for them to hold these beliefs—would have disguised a prejudice against spirituality. I therefore answered with a weak yes, because I have never personally experienced a divine presence in my own medical practice.

A Navajo medical anthropologist once explained to me that in her society, as in most traditional societies, divine spirits will intervene therapeutically by casting out bad spirits only if a healer has been prepared through spiritual knowledge and practice. I have clinically been able to acknowledge the truthfulness of this claim. Every week I encounter in my Boston practice patients who are possessed by the spirits of relatives murdered by the Khmer Rouge, who appear primarily in dreams. The bodies of these deceased relatives invariably were desecrated. I carefully obtain the full trauma story of the spirit possession and work with the patient to resolve the spirit's demands and wishes, which usually involve a proper Buddhist funeral ceremony. After these rituals occur the spirits disappear from the dreams, along with the patient's physical complaints.

A middle-aged Bosnian psychiatrist had a clear role for spirituality in his therapy. When he was a Muslim youth in the former

Yugoslavia, he initially rejected the strict Islamic religion of his parents, in particular his mother. Under Communism his parents had been considered primitive, old-fashioned, and poor, or *papak*, the "hooves of a cow." Later he became a well-known painter in Bosnia and then a medical doctor and psychiatrist. Following a dream in which Allah confronted his atheism, he went back to the mosque and began to pray. After his first prostration, he started to cry uncontrollably and let out a primal scream, which completed his rededication to his religion. He learned Arabic in order to read the Qur'an, and he reestablished close ties with his parents and neighbors, opening himself up to the faith of those generations of people considered old-fashioned and underdeveloped by the Communists who ruled his society.

When war started after the breakup of Yugoslavia in 1992, he was called up by the military to protect his people against the atrocities of the Bosnian Serbs. On the battlefield as a doctor, he was unarmed and yet no more than thirty meters from the front line. During one brutal battle, Serb bullets tore into the left side of his body. Before passing out, he sat down on the battlefield in a meditative pose, closed his eyes, and thought, "I am now a martyr and will soon enter paradise." He saw a ball of yellowish-white light without sharp borders engulf him and he began to rise up. He could see his soul separating from his body, and he felt relieved that death was painless. As this process was nearing its end, however, he found himself unable to speak the Islamic words that would allow him to enter heaven, "I bear witness that there is no God but Allah and that Muhammad is God's slave and messenger." He woke in a military field hospital with impaired use of his left arm due to nerve damage. Eventually he received surgery in America and recovered the use of his arm.

After the war ended in 1995 with the Dayton Peace Accords, he found himself in charge of caring for 120 seriously mentally ill patients who had been left behind in the mental hospital by the retreating Serbian forces. Their own people had locked them behind bars and left them under horrible conditions. He worked with each and every one of the Serb patients, trying to restore their mental health with medication and therapy and eventually returning them, in good condition, to the enemy side. As a doctor and human being, he was very satisfied with his work, and ultimately he was able to harmonize his Islamic beliefs with the Christian beliefs of his patients.

Today he works in Tuzla as a psychiatrist with people from all ethnic, cultural, and religious backgrounds, including Bosnian Serb, Croat, and Muslim. He asks all of his patients if they believe in God. If they say no, he proceeds with conventional psychiatric care. If they say yes, he tries also to open up that side of their lives. He prays privately with his Islamic patients in his medical exam room, as prayer is still not considered a standard psychiatric practice in Bosnia. He is strongly antinationalist, believing that those who use religion for political purposes are impostors creating great anxiety and conflict among people. This physician is fortunate to have found the spiritual power of self-healing in his own life, which he can then use in appropriate and sensitive ways in his medical practice.

HEALING IN EVERYDAY LIFE

The social instruments of healing are equally relevant for people facing serious health threats such as cancer. While considerable scientific information is emerging about the psychological and social activities that promote resiliency and reduce mortality in cancer patients, a systematic promotion of self-healing is still not routine in the treatment of these types of diseases. The social instruments of healing certainly cannot replace traditional treatment, such as chemotherapy and radiation, but an appreciation of self-healing could be integrated into the treatment process.

Persons confronting serious medical illness share many experiences with those affected by violence. Often the disease onset is sudden. A woman lives an uneventful life until a routine mammogram, followed by a biopsy, leads to the diagnosis of breast cancer. One day she is completely normal, and the next she must grapple with a life-threatening illness. The whole world of a person in this situation is completely transformed. Strong emotions, such as fear and sadness, flood the person, dominating her mood and radically influencing her behavior. The illness becomes a traumatic life event. Sometimes the side effects of treatment are more traumatic than the disease itself. Nausea, vomiting, weakness, and the disfigurement of surgery can become serious secondary traumas. Sometimes shame and humiliation are associated with the disease or its treatment, such as the hair loss from chemotherapy. The obvious difference between trauma survivors and persons with serious illness is that in the latter case a perpetrator rarely exists.

All the forces of self-healing found in traumatized persons are activated in people with serious illness. The social origins of traumatized persons' suffering often obscure the power of biological and psychological self-healing forces. In cancer and other seriously ill patients, the belief that genetic and other biological forces cause the illness hides the therapeutic power of the social forces of self-healing. Scientific appreciation of the interconnectedness of all self-healing forces—physical, psychological, and social—demands a unified, coherent plan of care and recovery.

Sarah, now a sixty-year-old college administrator, had just turned fifty when the diagnosis of cancer turned her life upside down. She had gone in for a checkup feeling perfectly well. When she experienced some pain during the gynecological exam her doctor ordered a routine ultrasound, which showed a golf ball–sized growth on one ovary. The diagnosis proved to be ovarian cancer, which is usually diagnosed late in its course. Remarkably, Sarah's cancer was at a very early stage. After surgery and chemotherapy her physician told her that although she would need to be monitored carefully, her prognosis was quite good.

But Sarah was devastated by the diagnosis; she felt her life was ending. Despite the doctor's outlook of cautious optimism, she was convinced that she would succumb to the cancer and could not stop thinking about impending death. She planned her funeral, carefully deciding on the music and who would deliver the eulogy. A year after her diagnosis, although there was no evidence of recurrence, she remained obsessively preoccupied with her mortality.

The turning point for Sarah came when a friend of a friend took her to an ovarian cancer support group meeting. There she met other women coping with the disease, including several in the late stages who were in fact close to death. Rather than deepening her worries about her own survival, exposure to these women galvanized Sarah to action. She became involved in a network of volunteers who provided moral support and material help, such as transportation, errands, and meals, to women with cancer who needed a hand. After working with the group for a few months, Sarah found that her preoccupation with her own death had ceased. In its place was a deeper connection with her spiritual self and a profound sense of gratitude for each new day that found her alive, healthy, and able to contribute. Ten years later, she remains free from cancer and is still involved in ovarian cancer advocacy work.

The social instruments of self-healing might seem relatively easy to mobilize and direct, with a wealth of opportunities for work, altruistic behavior, and spirituality already at hand. Yet a number of factors interfere with this rosy scenario. Those around us, including our families, neighbors, doctors, and therapists, may know little about the curative value of social activities. More significantly, since they have no knowledge of the inner workings of our minds and are not directly in touch with our traumatized world, only the most empathic of our relatives and neighbors will realize what is needed and thereby be able to help. These same people may in fact be afraid that the traumatized person's situation is hopeless and nothing can really be done.

Fortunately, few traumatized people have such monolithic, narrowly hopeless views of their posttraumatic state. While every human being lives and operates in a social world that can be hurtful, cruel, and violent, this same world can bring about salvation, joy, and nurturance. Traumatized people have the inner knowledge to use their social environment to repair the damage caused by violence. Although this effort may be great, the potential healing benefits of work, altruism, and spirituality are even greater.

Chapter 8

THE CALL TO HEALTH

I AM AFRAID of this patient." This thought often echoes in the minds of doctors and therapists, paralyzing the self-healing forces in traumatized persons. I have observed this fear in my own colleagues who, after listening to a patient's trauma story, flee from the examination room or withdraw into themselves in shock and bewilderment. I have experienced it myself. The fear is based on the irrational belief that the patient will never recover from his or her ordeal. Faced with such trauma, the health professional unwittingly taps into the annihilating energy of the perpetrator. And this energy can be terrifying. The doctor is unprotected and unprepared for this disturbing result.

A Renaissance painting by Raphael, *The Transfiguration,* on display in the Vatican Pinacoteca in Rome, captures on canvas the fear healers face in confronting serious illness. Commissioned in 1517 by Cardinal Giulio de' Medici for the French cathedral of Narbonne, this painting perhaps offers insight into the healing experience because Raphael himself fell ill and died while he was completing it.[1]

Raphael portrayed on the canvas two scenes from the New Testament. In the top scene Christ is transfigured into a heavenly spirit, surrounded by Moses, Elijah, and the disciples. In the lower half of the painting the disciples are attempting to heal a boy who is possessed by a demon. The boy is apparently having a seizure while being held by his father. The disciples' faces are filled with anxiety and dread because their healing has not stopped the boy's convulsions. The onlookers plead with the apostles for help and even show signs of anger at their ineffectiveness. This rendition of the apostles' failed healing experience reveals a social context of anarchy, confusion, and hopelessness. The illness—the demon within the boy—is completely in control.

The resolution to this crisis of healing comes not in the painting but in the Scriptures. After the disciples have failed to heal the child, Jesus himself drives the demon out of the child, instantly curing the boy:

> Then the disciples came to Jesus privately and said, "Why could we not cast it out?" He said to them, "Because of your little faith. For truly, I say to you, if you have faith as a grain of mustard seed, you will say to this mountain, 'Move from here to there,' and it will move; and nothing will be impossible to you." (Matthew 17:19–21)

Here Jesus is saying to his disciples that he is not the only source of healing. Human beings also have this great power if, like the mustard seed, they have faith in their own potential. The mustard seed, though tiny, can grow into a large plant if planted in the proper soil. Jesus is telling his disciples that, in planting the seed—or healing— they must not prejudge the growing environment—the patient. Some growing environments and patients can seem so debilitated and void of potential for change that the immediate tendency is to give up on them, without even trying. But it is also true that the least likely ground can produce a healthy plant—and that the sickest, most destitute patients can recover.

Raphael's *Transfiguration* is considered a splendid example among Italian Renaissance paintings of *incitamento devozionale*, "call to devotion," because of its spirituality and reverence. With its emphasis on *humanitas*, "love for humanity," the painting shows that mankind too is capable of replicating the divine transformation (upper panel) through the healing act (lower panel). To achieve this call to health, however, we must first overcome our very human fears.

A GOOD PROGNOSIS

For doctors and health professionals to move beyond their fears to a more positive and optimistic place, they must first become aware of the conditions that prevent them from seeing their patients in a different light. Rarely do healing professionals, who spend little time with their patients and are detached from their social realities, need to acknowledge their negative emotions toward their patients. Few therapists interact with patients within the patient's own social world. Therapists thus protect themselves from observing firsthand what is occurring to the patients in their homes and communities. The concrete realities of the traumatized life remain unseen.

Furthermore, for medical practitioners, the trauma story has become largely irrelevant to the healing process. Medical and psychiatric science isolate body parts and pieces of the mind, breaking up human disease into smaller and smaller units, until finally arriving at the genetic and molecular level. Within this frame of reference, knowledge of the patient's trauma story and corresponding natural world has no value—and any fear of the patient that may exist does not need to be confronted. While the tremendous power of this scientific model cannot be denied, it does not seem capable of relieving the suffering and injuries caused by one human being to another. As *The Transfiguration* illustrates, suffering is very much a part of a patient's community, including family, neighbors, and the healers themselves.

Ancient Greek and Roman medical practitioners had a possibly more useful way of going about their business. They understood that human beings are part of nature and that their illnesses and healing are part of the world around them. The ancient world's symbol for the god of healing, Asclepius, is a staff with a snake wrapped around it. The staff represents the walking stick of physicians, who went from house to house and village to village treating their patients. The snake was revered for its medical powers. It lived in the brush, where it came to know the healing properties of all plants and herbs; and the tunnel where it lived was the entrance to the underworld, Hades. As the snake shed its skin, it reenacted the casting off of illness in order to be reborn to a healthy new life.[2]

Ancient doctors were good medical scientists and craftsmen who focused on understanding the life history of an illness, from its inception and current presentation to its future course. Through hands-on experience with patients, early Greek physicians practically lived with the illness and therefore understood how it would play out in the body and mind of the patient if left untreated. In reaction to this knowledge, they actively supported and encouraged the healing process.

Ancient doctors also had a different view of prognosis than we have today. The modern role of prognosis is to gauge the probability of an outcome. In contrast, prognosis was used in ancient times to assure the patient that a certain outcome would occur. The physician knew intimately the course of the illness and could inform the patient and family of the results, thereby relieving their anxiety and fear, especially if the predicted outcome was favorable. Prognosis was primarily a psychological support to the healing process. Those who could not be cured and would die were referred to the temple or priests for religious and spiritual healing. This relationship between the healing power of nature and medicine is emphasized in an ancient Greek text on medical healing:

> By stitching and cutting, that which is rotten in men is healed by physicians. This too is part of the physician's art; to do away with that which causes pain, and by taking away the cause of his suffering to make him sound. Nature of herself knows how to do these things. When a man is sitting it is a labor to rise; when he is moving it is a labor to come to rest. In other respects too nature has the same qualities as has the medical arts.[3]

Ancient physicians did everything in their power to maximize natural healing and lessen the violence of illness on the patient's body and mind. They told the patient: "I know your illness and will help cure you or at least relieve your suffering." In contrast, the modern physician states: "You may have cancer, infection, or a host of nonserious or potentially fatal diseases. Depending on the diagnosis, you may be in luck and have a good outcome." Prognosis, however, can be used by modern doctors as the first step in establishing a trusting, therapeutic partnership that supports the natural healing capabilities of the patient. Enough is now known of the therapeutic trajectory of traumatized persons that those assisting in the healing process can be extremely optimistic. The fear of a poor outcome or bad prognosis is just that, a fear, which is not based on solid scientific facts and can now be properly disarmed by the healing practitioner.

In reworking their use of prognosis, doctors must also begin to challenge the conventionally held concept of health. Forming the bedrock of public health today is the definition established by the World Health Organization (WHO): "Health is a state of complete physical, mental and social well-being and not merely the absence of disease or infirmity."[4] This now-classic definition, generated by the UN after World War II, was considered extremely avant-garde at its inception because of its lack of emphasis on disease and its concern for physical and psychological well-being.

But this definition also codified a passive definition of health. A global transformation of this concept of health is now occurring, especially as the women's movement challenges the idea that people can be considered healthy because they have no disease, despite the fact that they are oppressed, have limited opportunities for education and work, or face routine domestic and sexual violence. Women in India recently wrote a new and more dynamic definition of health, which can be applied to all traumatized communities:

> Health is a personal and social state of balance and well-being in which people feel strong, active, wise and worthwhile; where their diverse capacities and rhythms are valued; where they may decide and choose, express themselves, and move about freely.[5]

This definition reveals health as a dynamic, active process consistent with the model of self-healing. According to this new definition, abused and oppressed people who continue to be violated cannot be considered healthy; violence must be eliminated and these people must be provided with opportunities to maximize their well-being and their potential for healing.

STEPS TO SELF-HEALING

In 2000 my clinic initiated a community experiment to promote health based upon the new philosophy of self-healing and the socially and psychologically expanded definition of health for traumatized persons. Adopting the philosophy of Douglas Bennett's "upside-down psychiatry," which gives the best health care to the poorest and most traumatized population, we launched this experiment in Lowell, Massachusetts, an industrial town that is home to almost forty thousand Cambodian refugees and is the second-largest Cambodian community in America. Our Harvard group knew from public health statistics that there was a high rate of diabetes and other stress-related diseases in the middle-aged and elderly Cambodians. Community leaders strongly supported the plan to recruit local survivors of the Cambodian genocide into classes that would maximize their psychological and social forces of self-healing.

Over a three-year period, a hundred community members voluntarily joined the health classes, mostly middle-aged and older men and women. All had lived through the Pol Pot genocide. Approximately one-third were seriously depressed, and most were untreated.[6] Each class consisted of about twenty-five people, who met weekly for two hours over a three-month period, with a small graduation ceremony at the end. The classes were conducted by Svang Tor and me and focused on coping with the major physical and mental health problems associated with violence. Participation in the class required a total commitment to and support of the principle of self-healing; an expectation of improvements in health regardless of their current state of well-being; and an acceptance of their role as our students, not our patients. They would be taught the skills for enhancing their own self-healing.

It turned out to be incredibly easy to get the Cambodian residents involved. Many were recruited from the social programs of the local Cambodian community centers. Few missed any sessions, although most started out highly skeptical that the classes could help them. None of them had been taught the basic principles of a healthy lifestyle in Cambodia, nor had they any idea of how their experiences of violence affected their physical and mental well-being. Nevertheless, even the most uneducated and elderly of these Cambodians rapidly and enthusiastically caught on to the principles once they were given guidance.

NUTRITION AND EXERCISE

Modern research has reinforced the major role of nutrition and exercise in maintaining and fostering well-being. Good nutrition and daily exercise are potent factors in reducing trauma-related upset and health problems. Exercise, for example, has been shown to be effective in treating depression in all age groups.[7] Exercise not only relieves stress but also increases muscle strength and promotes cardiovascular health. As part of our classes, we provided direct information about exercise and nutrition and suggested simple activities for even the oldest survivor. When students were told that the only person who could not profit from good nutrition and exercise is a corpse, they broke into laughter. Survivors appreciate learning about simple ways to improve their lives and well-being that do not probe or trigger deep emotions.

At first the students brought only doughnuts and soda as snacks to class. It became apparent that they took for granted their own healthy and delicious Cambodian cuisine, which relies heavily on fish, fresh fruits, and vegetables. Few remembered savoring the smells and tastes of common Khmer dishes; none associated historical and cultural pride with their traditional cuisine. For many of them, American junk food was better than Khmer food, partly because it was modern, new, quick, and easy, but mostly because it was American. They wanted to fit into their new country, even if only in a superficial way, by eating American food. After our discussion of good nutrition, the students began to bring bananas, grapes, oranges, and water to class without being asked. The emphasis on appreciating their own food culture and history generated not only increased feelings of well-being but also pride in their ethnic identity.

One exercise was called "tasting the banana." They were asked to break off a piece of banana, put it in their mouths, and slowly savor all the flavor and texture in this small bite. What a joy! The banana was delicious. They could not remember the last time they had actually tasted a banana—or any of their native foods. They were asked to enjoy all aspects of food preparation, from cooking their next traditional Cambodian meal to eating slowly and noticing every small detail about the dishes they had prepared, including the smells and tastes. The results of this assignment were always exciting, as the traumatized people reported fully enjoying a meal for the first time in ages. In situations of extreme violence, some of them had experienced starvation or had been forced to eat putrefied and damaged foods. Because of this background, food had lost its value as a cultural and social event. There was great health benefit in reviving their interest in traditional foods.

One of the goals of the classes was to help the students become more aware of the physical state of their bodies, but first they had to acknowledge the reality of what they had physically experienced. Violence and torture leave many visible and invisible physical scars. The body is imprinted by the history of its violence, with each body part and organ system bearing witness to the violence that has occurred. Sexual abuse, for example, is signaled by scars from the mutilation of breasts and genitalia, as well as by chronic pelvic inflammatory disease, hepatitis B, cervical cancer, and HIV/AIDS. The Cambodian students were taught that every form of trauma and torture has long-term physical consequences and that chronic stress can create a tense body that loses physical strength and flexibility over time. The women especially appreciated this class, since so many traumatized Cambodian women are culturally taught to be detached from their bodies. They are kept wrapped up in traditional clothing from head to toe in order to hide their bodies and their sexuality. The class encouraged women who had been injured, especially through sexual violence, to have their doctors address those injuries.

One of the primary class assignments was to walk every day for twenty minutes. This assignment caught on quickly and class members were soon meeting together for group walks. No sight was more inspiring than seeing the transplanted Cambodians walking with each other around the city of Lowell and its Victorian buildings, with joy on their faces because of the fresh air and physical exercise. For many women in the class, it was a revolutionary experience to feel their bodies in motion. Burdened with many chores and responsibilities at home, it took a doctor's order to get their family and community to allow them to have the hour off they needed to exercise without criticism or complaint. All enjoyed exercising and developing friendships with the other walkers.

LOWERING THE HEAT

As the Cambodians gathered for the health classes, their faces showed the marks of past and present traumas and the struggle for healing going on within them. They had been through life situations most of us could not imagine surviving. In the early 1990s, when our team collected data for the first time on the traumatic life experiences of the refugees in Site 2, the initial results astounded us. One thousand and four adults over eighteen had experienced a total of 16,000 major trauma events.[8] Since we had asked only if an event had occurred, not how many times, this number was an underestimate, as some refugees had experienced more than one event. The large number caused us to wonder what effects these events might have on the health of survivors over time. As it turned out, these experiences were the fire that kept the emotional pot on a steady boil.

The Cambodian survivors reported in Lowell that twenty years after Pol Pot their bodies and minds still boiled over with emotion every day from the suffering associated with their traumas. Everyone agreed that they had not come up with any measures for turning down the flames. None of the Cambodians understood how the stress from their life experiences had, and was continuing to have, a negative impact on their health and well-being. Survivors are actually shocked to learn that trauma-induced stress contributes to their hypertension, cardiovascular disease, and even cancer, all diseases that develop in greater proportion in survivors than in nontraumatized populations.[9] But it was not difficult for us to teach the Cambodians about how stress causes illness, because they could now see and recognize it in their own bodies and lives.

During the early 1950s, Thomas Holmes and Richard Rahe pioneered scientific research on the impact of life events on health and disease. In 1967, they published a scale for marking stressful life events, the most potent of which are:

EVENT	SCALE OF IMPACT
DEATH OF SPOUSE	100
DIVORCE	73
MARITAL SEPARATION	65
JAIL TERM	63
DEATH OF CLOSE PERSONAL FAMILY MEMBER	63

The death of a spouse, with a score of 100, is here considered the most stressful life event. With this scale Holmes and Rahe could then add up the scores of all stressful events experienced by a particular individual to come up with a total score, from which they could predict if that person would become ill. For example, a total score of between 150 and 199 over one year carried a 37 percent chance of becoming sick the following year, a total score of 200 to 299 carried a 51 percent chance, and a total score of over 300 carried a 74 percent chance.[10] Cambodians, similar to most people who have experienced extreme violence, have scores so high they are way over the top of this scale, with ominous implications for their health status.

The students were taught that everyday and extreme traumatic events initiate the classic fight-or-flight stress response. Also, there are many physiological reactions geared to help the individual survive, including hormones that make more energy available and the release of endorphins, the body's natural painkillers. When there is no relief from a trauma, the individual's stress response can overactivate, causing the system to break down. Survivors who cannot escape from this cycle become physically exhausted and hopeless, until their bodies and minds are eventually overwhelmed.

All of our students were shown how this process had been affecting their lives. They came to realize that even thinking about violence that occurred years ago reactivates the stress response, just as if the event were happening again. Each thought of the trauma and each new stress brings the pot to a boil, eventually causing serious illnesses to develop. We then focused on teaching them techniques for turning off the fire, such as engaging family and community elders in problem-solving and using relaxation techniques like prayer and meditation.

BETRAYAL AND FAMILY SOLIDARITY

Violence affects families not only physically through murder, disappearance, or the loss of home, but also emotionally, by creating enormous, seemingly irresolvable conflicts among family members. Traumatized persons generally have a belief, often secret and unexpressed, that someone close to them in the family or an important friend has betrayed them. The feeling of betrayal ultimately infiltrates all aspects of a survivor's life and personal relationships. The word *betray* as derived from its Latin root means literally "to turn over and by doing so make someone vulnerable to harm and/or injury." Its current sense is "to give up to, or place in the power of, an enemy by treachery or disloyalty." Enemies cannot betray their victims, only those in close, trusting relationships who have the kind of knowledge about someone that makes them vulnerable to harm. The students confirmed the centrality of betrayal in their lives.

From two decades of clinical experience I became aware that many situations involving small dishonesties or betrayals can be magnified into big, potentially deadly betrayals when historical circumstances suddenly change. Betrayal with a "little b" can become betrayal with a "big B." All the Cambodians in the class were struggling with "little b" betrayals that had become "big Bs." One woman told a story about her husband who, before the Khmer Rouge period, had been having an affair with a girlfriend whom he supported in another village. His wife knew about the situation but quietly tolerated it as a "little b" betrayal. When the Khmer Rouge took over their village, the husband was away with his girlfriend while his family was moved to a concentration camp; his fate was unknown to his wife. After the war ended, he was reunited with his wife and children, and it turned out that he had survived safely with his girlfriend in Thailand, while his family had suffered starvation, murder, and the death of many relatives. His wife was quietly enraged at her husband's betrayal, so much so that she could show him no love or support. His affair had turned into an unforgivable "big B" betrayal, and her anger came to have a decidedly negative impact on the whole family.

Feelings of betrayal that are not so clearly justified can also destroy a family. While in the Khmer Rouge camps one student's baby was dying of an illness that he as a medical practitioner could have treated with the proper drug, but the Khmer Rouge was giving the child useless medication. His wife begged him to find the right drug in the local infirmary, which had been abandoned, but the husband refused, knowing that he would be executed by the Khmer Rouge if he revealed his true identity. Their little son died. Shortly thereafter the couple escaped to the Thai border, both overwhelmed with grief for their son. At the border the wife refused to cross over with her husband, returning instead to assist her mother in a Khmer Rouge camp. He felt abandoned. Ultimately he arrived in the United States as a refugee, believing his wife had died in Cambodia. Two years later, when his wife arrived safely with her mother, they resumed their marriage, but soon split up because of the intense anger and rage they each felt for the other's betrayal.

The students came to see that the list of perceived betrayals is limitless, affecting almost all families that have experienced extreme violence. Women who have been raped are often blamed for "betraying" their husbands. Other possible betrayals in a survivor's life are the hoarding of food when relatives are dying of starvation, falsely accusing someone of acting against the perpetrators, and turning in others to the enemy. Like a worm hidden in an apple, these feelings of betrayal are usually secret and end up destroying both personal relationships and the individual's health and well-being.

The negative emotions associated with violence, along with the perceived betrayal of family members and friends, provide an unstable foundation for building a strong personal and cultural identity in children and adolescents. The students examined in the class how their children and other Cambodian young people find it almost impossible to take pride in a community that has been destroyed, oppressed, or humiliated. Locked in a state of victimization, the students discovered how common it was for them to recapitulate all the bad things that have happened in their society, ignoring the resiliency imparted from their cultural background and experience. They saw how difficult it is for their children to be proud of being a victim of genocide, leading the young people to have considerable ambivalence about their heritage.

All of these issues were openly addressed in the class, including the necessity for repairing significant personal and social relationships that had been damaged by betrayal. Long-standing anger toward relatives and friends was replaced by forgiveness. Lessons from African Americans, who have learned to build pride on a past consisting of slavery, racism, and oppression, were used to teach the survivors about how to reclaim cultural respect for their former experiences and ancestors. Positive aspects of the Cambodian experience were identified by the class and given priority over the traumatic events that occurred during the Pol Pot era. And the students were encouraged to share this newfound respect for their Cambodian identity with the young people around them.

FAILED MEMORIES

The sacredness of memories is a delicate issue to take up since even painful ones, especially those of loved ones who have been taken away by violence, help maintain a closeness to and continuity with the deceased. When our students were asked if they had memories of their traumatic past, most responded, "Yes, every day." They also revealed that these memories were often accompanied by nightmares. Both the memories and the nightmares left them physically and emotionally upset but also kept their loved ones in their hearts and minds.

When the Cambodians were asked to recall a disturbing memory that occurred at least once a week, all of them came up with at least one; many had more. A man in his early sixties told about a recurrent memory of when his son was dying in a Khmer Rouge concentration camp. He had medicine that he believed could save his son, yet the Communist soldiers would not allow him to leave his village and go to his son. If he tried to escape, he knew he would be caught and killed. A week later he was told his son had died. He has never recovered from this loss, and thinks about his son every day. This memory brings with it great sadness and regret.

The Cambodian survivors readily shared these memories with each other and acknowledged the upset caused by them. They did not realize, however, that if not brought under control, these failed memories could literally kill them. Once they grasped the idea that they were actually in charge of their traumatic memories, they were able to compartmentalize and ritualize them so that they only occurred at certain times and places. Once localized, such thoughts could be safely and freely expressed, and possibly given new meaning through a religious ceremony or a moment of private reflection. The father who thought frequently about his son successfully contained these recollections by only expressing them during weekend prayers at the Buddhist temple. Recording failed memories, nightmares, and highly emotional events in diaries and journals helped the survivors to extinguish or quiet their painful thoughts.

Bringing failed memories and nightmares under control led to the broader therapeutic activity of learning to control emotions. The students now had the firsthand experience of realizing that emotions can be contained and even eliminated if approached in a disciplined, systematic way. They learned to set emotional thresholds so that when their emotions got out of hand, they could rein them in and shut them off. The students were eventually able to say, "When I think about this, I become extremely upset. Now when I start having these thoughts I just turn them off immediately." They learned how to avoid places, thoughts, and behaviors that generated high emotions, which over time would lead to illness and a general lack of well-being. Coping with failed memories actually helped them improve their connections with their lost family and friends — by mastering their emotions they were able to fully appreciate the deceased without being distracted by their pain.

THE HEALING POWER OF LAUGHTER

After I had worked for eighteen months in the clinic with an older, depressed Cambodian woman who had been severely tortured and never showed any interest in her appearance, she showed up at a meeting with an attractive haircut, obviously done at a professional beauty salon. I commented that her haircut looked very nice, and she smiled. Then I said jokingly that after she had left the beauty salon, all of the older Cambodian men must have chased after her. The patient laughed in delight, sharing her pleasure at being found attractive again by others. At this moment, as she reflected upon her recommitment to her physical appearance, she became aware of the hopefulness of her situation.

I learned from my clinic experiences that introducing humor to survivors is a liberating experience for all, so I tried to bring humor into the health classes. To illustrate to the Cambodians how difficult it is for a doctor to hear about a patient's health problems through an interpreter, I used the childhood game of a telephone circle. During one class I whispered into the ear of the first Cambodian woman, "The dog likes candy!" The woman laughed aloud as she whispered it to the next woman sitting beside her, "The dog likes candy!" She thought a dog eating candy was a silly idea. Each whisper led to a chain reaction of smiles and laughter. Even the usually serious Cambodian men now laughed. The whisper proceeded around the room and until finally it ended where it began. Surprisingly, unlike the usual childhood outcome, where the initial phrase ends up completely distorted, the final whispered phrase remained unchanged: "The dog likes candy!" This was probably due to the intense interest of the Cambodians in the exercise. An elderly woman, who had just returned from the hospital following a stroke, remarked that this exercise added ten years to her life, explaining, "A laugh can cure illness because joy can take the sadness out of one's mind." All members of the class agreed.

As demonstrated by extensive research, laughter and humor are therapeutic. While this reality has found its way into cancer wards and into the treatment of other serious medical disorders, it has barely entered the doorway of modern psychiatry. Mental health practitioners are likely afraid that humor will be seen as insensitive to an already vulnerable person. Yet without humor and the joy it triggers, an additional aid to recovery is lost. It is hubris for psychiatrists to think that they can intellectually "understand" all of life's problems without the help of the comic arts, including puppets, mimes, humorous storytelling, and comedians.

The true place of laughter in recovery is a simple exercise like the daily walk. Norman Cousins, American editor and essayist, calls laughter "inner jogging." As researcher Robert Brody states:

> Once you are ready to laugh, the muscles in your face that control expressions start to contort. Muscles throughout your body contract like fists. Your vocal cord muscles, designed for intelligible sounds, cannot coordinate. Your glottis and larynx open, relaxed and ready to vibrate. Your diaphragm tenses up in anticipation of respiratory spasms. Air in your body billows until you feel pressure building in your lungs.... Once the laugh gets into full gear your breathing is interrupted for a station break. Your lower jaw vibrates. A blast of air gushes into your trachea, flinging mucous against the walls of your windpipe. Pandemonium! Out comes your laugh, in some cases clocked at 170 miles an hour.[11]

In addition to relieving stress and anxiety, laughter is now being shown by scientists to have positive physiological and autoimmune responses, which aid in the healing of physical and mental disorders.[12] Because laughter is contagious, it also brings pleasure to others.

The Cambodian survivors were told repeatedly that they needed joy and laughter in their lives to be healthy. At one point I wrote everyone in the class a prescription: "Enjoy yourself, have some fun over the next week." And they did, often for the first time in decades.

SOCIAL INSTRUMENTS OF HEALING

Traumatized persons rarely make the link between social activities and healing from violence, despite the fact that isolation seriously threatens physical and emotional well-being. Many of our students, especially the elderly, were alone most of the day. This situation was corrected by the small community formed by the class and by becoming involved with people at the local Cambodian center. Cambodians, like many survivor communities, are culturally oriented toward assisting others, especially family members and neighbors, which contributes to healing. However, most of these people had few material and financial resources to share. Some of them could not even treat a friend or neighbor to a cup of tea. Some were too physically and mentally exhausted to be helpful. Violence, especially if chronic and ongoing, creates not only physical fatigue but also emotional depletion. Few Cambodians understood that their lack of energy was due to the despair caused by both their humiliating abuses under the Khmer Rouge and by their struggle to adjust to the American way of life. Helping the students relate to each other in spite of their feelings of hopelessness was one of the first steps in rebuilding their vitality, so that they could participate in the social forms of healing.

Because of the many legal and economic barriers, the concept of work needed to be redefined if it was to contribute to self-healing for these survivors. Employment provides a stable source of identity, productivity, and income, but formal work was often not an option. Informal work activities were encouraged, such as gardening or farming, small-scale vending, self-employment, and under-the-table income-generating pursuits. The Cambodians rarely talked openly about their black-market dealings because if caught, they could be arrested and fined. Such activities included being a domestic servant or construction laborer, or working illegally in jobs with serious occupational hazards such as handling toxic chemicals.

We also encouraged our students to participate in spiritual activity. Although access to the local Buddhist temple was readily available, some Cambodians were reluctant to participate. Some women were afraid they would be stigmatized because of their sexual abuse.

Other students did not have faith in the ability of their religion's practices and rituals to address their problems. The most common barrier to spiritual practice was the survivors' chronic emotional turmoil, which prevented their ability to concentrate on prayer or meditation or participate in religious services. Whenever they entered a quiet contemplative place, their minds would be flooded with violent thoughts and images.

Though many trauma sufferers need the benefits of spirituality, some are so distressed that they cannot use this pathway to self-healing. These barriers to involvement in spiritual practices were identified in the class and resolved through group discussion and activities that helped them clear their minds and allow successful Buddhist chanting and meditation.

FROM EXTREME SITUATIONS
TO THE ORDINARY

Comparison of the emotional status of our one hundred students before and after their health training revealed a marked increase in energy and feelings of wellness, as well as a clear reduction in feelings of hopelessness, despair, and depression. Six months to a year after graduation the students were continuing the physical and mental exercises on their own. The program had actively enhanced their self-healing.

Few people who have been injured by violence have experienced anything comparable to what the Cambodians endured in the Khmer Rouge concentration camps, but the general principles of their recovery are relevant to all violence survivors. The self-healing approach is applicable to anyone who has suffered physical and mental damage, whether from separation and divorce; domestic and sexual violence; the unnatural loss of a child, spouse, or friend; or other common forms of trauma. Self-healing is a counterforce to the maladies caused by human aggression. The Cambodians demonstrated that resiliency and repair can be maximized through a systematic and concrete approach.

After my team's experience with the health classes, we modified and adapted the principles to more ordinary situations. In doing so, we chose the activities with care, so they'd be the most effective and accepted in a given culture or social class. Choices for exercise, for example, can be strongly influenced by gender, since females may prefer certain exercises, such as yoga, while males may prefer more vigorous activities. Fortunately almost everyone is comfortable with vigorous walking. Nutrition varies dramatically, with choices of healthy food being determined by cultural norms, sensitivities to food types, and tastes. It was also critical for us to be aware of the specific types and intensities of stress that exist in a given violent situation, for each is characterized by a range of trauma events. While situations of domestic violence differ markedly from serious job harassment, the associated stress and its impact on medical and psychiatric illness remains the same.

The story of Anthony, a businessman, illustrates how the health approach used in the Cambodian class can be applied to mainstream individual therapy. In many ways, Anthony's situation differed from those of our Cambodian students. He did not have the benefit of group support as he dealt with his traumatic situation. However, since he worked at a high-paying job, he was able to join a sports club and readily handled the areas of exercise, nutrition, and employment. As an American citizen, he did not have to deal with the stress of adjusting to a new society. He was a stable, secure middle-aged man with plenty of friends and many positive social relationships. But he had undergone trauma and was in need of self-healing.

Anthony and his wife divorced when their daughter was ten years old. The wife remarried and moved far away with her new husband and Anthony's daughter. Immediately after the move, the stepfather began physically abusing the child when he was drinking, which he did frequently. On one occasion, he seriously injured the teenage girl in a motor vehicle accident caused by his drunken driving. After the daughter left home for college, she revealed to her father a history of more than eight years of physical abuse. She brought her stepfather to trial on criminal charges of physical abuse and injury, but the stepfather received only a reprimand from the judge. A year later, the girl committed suicide.

Anthony was overwhelmed by rage toward the judge, the stepfather, and his ex-wife, who he felt had killed his daughter. He wanted revenge on all of them. Over five years in treatment with other psychiatrists, he was told that he needed to give up his feelings of rage and retribution. In contrast, when he came to me, I validated his feelings. The stepfather had done terrible things to his daughter, and that person needed to be punished. By allowing years of physical abuse of the child — a reality she denied — his wife had indeed betrayed their daughter. And the judge had reached a decision that was unfair and unjust, perhaps leading to his daughter's suicide.

Having acknowledged Anthony's deep feelings of betrayal and revenge, I then asked how he wanted to act upon them. My acknowledgment led him to an outpouring of grief, whereby he eventually arrived at the even deeper feeling that he himself had betrayed his daughter. As a business man, he had moved around constantly and spent little time with his daughter while she was growing up. He felt he could have discovered the physical abuse if he had spent more time with her. A betrayal with a "little b," spending all of his time involved in his job, had led to a betrayal with a "big B," not realizing a violent man was living in the same household as his child. At this point in his therapy, Anthony began to assess his tragic situation realistically and to come to terms with his grief and guilt.

The therapy followed the steps we had established in the Cambodian class. Anthony's mind, like his Cambodian counterparts, had become filled with repetitive nightmares of his daughter's suffering and his inability to stop the abuse. He acknowledged the need to reduce his nightmares and the failed memories of his daughter's suicide. Anthony was able to address his nightmares and eventually extinguish them by acknowledging that his dreams could never bring his daughter back to life or resolve his current sadness and guilt.

Eliminating suffering is not enough in any trauma case. The goal must also be to reestablish a life of pleasure and joy, an extremely difficult prospect. Anthony did not want to give up his suffering and replace it with a more positive outlook. Through his pain he kept the spirit of his daughter alive. His daily outbursts of rage toward his wife, her husband, and the judge made him feel like he was doing something to avenge his daughter. These emotions blotted out his ability to enjoy even the simple things in life. He was eventually able to regulate these painful emotions, not allowing them to flare up at any time of day or night. He could better love his daughter's memory by casting away the turmoil that was destroying his life. This step might have been easier for him in a group setting, since others can affirm the survivor's need to bring back harmony and pleasure.

Altruism, work, and spirituality, major components of any trauma recovery program, can also be dealt with in individual therapy. For Anthony, entering each of these social domains became easier and easier. He was always a hardworking man whose job focus had kept him alive after his daughter died. And he had a strong desire to help young people in trouble, which he eventually actualized while in therapy. Most important, Anthony as a Roman Catholic was able during confession to ask for forgiveness for neglecting his daughter. He learned to bring the traumatic memories of his daughter out of his nightmares and place them in his prayers in church, where he offered them up weekly as a blessing for her soul and asked God to help him forgive himself and his ex-wife for their failure to protect their child. While he was able to heal himself of his traumatic memories, at the end of his treatment Anthony's desire for the stepfather to be punished still remained strong. He also continued to maintain that the legal system had failed his daughter.

SOCIAL JUSTICE

One outcome that is difficult for traumatized persons to achieve either alone or together is social justice. Traumatized people hold a deeply personal as well as social definition of justice. For them, it is about a fair consideration of the individual situation, which can vary infinitely. In most societies, therefore, the justice demands of traumatized citizens are difficult to meet. Justice is political, not personal. Rarely does justice care for the personal pain and suffering of survivors; it is insensitive to their therapeutic needs. Criminal trials, truth commissions, human rights tribunals, and local courts are not set up to express concern for the recovery of the victim. Survivors and their healers are often faced with the fact that healing is either ignored or poorly supported—the ultimate goal for society is how to punish those who have committed violent crimes. In countries in which politically motivated violence continues unabated, concern both for social justice and personal healing is absent and actively opposed.

Doctors' fears of the traumatized person can be overcome by recognizing the wealth of recovery resources that their patients can mobilize. The remarkable achievements of the Cambodian refugees and of individual survivors such as Anthony demonstrate that a systematic recovery approach, based on a disciplined, daily effort, works better than a hodgepodge of half-hearted, inconsistent efforts by doctors and traumatized people. This self-healing model and its accompanying techniques can be widely applied in situations of extreme and ordinary violence. If society's appointed healers give up their fears and plant the mustard seed of health within all sick persons, remarkable results will occur.

Chapter 9

SOCIETY AS HEALER

THE INDOCHINESE PSYCHIATRY CLINIC (IPC) in Brighton, Massachusetts, was young, only eight years old, and just beginning to flourish. Its staff of sixteen doctors, social workers, psychologists, and Indo-Chinese paraprofessionals successfully served the region's most emotionally disturbed individuals within the newly arrived refugee communities. The clinic had more than 160 patients. The state of Massachusetts publicly supported it. And then one day the telephone rang with an urgent message from the state's commissioner of mental health, informing us that because of budget cuts, the clinic must close within two weeks. All patients had to be discharged, despite the fact that alternative clinical services for them did not exist. The entire staff was to be laid off.

My staff and I were devastated by this order. It felt as if we were being asked to take our patients off of desperately needed medical and psychiatric care, comparable to being told to remove someone from dialysis. I could not imagine being asked by our government to abandon the care of our patients. Twenty psychiatric clinics in all, serving the poorest people in the state, were on the chopping block. Having suffered many earlier fiscal crises over the clinic's brief history, I also felt a strange relief that maybe it was time for me to give up my job of directing the clinic. It would certainly be easier and financially more lucrative to provide mental health care to a less socially disadvantaged population.

Out of my confusion I called my mentor and former teacher at Yale, Professor Boris Astrachan, for advice. I explained to him that there was nothing I could do to save the clinic because of the state's financial crisis. I had to give up.

After I had finished speaking, there was a long silence, until Professor Astrachan exclaimed in a loud voice, "Bullshit! Don't you ever believe that any political decision is just about money. It is always about values and principles. Go back to your community of clinic supporters and patients and have them help you fight this decision, because it is unfair and morally wrong. The state has a responsibility to care for its sickest citizens; it is morally irresponsible to abandon those already in treatment."

His words energized me and the staff, so we went to our patients and asked them to help us save the clinic. Their response and the reaction of the local Indo-Chinese communities to our request were overwhelming. Thousands of them called the governor's and commissioner of mental health's offices to make one brief comment, "*IPC yes!*" since most could not speak English.

A few days before the clinic doors were to close the *Allston-Brighton Citizen* published an editorial titled "Indochinese Center Must Stay":

> The devastating cut in state aid to the Brighton-based Indochinese Psychiatry Clinic cannot be matched for callousness.

The nationally-acclaimed center faces imminent collapse following a recent announcement that all state funding, roughly $290,000, will be withdrawn from the center.

The clinic has done innovative and life-saving work on behalf of Cambodian, Laotian and Vietnamese refugees in our community. Most notably, it has provided important healing opportunities for Indochinese residents who suffered torture at the hands of political madmen in their countries of origin.

Through the work of the center's medical staff and specially trained Indochinese counselors, hundreds of such individuals have been helped to renew their once shattered lives and become useful members of this community. Stripping funds for continued operation of the center is just another form of brutalization.

State Sen. Michael Barrett and Rep. Kevin Honan have vowed to fight for the center's continued existence. The citizens of Brighton should join with their representatives and vigorously protest the closing of this humane and valuable community asset.

Officials of the state Department of Mental Health should know that we fight for our own in Allston-Brighton. It makes no difference whether the victims are longtime residents or relatively powerless newcomers.

The state's leadership was clearly swayed by the outpouring from our clinic supporters. On the day of the planned closure, eighteen clinics were shut down, never to reopen, except for ours and a clinic for the mentally ill and hearing-impaired. Even after this decision, the phone calls in support of IPC continued unabated. A few days later the governor's office called to ask us to please stop the calls because they were interfering with their work.

Astrachan's admonition was correct: The decision by politicians and policy makers on how to use limited resources is always a value judgment. Unfortunately, the health and mental health of traumatized people are usually considered by society to be very low priorities. The personal healing of trauma-related illness, whether from torture or domestic violence, is considered an individual matter to be solved privately by the victim. Rarely in even the most enlightened democratic societies is the healing of trauma considered a social and political responsibility. In the most extreme cases of populations devastated by war, post-conflict governments and international aid agencies focus primarily on the repair of roads, buildings, and financial infrastructure. Damaged individuals, in particular those with psychological damage, are left to fend for themselves.

The idea that no relationship exists between personal healing and societal recovery is pure fiction. Yet its perpetuation allows the daily occurrence of poverty-related violence, whether from gangs, drugs, prostitution, or the sexual abuse of children and women, to be neglected as a social priority. Thankfully the attitudes that underlie this neglect are slowly dying. Scientific validation of the power of self-healing in traumatized persons is on the verge of spawning a revolution in health care. The recognition of self-healing as a biological, psychological, and social response to violence is breaking down negative social attitudes that marginalize traumatized persons. Those governing society now need to link social and medical institutions with the forces of self-healing. It is not possible to work for this development in authoritarian societies, where political oppression and related economic and social violence are too widely prevalent to offer chances for reform. Democratic societies offer the best possibility of change.

OBLIGATION VERSUS DEPENDENCY

Language itself can actively work against society's relationship to the traumatized person. The 1995 earthquake in Kobe, Japan, highlighted this reality. The Japanese people have a well-developed language for discussing their personal relationships. In *The Anatomy of Dependence*, the Japanese psychoanalyst Takeo Doi described the central importance of *amae* or dependency in Japanese interpersonal relationships. *Amae* can be defined as the desire to be loved in the way an infant is loved by the mother. It is common and accepted for adults to *amaeru*, or behave self-indulgently, in looking for motherly love from others with whom they feel they have a special relationship. The Japanese language has many terms for describing the psychological state of failing to *amaeru*, such as *suneru* (sulking), *higama* (feeling that one is being treated unfairly), *hinekureru* (feigning indifference to others instead of showing *amae*), and *uramu* (showing hatred or resentment because of being rejected). Whether it is obvious or not, the Japanese are always concerned about others' reactions to the state of *amae*.

Interpersonal relationships in Japan are regulated not only by the need to be affectionately cared for by others but also by *on*, or obligations. One common type of obligation is *giri*, or those obligations that have to be repaid exactly in kind and within a certain time period. *On* stresses the psychological burden that accompanies receiving a favor, while *giri* stresses the interdependence created by obligations.[1]

The Japanese are extremely sensitive to and closely monitor the impact of their actions on others. While tragic events increase the need for loving support, most Japanese survivors of the Kobe earthquake felt they could not burden their families with their enormous physical and emotional needs, because they could not honor their *giri* to repay favors with an exact equivalent. Asking strangers for help was even more out of the question. The situation created a crisis for normal interpersonal interactions in Japan. The positive dependency encouraged by *amae* could not be properly extended to the hundreds of thousands of people who lost their homes and their loved ones in Kobe because the survivors needed too much help.

A loosening of obligations through public recognition and discussion of the problem would have helped earthquake victims avoid the shame and embarrassment of being selfish, as defined by traditional standards. Only by modifying *giri* could injured and depressed people have received greater family and community support. Although some minor changes in social relations did occur, the extraordinary needs of the earthquake survivors and their resulting debt still could only be managed by the government. The Japanese government in Kobe took up this obligation and while doing so also became sensitive to the psychological problems of the earthquake survivors, providing them with mental health support.

Kobe was a historic watershed for Japanese society as citizens throughout the country saw for the first time the necessity to help those in need without blaming and criticizing them for lacking traditional Japanese stoicism. Thousands of ordinary citizens flooded into the earthquake disaster zone to volunteer their assistance. This revolution in caring for traumatized people that started in Kobe has continued to blossom in Japan. Today, after a disaster in Japan you would never find the SMILE stickers that the local authorities posted on telephone poles and buildings throughout the city of Kobe, exhorting the city's survivors to passively accept their fate without expressing any negative emotions.

The Kobe lesson can be extended to the United States. Americans live in a multicultural society whose bedrock is self-reliance and resilience, in contrast to the Japanese emphasis on *amae*, or dependency. In New York City immediately after the September 11 attacks, the city witnessed incredible solidarity across cultural and ethnic groups. One New Yorker could ask almost any other New Yorker for help and it was readily given. But this solidarity diminished over time, probably because the new boundaries and lower thresholds for dependency and support that spontaneously occurred after September 11 were not formally recognized and established. Politicians did not fully appreciate this potential for a transformation in social relationships. They made a great mistake when they failed to promote collective healing and instead told people *not* to sacrifice and to conduct their business as if nothing had happened.

This error in political judgment was based upon ignorance of the power of self-healing to create a powerful new social reality. Social discomfort and tension arose as African Americans began to publicly express their reactions, including some who felt the experience of terrorism was similar to their feeling of powerlessness in dealing with the chronic violence of racism. Suddenly white people were for the first time subject to the violence that African Americans have long endured. African Americans were not provided the opportunity to teach the general public the lessons they had learned that allowed them to cope with racism.

Societies often do not want to acknowledge the physical and mental health damage caused by extreme violence because they would then have to acknowledge that violence existed before the catastrophic situation. Such avoidance protects the society from widening its awareness of chronic low-grade violence and its causes. The terrorist attacks in New York City elicited the fear of exposing the real level of violence that existed prior to September 11. That hidden violence emerged unintentionally in a study of more than eight thousand New York City public school students in grades four through twelve conducted six months after the attack. The ethnic distribution of students was approximately one-third Hispanic and one-third African American, with Caucasians and Asians in the minority at about 13 percent each. About one-quarter of the students had at least one major psychiatric problem; one-tenth had symptoms consistent with posttraumatic stress disorder; and 5 percent of the adolescents had severe alcohol abuse that impaired their daily functioning.

These high levels of psychiatric distress could not be attributed solely to the attacks, because nearly two-thirds of the children had been exposed to one or more traumatic events prior to September 11. Two out of five students, for example, had seen someone killed or seriously injured. One out of four children reported the violent or accidental death of a close friend. One out of four children reported the violent or accidental death of a family member. And one out of seven children had themselves been seriously hurt in a violent or accidental situation.[2]

This level of exposure to violence was not terrorist-related. New York City public school children are actually faced with violence almost every day, which contributes to their high levels of psychiatric problems.

The attacks on the Twin Towers overshadowed the chronic violence affecting American society. Such endemic violence may be related to ethnicity, gender, poverty, and economic exploitation. Many leaders are afraid, especially when faced with catastrophic situations, to pursue these issues. Violence in New York City's public school population is a Pandora's box; no one in power wanted to open it. So damaged people remain damaged, as new fears of international terrorism are layered upon a life already riddled with violence. One of the great tragedies of September 11 was to ignore this opportunity to confront the low-grade violence affecting American society. The social realities of neighborhood violence could have been radically transformed by linking our country's fight against terrorism to a fight against economic and criminal violence.

MEDICAL ARROGANCE

Modern medical and mental health practitioners and institutions have been unable to show leadership in establishing self-healing as a central element in the relief of suffering. The medical profession's narrow focus on the biological causes of disease, and its conflict of interest based on profits reaped from the pharmaceutical industry, have skewed it away from less profitable holistic approaches. Even if the majority of medical healers had noble motives and goals, barriers would still remain to acknowledging and aiding self-healing.

Practitioners stand watch at the doors of conventional medicine, keeping traumatized people out of effective medical and psychiatric care, because they fear that their skills, knowledge, and institutions are not sufficient to contain the pain and suffering unleashed by violence. The hurt seems so big that it has no boundaries, unlike other serious illnesses, so they leave the survivors to handle it on their own. Because of doctors' theoretical hubris and the grandiosity of their models, they cannot acknowledge this situation nor can they form a full partnership with the trauma sufferer. In my clinical experience, it is common for the medical doctor to avoid knowing anything about the patient's traumatic life history even after years of providing care. Doctors feel the need to dominate the relationship. They are thus unable to harness the therapeutic power of self-healing. To admit that the patient's own resources are the major pathway to healing would demand humility.

In contrast, mental health practitioners place emphasis on the trauma story when treating survivors of violence. But rarely do they obtain and use all four elements of the trauma story (the facts, the cultural meaning of trauma, looking behind the curtain, and the listener-storyteller relationship). Such a narrow focus of therapeutic support can sometimes go awry. Brutal facts of the trauma story end up overemphasized or even fetishized, as though the telling of the experiences has almost magical powers to cure the patient's suffering. The therapist encourages the patient to repeat the story over and over, in hopes that the associated outpouring of emotions will eliminate the symptoms. Psychotropic drugs are also usually helpful in reducing symptoms. But the concrete realities of the patients' daily lives and their use of the social instruments of healing are usually ignored. One study of the therapeutic approaches of professional healers, including mental health practitioners, in Cambodia and Bosnia found striking similarities in both countries. While all these practitioners approached their patients from their own theoretical frames of reference, they believed universally that the major problems facing their clients were violence and poverty. But since they had no training, skills, or resources for dealing with poverty and violence, they simply ignored these issues. In this way, their therapy remained isolated from the traumatized patient's social world.[3]

Yet some health professionals have begun to use more innovative methods that acknowledge the importance of self-healing. Practitioners in the Peter C. Alderman Masterclass actively support the resiliency of their patients. They also focus on their own need for encouragement and self-care in the face of treating patients who have experienced extraordinary violence. These heroic practitioners have discovered that the greatest barrier to their work is the potential harm to their own well-being from their overwhelming empathy and compassion for their patients. Instead of keeping the patient at a distance, they have implemented a program of self-care, supported by the Masterclass. This program acknowledges the practitioners' scientific respect for the empathic relationship, which transfers the pain experienced by the patient into the mind and body of the clinician. The problem arises when the accumulation of suffering by the practitioner leads to unhealthy consequences, including physical illness, exhaustion, and depression. To counteract this, Masterclass participants focus on the sharing of difficult cases during their meetings in Italy and then informally with their colleagues at home. This program improves the health and well-being of the practitioner and fosters a positive doctor-patient relationship. If the doctors neglected the power of self-healing within themselves, they would also be neglecting it within their patients, and then they both would be lost, as the emotional distress shared in their relationship would become overwhelming. Unfortunately, many medical and mental health practitioners live in a macho professional world that never allows them to acknowledge their own vulnerability and need for self-care.

GOOD INTENTIONS LEADING TO BAD OUTCOMES

Good people and institutions can sometimes do bad things. This certainly characterizes many international humanitarian relief organizations that are trying to help traumatized persons, especially refugees and other survivors of violent conflict. I became aware of this discrepancy between good intentions and bad outcomes very early in my refugee work. In 1990 I received a secret letter from Cambodian refugees living in Site 2, who were caring for the most psychologically damaged residents of the camp, independent of the camp authorities. Written in Khmer, the letter was smuggled out of the camp by a relief worker and clandestinely faxed to my clinic in Boston. In writing the letter my Khmer friends had risked their lives, because they had been warned by the Thai authorities that they would be severely punished if they told anyone about camp conditions, especially outsiders. This letter began:

> *January 5, 1990 2 p.m.*
> *Almost all Cambodians who live in Site 2 camp have mental illness. Some have serious illness and some have not. These mental illnesses are caused by living in the camp too long, and by the corruption of the people who have power in this camp. Like a recitation from Grade 3, "The Wild Ox: The small eat little and the big eat a lot."*

Contrary to what the United Nations and Thai camp authorities were reporting officially to the world, long-term confinement and corruption were creating mental illness in the Khmer population. Surprisingly, the letter did not mention the Pol Pot genocide of 1975 to 1979. Apparently confinement and corruption had eclipsed the violence of the Pol Pot period as a major trauma.

The letter went on:

> *These leaders dispute one another over who has more power. This power leads these leaders to corruption because they think that when they have the power, they have money. Where do they get the money from? They all get the money from the relief agencies. They use the people as a means to get the money. They complain to these agencies that they need this and that for their people. These agencies agree to*

give assistance without knowing that the camp leaders used
the people's names as their cover to get money for themselves.
But the people are still suffering and are deprived of
necessities. You feel that you can do nothing except to watch
these acts of corruption occurring. You only feel hurt by these
betrayals.

The leaders are very smart at making profits. The rights and
powers are with the people. To do something, though, without
their permission is wrong. Here, they say, we have democracy,
but they practice dictatorship. Look at the president of the
camp, president of Khmer Women's Association, section leader,
school director, police chief, president of the hospital; there have
been no changes in those positions for ten years. Even if the
people do not like them, the people can do nothing. These are
the causes of the mental illness.

After their humiliation under the Khmer Rouge regime the refugees were still being imprisoned, exploited, and betrayed by an
internationally supported and financed "democratic" Cambodian
regime within the camp. Even without the letter, the international
aid community could not claim ignorance of this situation. By
agreeing to work under the policy of "humane deterrence" imposed
by the Thai government, whereby people are given just enough resources to survive, the UN and other relief organizations had made
dangerous compromises. Unfortunately, the nature and extent of
these compromises will never be known because the records of the
United Nations Border Relief Operations, which ran the camps, have
been destroyed.

The denial by international aid workers that they were servicing
a violent, inhumane confinement is hard to understand, but the letter provides some insight:

Most of the foreigners believe that Khmer people don't want
to go anywhere and that they love their country and have a
good life in the camp. Khmers help each other very well.
Khmers love each other. It is true because the foreigners help
only the power people. Khmers are afraid to speak.

The Khmer were clearly afraid to trust their caretakers with their trauma stories. In general, the humanitarian and UN relief workers, while materially helping many Khmer to survive, did not enter into full listener-storyteller relationships. Although some aid workers were sensitive to the mental health problems of the Khmer, these people had little impact on the camp's policy of humane deterrence, which was generating considerable emotional distress. A tremendous opportunity for recovery from the Pol Pot genocide was lost.

The letter ended with a prediction of catastrophe:

For my own idea, if everything is still going on for another
five years, all Khmers will become crazy. Khmers need
treatment or almost all of them will die from severe
depression and from feeling that their lives are hopeless.

While Site 2 eventually closed in the early 1990s as the residents returned home to Cambodia, its reality is being replicated today in Asia, Africa, the Middle East, and Latin America. Seven million of the world's nearly twelve million refugees have been warehoused in refugee camps for more than a decade.[4] Refugee camps and settlements epitomize the almost universal waste of the healing potential of traumatized people. In its desire to protect and care for refugees, the international community has created environments that maximize almost every negative social factor that fosters illness, such as chronic unemployment and unremitting violence. Similar contradictions can be found at local and community levels, where political compromises are accepted that affect the society's most basic values. In the case of refugee assistance, humanitarian relief organizations must take up strong positions against situations that are clearly wrong.

HUMAN RIGHTS VERSUS HEALING

A major conflict exists today between the focus on human rights and the need to care for traumatized persons. After the violence ends, survivors all over the world want to achieve social justice. Publicly addressing social justice should enhance survivors' recovery by mirroring their own therapeutic struggles. Forensic activities and the prosecution of war criminals are great advances in human rights law. It seems likely that the Truth and Reconciliation Commission in South Africa and the tribunals regarding the former Yugoslavia at The Hague, which are modern experiments in establishing social justice in post-conflict societies, will be of great therapeutic value to local citizens. However, such therapeutic benefits have not yet been empirically demonstrated.

The social acceptance of public testimonies in some countries may take decades, as it did in Chile regarding the Pinochet regime. The protracted course of bringing perpetrators to justice results in a failure to provide closure for their victims. The long-anticipated death of Pol Pot in 1998 seems to have provided little relief to the Cambodian diaspora in America. A few Western journalists witnessed Pol Pot's trial by the remaining Khmer Rouge cadre. Shortly thereafter, he died a sick and broken man, bizarrely cremated on a pile of abandoned tires topped by his favorite chair. The proposed trial under the current Cambodian strongman, Hun Sen, of the remaining aged Khmer Rouge leaders threatens to reopen a period of massive public grief and suffering. Because the potential negative therapeutic consequences of this trial are high, the international community must guarantee mental health support for those who testify.

At the minimum, truth commissions need to provide psychological support, including counseling, to the thousands of survivors who tell their trauma stories in this political and legal context. It is worrisome that the psychological support of victims has been so limited, often nonexistent.

It is also distressing that in their pursuit of justice human rights workers are concerned only with proving a violation of human rights law, with little regard for the effects of this violence on the survivor's health and well-being. The legal system's interest in the recovery from violence is rarely witnessed.

Societies make a grave error when they emphasize obtaining the details of killings and other crimes over the mission of self-healing. The international human rights community in Srebrenica, for example, has created a museum of horror with its monuments and graves. Everywhere you go in the province you are confronted with the evidence of the massacre of local civilians. Certainly the bodies of disappeared persons should be identified and returned to their families: restoring even a small bone to a family seems critical to fostering their grief process and subsequent healing. However, local villagers feel that the energy expended to establish these details of death has been greater than that put toward helping individuals in their self-healing process. The lack of concrete health and mental health services in the province is a clear indication of this.

In the early 1980s this conflict between groups involved with human rights and mental health was sometimes extreme. One woman, while fleeing into Site 2 from Cambodia, was brutally assaulted by unknown guerilla fighters. Her husband was murdered, she was raped, and both her hands were amputated. After the clinical team at the refugee clinic had worked out a mental rehabilitation and counseling strategy for her, they brought a picture of her to a human rights agency, asking for assistance in supporting her treatment. The agency responded that since this was not a human rights violation but a crime conducted by bandits, it could not help. My medical point of view is that deciding whether legal codes had or had not been broken is irrelevant to aiding someone recover her physical and mental health.

This scenario could no longer occur today in regard to sexual abuse. Coined in 1907, the phrase *crimes against humanity* was left unspecified until World War II, when the International Military Tribunals for Germany and Japan defined such crimes as "murder, extermination, enslavement, deportation, or other inhumane acts committed against a civilian population." Sexual violence was largely ignored until the 1990s, when the massive rapes that had occurred during the conflicts in Rwanda and the former Yugoslavia came to public attention.

> Large-scale genocidal behavior, including massive rapes
> and gender violence, in the former Yugoslavia and Rwanda
> in the early to mid 1990s has led to the expansion of pro-
> tection against systematic wartime rape under interna-
> tional law.[5]

The protection now includes providing medical and mental health care to sexually violated persons.

Just as human rights law has done in the case of sexual violence, it must now shift its focus away from strict legal definitions and extend a commitment to providing universal medical and mental health care to all victims of violence. The design and implementation of healing responses, currently at the whim of governments, international development agencies, and the United Nations, must be systematically funded and legally mandated. Human rights activists and their humanitarian aid colleagues must link their work to the healing process. They must ask: "How are my projects and policies affecting the health and well-being of survivors? Are these projects promoting the self-healing of the communities and persons being served?" Unless attention to the psychological and social welfare of survivor groups informs all human rights work, relatively wealthy humanitarian aid environments will come to exist alongside inadequate and failed healing programs.

MAINTAINING A SICK SOCIETY

In the spring of 2004 a young Muslim man named Jusuf, who had fought as a boy in the Muslim defense force in Bosnia, was working on a development project in Srebrenica province. He was attempting to teach Serb and Muslim farmers how to process local cheese so that it could be successfully marketed in Bosnia. This young man was extremely idealistic and worked long hours to achieve his mission, but the horror of Srebrenica haunted him. He felt the undercurrents of animosity flowing through the community, in spite of the denial by the local Serb population and the national authorities that any violence had occurred.

Jusuf reported on the psychological well-being of the local population as he found it:

> My first trip to Podrinje region was a very deep experience for me. I felt hopeless in this new world and it seemed I had become a missionary. When I introduced the cheese project to local Serb authorities they pretended they had not heard my Muslim name. They ignored me.

Even in attempting to bring a practical economic project with no controversial issues of human rights into the region, he felt like a missionary from the outside world. Despite being ignored by Serb authorities, Jusuf expressed his openness to reconciliation:

> My task in the project was to provide a market for the local cheese producers. I was afraid, but I also felt my work was important for these people. I felt among the local Serb people their resistance and they were not friendly. But I decided to honor all people no matter their nationality. I decided to have an open heart towards everybody and to proceed with implementing my work.

On the other side, Jusuf's own people, the Muslims, demanded that he acknowledge the violence they had experienced:

> People felt my openness and dedication to my task. I understood those people were very simple, smart, and steady. I also understood that Bosnian Muslims identified themselves with the victim role. Whenever I started to behave normally to them, they reminded me to be conscious that they were genocide survivors.

Jusuf felt this victim mentality had been fostered by the international aid community:

> The people in Srebrenica of both nationalities are very suspicious. They will listen to you very carefully and after you think they have accepted the idea, they simply ask for a donation. They ask you many times. I think these people, especially the Bosnian Muslim population, are very dependent on humanitarian aid. They always expect donations.

When survivors ask for donations nine years after the seminal traumatic event, it is a warning sign that the self-healing process related to work and altruistic behavior may be seriously impaired. The official denial of violence contributes directly to this condition, leaving a place in which fear grips all residents of Srebrenica:

Srebrenica is very devastated. The roads are bad and in wintertime completely closed. In the villages there is no supply of clean drinking water during the summer. The town is neglected but I feel what this town is missing the most is people. This town is missing its physicians, engineers, teachers, and intellectuals. Before the war, Srebrenica was a very developed town. The people were educated. Now those who were educated did not come back.

They are afraid the peace is very fragile and they will have to escape over the hills again. I think the educated people are frightened for their lives and their children's future. They do not want to return. They mention that Srebrenica salaries are very low, which is true, but in my opinion fear is the main obstacle for educated people returning home.

Even today the fear in Srebrenica is tangible, magnified by the monuments and graves. The mind is left to dwell on mass executions. The Serb and Muslim people who remain are afraid to commit to a future with each other. As a result there is no future for their children. Neither side has agreed to cooperate in establishing a new society that could bring prosperity and a good life to all. Instead, life in Srebrenica remains joyless and despondent, without the coffee shops, parks, and playgrounds filled with adults and children that are characteristic of other Bosnian villages. As Jusuf summed up the situation, "I feel that Srebrenica society is very ill."

HEALING FOR THE TWENTY-FIRST CENTURY

Imagine a scenario in which the self-healing capacities of individuals are harnessed into a major social force. The collective contribution of traumatized citizens could be enormous. A new synergy would develop between trauma sufferers and society. There is hope for a community in which the marginalized survivors are welcomed back, just as Philoctetes, having been rescued by the Greeks from his abandonment on Lemnos, came back to help win the Trojan War.

When mass violence occurs, there is damage not only to individuals but to entire societies, indeed to the world. The victims of September 11 and their families and friends suffered horrible losses, but even those of us who watched the television footage suffered, whether by experiencing depression, anxiety, a loss of faith in humanity, empathic overload, or emotional withdrawal. As a consequence, healing must occur not only within individuals but also within societies, with society as the healing agent. The trauma sufferers need society's assistance in the self-healing process, and in turn they help society heal by sharing their stories, experiences, and wisdom. Personal and social healing are united in a reciprocal and mutually advantageous relationship. Through the journey of self-healing that each one takes, survivors can teach the rest of us how to recover from injury in a violent world.

This radical shift in society's view of traumatized persons must begin with the survivors themselves through the sharing of their stories. Yet revealing the full trauma story, not just the brutal facts, takes courage on the part of the survivor, especially in societies and communities where violence is endemic. Shame and embarrassment are inevitable accompaniments to physical and emotional injuries. Survivors' willingness to speak out depends on their faith that they can transform the negative emotions that have been implanted in their consciousness by violence. In order to normalize the self-healing process, traumatized people need to share both in groups of peers, which are the safest environment, and in political contexts, which are the most dangerous. Shifting from private thoughts to a public discourse allows for clarification of ideas, group support, and more effective problem-solving. Speaking out on the effects of violence in other societies and communities may be easier than doing so in one's own, because of how hard it is to discuss controversial local abuses. This is apparent in the reluctance of Americans, past and present, to address the negative psychological consequences of two momentous events in our country's history: the ethnic cleansing of Native Americans and the institution of slavery.

Trauma survivors can transform social and cultural barriers to self-healing by making it a meaningful concept in our vocabulary. Vietnamese combat veterans have already shown the way in this area by educating the world about posttraumatic stress disorder (PTSD), which has come to be universally understood as a realistic assessment of the psychological damage that can be inflicted upon soldiers who engage in life-threatening combat. The use of the term is now a call to action for preventing and treating the condition. During World War I the new term *shell shock* brought social compassion to soldiers who emotionally broke down during fighting. Similarly, when a woman is described as a victim of domestic violence, people become more capable of reaching out with nonstigmatizing help. Self-healing terminology related to violence needs to enter similarly into the public discourse.

Research must also play a major role in any modern-day plan to promote self-healing after traumatic life events. Scientific investigations now focus on illness and on detailing the negative consequences of traumatic events. When a tragic event occurs, science wants to know the pathological effects that follow at the biological and sociological levels. A major reorientation must occur, similar to the call in the 1950s for an upside-down psychiatry to abandon punitive approaches to the mentally ill person. In fact, traumatized persons are extremely resilient and find ways to cope with often incomprehensible situations. Instead of focusing on survivors' pathology and disease, we should be examining their survival and self-healing strategies. This needs to be a science of resiliency and wellness.

Professionals and volunteers who care for traumatized people must also assess whether their efforts are actually helpful. After every new catastrophe people with compassion and good intentions actively seek to help others. But rarely are the consequences of these humanitarian efforts evaluated. It is assumed that psychological and social interventions are helpful at best, benign at worst. However, misguided attempts at psychosocial assistance to traumatized persons can be extremely destructive, short-circuiting the self-healing process and creating real disease and illness. It is essential that all assistance be evaluated as to its ultimate beneficial or harmful impact on individuals and the community.[6] Not everyone who has been injured by violence wants to be aided in a way that may be culturally insensitive or disruptive to their natural self-healing capacity. For example, traumatized persons resent the automatic assumption that their history of violence requires that they undergo therapy in order to be normal.

Engaging traumatized persons in their own recovery must become a mantra of social recovery. In 2003 I visited a clinic on the outskirts of Lima, Peru, in order to train the local medical professionals in the mental health care of patients tortured by Shining Path guerillas. The clinic was located in a shantytown of 180,000 mostly Indian people fleeing the violence of the Andes and seeking work in Lima. The town was reminiscent of Site 2, in that thousands of wooden shacks had been built on a landscape that looked like the surface of the moon, with craters and hills devoid of vegetation. There were no parks, plants, electricity, or running water. Sewage ran down the dirt streets. Adolescents were aimlessly milling about. I asked the doctors at the clinic why the teenagers could not be mobilized into using their idle time to build sewers and physically improve the community. No one had an answer.

Similarly, on the other side of the world in Aceh province, Indonesia, twelve weeks after a tsunami killed hundreds of thousands of people and destroyed roads, houses, and bridges, adolescents and young adults were left idle. In spite of an enormous outpouring of international money and support, these traumatized young people were not enlisted into any meaningful community service. This inability to engage people in the rebuilding of their own future is unconscionable.

Facilitating the entry of the full trauma story, one of the most exciting dimensions of self-healing, into the social dialogue is another essential goal of recovery, but this can be an extraordinary challenge. In modern society there is rarely an opportunity for people who have experienced violence to tell their story as my father would do, sitting at the center of a family gathering in a small Italian community, teaching the young people through an oral history of real-life experience. Video games and movies seem so much more exciting than the slower pace of the storyteller.

Yet the trauma story remains a structure of great beauty embedded within our diverse cultural and social environments. In spite of the distortions and exploitations of traumatic life experiences by the media and others, the personal stories of our friends and families remain the most powerful. The news and entertainment media, particularly in America with its great power and influence, need to be engaged in a self-analysis of why they fail to present a realistic picture of violence, as well as how they can broadcast to the public the healing experiences of traumatized people and professional helpers.

The prevailing view that stories of healing and recovery will not generate enough national attention and are thus unprofitable may be wrong, and is unsubstantiated by data.

At times our cultural obsession with images of violence verges on a form of pornography. As one reporter described the television news, "If it bleeds, it leads." Yet society is cheating itself with these cheap graphic images of someone else's suffering. The media need to be encouraged to present the full trauma story, not just the horrors. Opportunities for the production of creative television and radio shows that present the complex world-in-transition of the traumatized person are limitless. In Peru more than sixty thousand persons were murdered by the Shining Path, in some cases by former government agents. Public television later told the stories of individuals and families who had testified at the Truth and Reconciliation Commission, which not only revealed the extent of atrocities committed, but more importantly achieved public insight into the transformation of lives damaged by violence.

Community-access television, radio, and the Internet can create a flourishing environment for storytelling and dialogue. Multiple stories can be shared in communities in many diverse and creative ways. National oral history archives can collect trauma narratives from survivors of such catastrophes as September 11, East Timor, Srebrenica, and Rwanda. Countries can send oral historians, anthropologists, and ethnographers into the field to collect the narratives of traumatized persons and communities. Musicologists and photographers can record their societies' cultural and material history. Recording booths, such as those experimented with in New York City, can be placed in key public locations to spontaneously capture the life histories of citizens as they strive to normalize their lives.

The arts come closest to symbolically representing human tragedy, because their methods of expression are similar to the visual picturing that occurs during the storytelling process. Modern films, plays, paintings, and sculpture can aid individuals and society in transcending the negative impact of human aggression. Picasso's icon *Guernica,* inspired by the Nazi bombing of Guernica in 1937 during the Spanish Civil War, powerfully portrays the violence and brutality of Francisco Franco's fascism. This painting, which was housed at the Museum of Modern Art in New York until 1981, when it was sent to Spain, inspired the efforts of an entire generation to prevent nuclear annihilation during the Cold War. Yet citizens do not need the great museums to discover their own healing traditions, for every community has local works of art that can clarify its own perspective on violence.

The Peter C. Alderman Foundation, created by parents whose son was killed in the attack on the Twin Towers, aims to develop an archive focused on healing near the site of Ground Zero. This athenaeum, as part of our vision, will collect and make available to the public an interactive display of narratives on self-healing and survival from traumatized persons, medical professionals, and traditional healers throughout the world.

The public commission of artworks could offer deeper cultural and social insights into violence and its healing. An Italian art impresario is currently designing an "art stop" in Rome that will include ancient Roman, Renaissance, and modern works of art that speak to us about the human responses to aggression. The "art stop" will be a self-guided walking tour to attractions such as the Coliseum, an ancient place of torture and barbarism; Raphael's *Transfiguration*; and the Etruscan fresco from the Tomba François, which displays (and warns against) the internecine destruction of Etruscan city-states. Each stop will have an accompanying written historical text, and perhaps an audiotape, addressing the issues expressed in the art that concern survival and self-healing from violence in our modern world. Other communities could create similar places of artistic reflection, leading to a public and private dialogue on violence and healing.

Similarly, local art can be integrated into places of healing. In Siem Reap, Cambodia, we were able to turn to local art to illustrate our clinic's mission as a healing place for the effects of violence. This art was not known before to the clinic's Cambodian staff. Guides at the nearby Angkor Wat temples pointed us to many beautiful bas-reliefs of healing scenes, especially on the Bayon Temple of the late twelfth to thirteenth centuries. In one bas-relief a patient from a noble family is resting on a big pillow while being comforted by a healer with his hand on the patient's head. The images and locations of these sculptures are now shared among patients and staff and have become a centerpiece of the clinic's artistic heritage, revealing the ancient Khmer's sensitivity to the healing of violence.

Violence can lead us on an unexpected journey into a strange land where, like Philoctetes, we have committed no crime, but have been abandoned and ostracized by society. Even our professional healers are capable of exploiting and abusing us. But we now know that located within our own bodies and minds is a powerful force, bursting to find expression, that is capable of healing any injury. The invisible wounds of violence are no longer invisible, and the invisible processes of self-healing are now evident. As new scientific discoveries are made, they will continue to show the tremendous power to heal that has been built into human beings over time. If society learns to use this empirical knowledge, no longer relying on social fictions and half-truths, the modern age can be an exciting one, where the effects of violence need no longer be feared, and we can welcome back into our communities those who have had to sojourn alone in the land of violence.

EPILOGUE

IN 1990 A MIRACLE OCCURRED in Thailand. The military supreme command had just about made the decision to move the 160,000 Site 2 residents—every man, woman, and child—away from the Thai-Cambodian border to a safer area, far removed from the daily exchange of rockets between the Vietnamese army and Cambodian guerillas. However, there was an ominous side to this plan. The rice fields where the refugees were to be relocated lay under a foot of water. Rumors spread throughout the camp, causing great consternation among the residents and relief workers.

I heard the rumors while on a mental health mission to the camp and immediately sent a message to the Thai general in charge, a man with a fierce and intimidating reputation. We explained to him that this relocation order, if carried out, would jeopardize the lives of camp residents, because of the health risks involved in building bamboo shacks in a malaria-infested rice paddy.

After we made our plea, the general forcefully reported back to us with some anger, "I was expecting you to argue against my order by accusing me and the Thai government of perpetrating human rights violations on the Cambodian refugees. I am the general responsible for the national security of Thailand. You are not. And I do not care what you have to say on this sensitive topic. If you had addressed me politically on this issue, I would have had you detained and immediately kicked out of Thailand and never allowed back."

We knew that in response to a human rights complaint by Amnesty International, Thailand had forcibly sent that organization out of the country and not allowed it back. The Thai general went on, "Now, however, because you have presented to me a medical argument against my decision, I will obey and cancel the order. You are medical people and know what is right for the health of the camp residents. I'm a military man, not a doctor. I only know what is best for the safety and protection of Thailand and its people."

Thousands of lives were saved on that day. Throughout the years, I have met many individuals in top political positions who have made policy decisions that had a significant impact on the mental health of traumatized persons. These policy makers usually did so because they or a family member had been damaged by the psychological consequences of violence. They knew the complexity of the trauma story firsthand and were courageous enough to follow its message.

But traumatized people cannot rely on political miracles to ease their suffering, as our nation witnessed when people died in the hurricane-flooded streets of New Orleans. Social reform needs not only the actions of enlightened leaders but also a widespread change in attitudes and practices. Because they are out of touch with the reality of their citizens, the political players maintain the neglect of the invisible wounds of violence and deny the social benefits that can accrue from the wisdom of survivors. Many traumatized persons

and their relatives, friends, and helpers have given up on society acting as a healing force because those who govern remain aloof and
critical of them. Yet this pessimism must be overcome and social reform must be launched, because the globalization of violence means
that every community has a mandate to deal with a dangerous world
that offers few spaces of safety.

At the level of healing that takes place between survivor and
healer, the reform is well advanced. Victims of violence are demonstrating that they can get better after their hurt, and their positive
healing results are being validated by science. The age of Philoctetes's
ostracism to the island of Lemnos because of the incurability of his
suffering is drawing to a close. A new age is emerging in which the
conventional medical system is being connected to the self-healing
of traumatized people.

Four simple questions summarize this therapeutic reform, providing a guide to assess the extent of self-healing in anyone. A family member helping a sexually abused relative, a parent caring for a
troubled child, a political asylum seeker assisting a tortured spouse,
and a doctor examining a traumatized patient can ask these basic
questions. The answers reveal what is being done and what still needs
to be done in the recovery process. The questions are:

What traumatic events have happened?

How are your body and mind repairing the injuries sustained
    from those events?

What have you done in your daily life to help yourself recover?

What justice do you require from society to support your
    personal healing?

I have taught mental health professionals and pastoral counselors how to use these questions in interviews. This process has

helped them achieve the beneficial effects of self-healing in their work. Traumatized persons can also profit in their own recovery efforts by systematically responding to these queries, writing down their answers, reviewing their responses, and formulating for themselves a recovery plan. I have seen this self-reflection develop into a daily meditation that leads to improved health, reduced hopelessness, and a restored sense of control over traumatic memories and emotions.

The fear of healers, as represented so powerfully in Raphael's *Transfiguration*, still needs to be addressed and overcome. Despite solid biological and sociological evidence confirming the power of self-healing and its contribution to personal resiliency, autonomy, and productivity many doctors continue to feel that survivors can't be helped. Our fear of the violated remains strong. Overcoming this fear and moving forward depends upon the universal human capacity for empathy. This ability for interconnectedness allows us to assist others as they move into new and hopefully better worlds. Empathy allows us to see that some traumatized people need to talk, others to deny, and still others to be relieved by medication. The traumatic world is not a static one, stuck in the miseries of the past, but is dynamically changing and evolving. Current therapeutic concepts that attempt to recover the life that *used to be* need to refocus their energies on to a life that is *becoming*.

Society and the professional healer can be part of this exciting transformation. Slobodan, a Serbian medical doctor in Srebrenica, epitomized the willingness to participate in the healing process through his work with Muslim patients. For a number of years after the war ended in 1995, only male Muslim patients would come to Srebrenica's health clinic for treatment, always accompanied by armed police escorts. There was a general fear in the Muslim community that they would be hurt or rejected by the clinic's doctors and nurses, all of whom were Christian Serbs. To the local Muslim population, these Serbs were contaminated by the recent massacre, even though none of them had participated in it. To make personal contact with the Muslim villagers, Slobodan took off his white coat and sat outside the clinic, casually drinking coffee. Local citizens, initially only Serbs, gathered around him to drink coffee and make conversation, which usually centered on their medical complaints. Then one day he had a breakthrough. An elderly Muslim woman approached him to share her physical complaints. His Serb acquaintances protested that he should not help her since she was an "enemy." He responded, "Why are you afraid of such an old lady?" Slobodan then escorted her into the clinic for treatment. This was a turning point for the clinic's relationship to the Muslim community.

The concept of self-healing demands a shift away from emphasizing illness and damage to appreciating natural healing processes. Modern healers, like their ancient Greek counterparts, must accept that their job is to aid the human organism's intrinsic drive to recover from the physical and mental injuries caused by violent acts. Self-healing emphasizes resiliency and well-being. In fact, it is precisely because of the self-healing response that relatively few people actually develop pathological and chronic disease states, such as severe PTSD, after violent experiences. As medicine has profited from intensive study of the normal process of physical wound healing, so it could similarly profit from a deeper understanding of the normal processes underlying the healing of trauma's invisible wounds.

Understanding these processes requires a radically different appreciation of the social role of the trauma story. The toxic trauma story that is constructed out of horrifying facts and disturbing emotions is a misplaced focus for therapists, the media, and other public interests. Telling the story of violence in this way is dangerous not only to the trauma survivor but also to society as a whole. The distorted emphasis can make survivors ill and contribute to a perverted collective memory of traumatic events, as shown by the international human rights community's obsession with mass graves in Srebrenica in lieu of focusing on reconciliation between Bosnian and Muslim neighbors. Similarly, the television images of the catastrophic displacement of thousands of persons in Louisiana after Hurricane Katrina will fade away after a few months, leaving behind the untold stories of hundreds of thousands of New Orleans residents struggling to rebuild their homes and jobs. Survivors feel exploited and demoralized as public attention shifts away from them once the concern exhibited during the immediate aftermath of a disaster fades.

When it comes to human suffering, public denial is great. Consequently, as socially responsible citizens we must learn what the full trauma story has to teach us about survival and healing. Listening takes discipline and patience to get beyond the details of brutal events to the story's deeper level of communication. It takes motivation to have enough interest in and involvement with persons affected by violence to appreciate that trauma stories and trauma survivors are primarily teachers. I have seen public television in Peru teach about recovery from violence to hundreds of thousands of citizens by broadcasting dramas based on the testimonies of the truth commission. I have seen the offices of doctors and social agencies in Boston turned into classrooms, with the survivors as the teachers. When professionals ask, "What can you tell me about what you learned from your experiences? How can other people in your family and community learn from your insights and knowledge?" useful information pours forth from the survivors. These people lay to rest our fear that the pain of trauma will be boundless and insupportable.

Evolution has created a biological necessity for all members of the human species, including children and adolescents, to contribute their life experiences to our collective survival and well-being. It is a public responsibility to learn what traumatized people have to teach, just as it is the responsibility of traumatized people to insist on teaching. Survivors demand trusted, disciplined leaders; quick and effective relief efforts; and a responsive authority figure, such as a medical doctor, who can provide protection and support. These and the many other lessons that can be learned from traumatized persons are priceless.

The trauma survivor reminds us all of our own vulnerability to tragedy and of the potential for society to abandon us. We know that society's neglect can have a greater impact on the fate of the trauma survivor than the violent injury itself. But another way is possible, as the story of victimization becomes a story of courage and the story of damage becomes a story of recovery.

In this book I have celebrated the capacity of human beings to overcome life's most horrific events as well as those traumatic experiences common in everyday life. Self-healing is found not just in the torture survivor and the families of the disappeared, the refugee and the earthquake survivor, and others who have experienced extreme violence, but in all of us. Human beings in our age, as well as over the centuries, have revealed their power to overcome human aggression and life's calamities. Yet in showing this resiliency, they have also been subject to every conceivable form of abuse and social punishment by the forces of oppression. Perpetrators will continue to fight anyone capable of resisting their goals. But we must persevere.

I am optimistic that the personal healing of traumatized people has been permanently transformed and will not revert to the hopeless attitudes and harmful practices promulgated by previous generations. But the social world in many places is still neglectful or even hostile toward these new ideas. Because my father knew this truth, his perspective on self-healing captured its essence: "See reality clearly, but never give up your dream."

ACKNOWLEDGMENTS

My work and ideas have been nurtured over the years by many sources. My mentors have included Professor Fritz Redlich, the first psychiatrist to become dean of Yale Medical School; the distinguished Yale social psychiatrist Professor Boris Astrachan; the English pioneer in the reform of the mental hospital, Professor Douglas Bennett; and the great internationalist, Professor Eugene Brody, former secretary-general of the World Federation for Mental Health. While my academic fathers promoted my scientific rebelliousness, my academic mothers, the child psychologist Dr. Nina Murray of Harvard; Dr. Patricia King, director of the Schlesinger Library at Harvard; and Ms. Sheila Biddle of the Ford Foundation, provided me with the courage to move ahead with my work in spite of conventional criticism.

I am indebted to James Lavelle, LICSW, the cofounder of our Harvard clinic, who helped build the clinic into an internationally renowned program. James's pragmatic wisdom has been invaluable. Our Cambodian colleague, Ms. Svang Tor, joined us during the clinic's early days and we have been working side by side ever since, caring for tortured and traumatized people. Many other wonderful clinicians have been an essential part of our clinical team including Dr. Ronald White, the psychiatric nurse practitioner Marguerita Reczycki, and the Vietnamese social worker Thang Pham.

I have had the privilege of spending thousands of hours in illuminating dialogue with Italy's foremost psychoanalyst, Professor Franco Paparo. Professor Massimo Ammaniti and his wife, Fausta, and Professor Giovanni Muscettola, through their generosity and support helped me reconnect with a society that has been a fountain of humanism and creativity in my work. I am indebted to the brilliant insights of my Croatian, Bosnian, and Australian colleagues, Drs. Narcissa Sarajlić, Aida Kapetanovic, and Derrick Silove. Professor Yasushi Kikuchi, Japan's foremost cultural anthropologist, has served as an ethnographic guide in all the societies that I have served.

Immediately after the September 11 tragedy, the Reverend Dr. Frederick J. Streets, Yale's chaplain, provided our clinical mission to New York with spiritual nurturance and support. Rev. Street's love of the healing experience has been an inspiration since we first became colleagues at Yale in the early 1970s. Dr. Riccardo Colasanti, a Roman Catholic brother and a leader of Caritas Rome, has also been a wonderful spiritual influence.

Since September 11, Lynn Franklin's belief in the importance of this book has been sustaining. She has been a literary agent par excellence. I thank the following editors for their assistance. Jane Isay, who acquired this book for Harcourt, had the brilliant suggestion of focusing the book on the healing experience. I am indebted to Jenna Johnson, my Harcourt editor, for her insightful direction and advice during all stages of this book's production. My manuscript editors, Virginia LaPlante and Kathleen Gleeson, did a superb job. I warmly appreciate the honest and helpful comments on the original book manuscript by Kathleen Rey Caridad, Robina Bhasin, Kris Guyot, and Micaela Iovine.

My deepest appreciation goes to all the storytellers who have shared their most intimate life experiences with me. I have been honored as a doctor and a human being to participate in the knowledge, wisdom, suffering, and recovery of so many heroic people around the world. Dr. Bakir Nakas and Mrs. Elizabeth Alderman stand out for their bravery in telling their stories without the protection of using an anonymous voice. All other names of traumatized storytellers have been disguised to hide their identities. I would like to offer a special dedication to Fataneh Moghtader, who read a little bit of this book every night for comfort while slowly being taken away by her illness. Her devotion to my work touched me deeply.

I have been moved more than I had expected in reliving the Italian immigration history of my family. My mother and father remain to me heroes for overcoming unbelievable violence to raise a family in the United States. My wife, Dr. Karen Carlson, and my children, Nicholas and Christopher, are now part of that legacy. Karen's professional passion for the health of women has been an inspiration. Her devotion to this book through every stage of its creation was an extraordinary gift of love. It was equaled by Nicholas's and Christopher's pride in Mom and Dad finally completing this herculean task.

ENDNOTES

PROLOGUE

1. Seth Mydans, "Fear of Disease," *New York Times,* December 28, 2004, A1.
2. Richard F. Mollica, "Invisible Wounds: Waging a New Kind of War," *Scientific American* 282, no. 6 (June 2000): 54–57.

CHAPTER 1

1. August B. Hollingshead and Frederick C. Redlich, *Social Class and Mental Illness: A Community Study* (New York: John Wiley and Sons, 1958).
2. Douglas Bennett, "The Chamberwell District Rehabilitation Service," in *Handbook of Psychiatric Rehabilitation,* ed. J. K. Wing and Brenda Morris (Oxford: Oxford Medical Publications, 1981).
3. E. Mapother, "Mental Hygiene in Adults," *Journal of Roy San Institute* 3 (1929): 165–75.
4. Richard F. Mollica, "Upside-Down Psychiatry: A Genealogy of Mental Health Services," in *Pathologies of the Modern Self: Postmodern Studies on Narcissism, Schizophrenia, and Depression,* ed. David Levin (New York: New York University Press, 1988): 363–84.
5. Gordon D. Fee, *New Testament Exegesis,* rev. ed. (Louisville, KY: Westminster/John Knox, 1993).
6. Herbert G. May and Bruce M. Metzger, eds., *The New Oxford Annotated Bible with the Apocrypha* (New York: Oxford University Press, 1977), 1223.

7. Richard F. Mollica and Y. Caspi-Yavin, "Measuring Torture and Torture-Related Symptoms," *Psychological Assessment: A Journal of Consulting and Clinical Psychology* 3, no. 4 (December 1991): 581–87.

8. Anne Fadiman, *The Spirit Catches You and You Fall Down* (New York: Farrar, Straus and Giroux, 1997).

9. Richard F. Mollica, "The Trauma Story," in *Post-Traumatic Therapy and Victims of Violence,* ed. F. M. Ochberg (New York: Brunner/Mazel, 1988).

10. Sappho, "Pain penetrates" in *Sappho: A New Translation,* trans. Mary Barnard (Berkeley: University of California Press, 1958), part 4, no. 60.

CHAPTER 2

1. Sophocles, *Philoctetes,* trans. R. G. Ussher (Oxford, England: Aris & Phillips, 2001).

2. Ibid, 35.

3. International Council of Scholars, *Encyclopedia of World Art,* vol. 4 (London: McGraw Hill, 1961), 308–9.

4. Richard F. Mollica, "Traumatic Outcomes: The Mental Health and Psychosocial Effects of Mass Violence," in *Humanitarian Crises: The Medical and Public Health Response,* ed. J. Leaning, S. M. Briggs, and L. Chen (Cambridge, MA: Harvard University Press, 1999).

5. Thomas Merton, *Contemplative Prayer,* introd. Thich Nhat Hanh (New York: Doubleday, 1996), 9–14.

6. Ibid, 101.

7. Richard F. Mollica and Linda Son, "Cultural Dimension in the Evaluation and Treatment of Sexual Trauma," *Psychiatric Clinics of North America* 12, no. 2 (June 1989): 372–74.

8. Sophocles, *Philoctetes,* Ussher, 35.

9. Ibid.

10. Sophocles, *Philoctetes,* ed. T. B. L. Webster (1970; reprint, Cambridge, England: Cambridge University Press, 2002), 79.

11. David Spiegel, "Healing Words: Emotional Expression and Disease Outcome," *Journal of the American Medical Association* 281, no. 14 (April 14, 1999): 1328–29.

12. Lynn C. Franklin, *May the Circle Be Unbroken: An Intimate Journey into the Heart of Adoption* (New York: Harmony Books, 1998).

13. J. M. Smyth, A. A. Stone, A. Hurewitz, and A. Kaell, "Effects of Writing about Stressful Experiences on Symptom Reduction in Patients with Asthma or Rheumatoid Arthritis: A Randomized Trial," *Journal of the American Medical Association* 281, no. 14 (April 14, 1999): 1304–9.

CHAPTER 3

1. D. C. Henderson, P. van de Velde, R. F. Mollica, and J. Lavelle, *The Crisis in Rwanda: Mental Health in the Service of Justice and Healing* (Cambridge, MA: Harvard Program in Refugee Trauma, 1996).
2. A. E. Goldfeld, R. F. Mollica, B. H. Pesavento, and S. V. Faraone, "The Physical and Psychological Sequelae of Torture: Symptomatology and Diagnosis," *Journal of the American Medical Association* 259, no. 18 (May 13, 1988): 2725–29.
3. Lydia Polgreen, "Painful Legacy of Darfur's Horrors," *International Herald Tribune,* February 12 and 13, 2005, 1 and 4.
4. Alfred de Vigny, *Oeuvres Poetiques* (Paris: Garnier Flammarion, 1978).
5. Jean-Jacques Rousseau, *On the Social Contract,* Book 1, trans. G. D. H. Cole (Mineola, NY: Dover Publications, 2003), 1.
6. David P. Chandler, *Brother Number One: A Political Biography of Pol Pot* (Boulder, CO: Westview Press, 1992), 143.
7. Ytzhak, "Osama bin Laden Turns to Poetry," *Victoria Independent Media Center,* September 20, 2003, http://victoria.indymedia.org/news/2003/09/16949.php.
8. United States Department of Defense, "Transcript of Usama bin Laden Video Tape," December 13, 2001, http://www.defenselink.mil/news/Dec2001/d20011213ubl.pdf.
9. Osama bin Laden, "Letter to America," *The Observer,* November 24, 2002, http://www.observer.guardian.co.uk/worldview/story/0,11581,845725,00.html.
10. Osama bin Laden, "Bin Laden tape: Text," BBC News, February 12, 2003, http://news.bbc.co.uk/2/hi/middle_east/2751019.stm.
11. David Trimble, "Nobel Peace Prize Acceptance Speech" (Oslo, December 10, 1998), http://cain.ulst.ac.uk/events/peace/docs/nobeldt.htm.

CHAPTER 4

1. Richard F. Mollica and Russell R. Jalbert, *Community of Confinement* (Alexandria, VA: Committee on Refugees and Migrants, The World Federation for Mental Health, February 1989).
2. Dennis S. Charney, MD, "Psychobiological Mechanism of Resilience and Vulnerability: Implications for Successful Adaptation to Extreme Stress," *American Journal of Psychiatry* 161, no. 2 (February 2004): 195–216.
3. B. A. van der Kolk, M. S. Greenberg, S. P. Orr, and R. K. Pitman, "Endogenous Opioids, Stress Induced Analgesia, and Posttraumatic Stress Disorder," *Psychopharmacology Bulletin* 25 (1989): 417–21.

4. Joseph E. LeDoux, "Emotion, Memory, and the Brain, " *Scientific American,* spec. ed. (April 1, 2002): 62–71.

5. Ibid.

6. Steven M. Southwick, Meena Vythilingam, and Dennis S. Charney, "The Psychobiology of Depression and Resilience to Stress: Implications for Prevention and Treatment," *Annual Review of Clinical Psychology* 1 (April 2005): 255–91.

7. Guido Majno, *The Healing Hand,* 3rd ed. (Cambridge, MA: Harvard University Press, 1982).

8. Stanley Jackson, *Care of the Psyche: A History of Psychological Healing* (New Haven: Yale University Press, 1999).

9. William Osler, *Aequanimitas* (New York: Norton, 1963).

CHAPTER 5

1. Primo Levi, *Survival in Auschwitz and The Reawakening: Two Memoirs,* trans. Stuart Woolf (New York: Summit, 1958), 60.

2. I. Agger, "The Female Political Prisoner" (paper, Eighth World Congress of Sexology, Heidelberg, June 14–20, 1987).

3. Jodi Halpern, "What Is Clinical Empathy?" *Journal of General Internal Medicine* 18, no. 8 (August 2003): 670–74.

4. Herbert M. Adler, "The Sociophysiology of Caring in the Doctor-Patient Relationship, " *Journal of General Internal Medicine* 17, no. 11 (November 2002): 883–90.

5. Richard F. Mollica, Y. Kikuchi, J. Lavelle, and K. Allden, *The Invisible Human Crisis: Mental Health Recommendations for Care of Persons Evacuated and Displaced by the Hanshin-Awaji (Kobe Earthquake)* (Harvard University and Waseda University, April 1995).

6. Sumako Harada, *From the Crumbled City: Tanka and Haiku of the Kobe Earthquake,* 1, A.

7. Beverly Raphael, J. P. Wilson, eds. *Psychological Debriefing: Theory, Practice, and Evidence* (New York: Cambridge University Press, 2000).

CHAPTER 6

1. Sigmund Freud, *The Interpretation of Dreams* (New York: Basic Books, 1955), 4–5.

2. Jonathan Winson, "The Meaning of Dreams," *Scientific American,* special ed. (April 1, 2002): 54–61.

3. Ibid., 60.

4. Ibid.

5. Richard F. Mollica, K. Rey, and M. Massaglia, "Longitudinal Study of Memory Consistency among Bosnian Refugees" (Unpublished manuscript, 2005).

6. Richard F. Mollica, N. Sarajlić, M. Chernoff, et al., "Longitudinal Study of Psychiatric Symptoms, Disability, Mortality, and Emigration Among Bosnian Refugees," *Journal of the American Medical Association* 286, no. 5 (August 1, 2001): 546–554.

7. Richard M. Wenzlaff and Daniel M. Wegner, "Thought Suppression," *Annual Review of Psychology* 51 (February 2000): 59–91.

8. Michael C. Anderson, Kevin N. Ochsner, Brice Kuhl, et al., "Neural Systems Underlying the Suppression of Unwanted Memories," *Science* 303 (January 9, 2004): 232–35.

9. Barry Krakow, M. Hollifield, L. Johnston, et al., "Imagery Rehearsal Therapy for Chronic Nightmares in Sexual Assault Survivors with Posttraumatic Stress Disorder," *Journal of the American Medical Association* 286, no. 5 (August 1, 2001): 537–45.

10. W. Gordon Lawrence, *Introduction to Social Dreaming* (London, England: Karnac, 2005).

11. Evan S. Connell, *Son of the Morning Star: Custer and the Little Bighorn* (1984; reprint, New York: Promontory Press, 1993), 64.

12. Brian MacQuarrie, "Reservation Where 10 Died Has Long Known Pain," *Boston Globe*, March 24, 2005, 1, 21.

13. Ron Balamuth, "Childreamatrix: Dreaming with Preschool Children, or Bootlegging Dreams into the School Years," in *Experiences in Social Dreaming*, ed. W. Gordon Lawrence (London, England: Karnac, 2003).

CHAPTER 7

1. Justin Kaplan, ed., *Bartlett's Familiar Quotations* (Boston: Little, Brown and Co., 1992), 537.

2. Charles Darwin, *The Origin of Species* (London: Murray, 1859; reprint, New York: Gramercy, 1979).

3. Edward O. Wilson, *Sociobiology,* abridged ed. (Cambridge, MA: Harvard University Press, 1980), 126.

4. Marlise Simons, "Officers Say Bosnian Massacre Was Deliberate," *New York Times International,* October 12, 2003, 10.

5. Chet Raymo, "Prying Open Darwin's 'Black Box,'" *Boston Globe*, July 19, 1999, C2.

6. Alison Jolly, *Lucy's Legacy: Sex and Intelligence in Human Evolution* (Cambridge, MA: Harvard University Press, 1999).

7. Sally Satel and Christina Hoff Sommers, "The Mental Health Crisis That Wasn't: How the Trauma Industry Exploited 9/11," *Reason* 37, no. 4 (August/September 2005): 48–55.

8. Seth Mydans, "Thai Villagers Haunted by Tsunami's Missing," *International Herald Tribune*, February 9, 2005, 2.

9. Swedish Integration Board, "Rapport Integration" (2003), 83.

10. Quoted in A. S. L. Farquharson, trans., *The Meditations of Marcus Aurelius Antoninus* (1989; reprint, Oxford: Oxford University Press, 1998).

11. Harold Koenig and Harvey Jay Cohen, eds., *The Link Between Religion and Health: Psychoneuroimmunology and the Faith Factor* (Cambridge: Oxford University Press, 2002).

12. Desmond Mpilo Tutu, *No Future Without Forgiveness* (New York: Doubleday, 1999).

13. Michael H. Monroe, D. Bynum, B. Susi, et al., "Primary Care Physician Preferences Regarding Spiritual Behavior in Medical Practice," *Archives of Internal Medicine* 163, no. 22 (December 8, 2003): 2751–56.

Chapter 8

1. Giorgio Vasari, *Lives of the Most Eminent Painters*, ed. Marilyn A. Lavin and trans. Mrs. Jonathan Foster (New York: Heritage, 1967), 59.

2. Gerald D. Hart, *Asclepius, the God of Medicine* (London, England: Royal Society of Medicine Press, 2000), 41–51.

3. Owsei Temkin and C. Lilian Temkin, eds., *Ancient Medicine: Selected Papers of Ludwig Edelstein* (Baltimore: Johns Hopkins Press, 1967), 229.

4. World Health Organization, Official Records, Number 2, "Preamble to the Constitution of the World Health Organization" (New York, July 22, 1946), 100.

5. Indu Capoor, Centre for Health Education, Training and Nutrition Awareness (CHETNA), Gujarat, India. October 29–November 11, 2001. Lecture, Fulbright New Century Scholars Program, Bellagio, Italy. Power of Definition in Global Health, http://www.cies.org/ncs(2001).

6. Grant N. Marshall, Terry L. Schell, Marc N. Elliott, et al., "Mental Health of Cambodian Refugees 2 Decades after Resettlement in the United States," *Journal of the American Medical Association* 294, no. 5 (August 3, 2005): 571–79.

7. D. A. Lawlor and S. W. Hopker, "The Effectiveness of Exercise as an Intervention in the Management of Depression: Systematic Review and Meta-Regression Analysis of Randomised Controlled Trials," *British Medical Journal* 322, no. 7289 (March 31, 2001): 763–66.

8. Richard F. Mollica, K. Donelan, S. Tor, et al., "The Effect of Trauma and Confinement on Functional Health and Mental Health Status of Cambodians Living in Thai-Cambodia Border Camps," *Journal of the American Medical Association* 270, no. 5 (August 4, 1993): 581–86.

9. Brent Q. Hafen, Keith J. Karren, Kathryn J. Frandsen, and N. Lee Smith, *Mind/Body Health* (Needham Heights, MA: Allyn and Bacon, 1996), 41–43.

10. Thomas Holmes and Richard Rahe, "The Social Readjustment Rating Scale," *Journal of Psychosomatic Research* 11, no. 2 (August 1967): 213–18.

11. Quoted in Hafen, *Mind/Body Health,* 552.

12. R. Martin, "Sense of Humor," in *Positive Psychological Assessment: A Handbook of Models and Measures,* ed. S. J. Lopez, C. R. Snyder (Washington, DC: American Psychological Association, 2003): 313–26.

CHAPTER 9

1. Takeo Doi, *The Anatomy of Dependence,* trans. John Bester (New York: Kodansha, 2001), 29–30.

2. Applied Research and Consulting, Columbia University Mailman School of Public Health, and New York State Psychiatric Institute, *Effects of the World Trade Center Attack on NYC Public School Students* (New York, May 6, 2002).

3. Susan D. Kelley, L. McDonald, and R. F. Mollica, *Psychosocial and the Concrete Realities of Psychosocial Practice at the Field Level in Bosnia and Cambodia* (Cambridge, MA: Harvard Medical School, July 2004).

4. Merrill Smith, ed., *Warehousing Refugees: A Denial of Rights, A Waste of Humanity* (Washington, DC: World Refugee Survey, U.S. Committee for Refugees, 2004), 11.

5. Tara Gingerich and Jennifer Leaning, *The Use of Rape as a Weapon of War in the Conflict in Darfur, Sudan* (Boston, MA: U.S. Agency for International Development/OTI, October 2004), 10–11.

6. Richard F. Mollica, B. Lopes Cardozo, H. J. Osofsky, et al., "Mental Health in Complex Emergencies," *The Lancet* 364, no. 9450 (December 4, 2004): 2058–67.

BIBLIOGRAPHY

Adler, Herbert M. "The Sociophysiology of Caring in the Doctor–Patient Relationship." *Journal of Internal Medicine* 17, no. 11 (November 2002): 883–90.

Agger, I. "The Female Political Prisoner." Paper. Eighth World Congress of Sexology. Heidelberg, June 14–20, 1987.

Alighieri, Dante. *The Divine Comedy*. Translated by James F. Cotter. Warwick, NY: Amity House, 1987.

Anderson, Michael C., Kevin N. Ochsner, Brice Kuhl, Jeffrey Cooper, Elaine Robertson, Susan W. Gabrieli, Gary H. Glover, and John D. E. Gabrieli, "Neural Systems Underlying the Suppression of Unwanted Memories." *Science* 303 (January 9, 2004): 232–35.

Applied Research and Consulting, LLC, Columbia University Mailman School of Public Health, and New York State Psychiatric Institute. *Effects of the World Trade Center Attack on NYC Public School Students*. New York, May 6, 2002.

Balamuth, Ron. "Childreamatrix: Dreaming with Preschool Children, or Bootlegging Dreams into the School Years." In *Experiences in Social Dreaming*, edited by W. Gordon Lawrence. London, UK: Karnac, 2003.

Bennett, Douglas. "The Chamberwell District Rehabilitation Service." In *Handbook of Psychiatric Rehabilitation*, edited by J. K. Wing and Brenda Morris. Oxford: Oxford Medical Publications, 1981.

Bertram, Christopher. *Routledge Philosophy Guidebook to Rousseau and The Social Contract*. New York: Routledge, 2003.

Bin Laden, Osama. "Letter to America." *The Observer*, November 24, 2002. http://observer.guardian.co.uk/worldview/story/0,11581,845725,00 .html.

Carroll, Lewis. *Alice's Adventures in Wonderland & Through the Looking-Glass*. New York: Signet Classics, 2000.

Chandler, David P. *Brother Number One: A Political Biography of Pol Pot*. Boulder, CO: Westview Press, 1992.

Charney, Dennis S. "Psychobiological Mechanism of Resilience and Vulnerability: Implications for Successful Adaptation to Extreme Stress." *American Journal of Psychiatry* 161, no. 2 (February 2004): 195–216.

Connell, Evan S. *Son of the Morning Star: Custer and the Little Bighorn*. 1984. Reprint, New York: Promontory Press, 1993.

Darwin, Charles. *The Origin of Species*. London: Murray, 1859. Reprint, New York: Gramercy, 1979.

De Vigny, Alfred. *Oeuvres Poetiques*. Paris: Garnier Flammarion, 1978.

Doi, Takeo. *The Anatomy of Dependence*. Translated by John Bester. New York: Kodansha, 2001.

Fadiman, Anne. *The Spirit Catches You and You Fall Down*. New York: Farrar, Straus and Giroux, 1997.

Farquharson, A. S. L., trans. *The Meditations of Marcus Aurelius Antoninus*. 1989. Reprint, Oxford: Oxford University Press, 1998.

Fee, Gordon D. *New Testament Exegesis*. Revised ed. Louisville, KY: Westminster/John Knox, 1993.

Franklin, Lynn C. *May the Circle Be Unbroken: An Intimate Journey into the Heart of Adoption*. New York: Harmony Books, 1998.

Freud, Sigmund. *The Interpretation of Dreams*. New York: Basic Books, 1955.

Gingerich, Tara, and Jennifer Leaning. *The Use of Rape as a Weapon of War in the Conflict in Darfur, Sudan*. Report. Boston, MA: US Agency for International Development/OTI, October 2004.

Goldfeld, A. E., R. F. Mollica, B. H. Pesavento, and S. V. Faraone. "The Physical and Psychological Sequelae of Torture: Symptomatology and Diagnosis." *Journal of the American Medical Association* 259, no. 18 (May 13, 1988): 2725–29.

Goodman, Nelson. *Ways of Worldmaking*. Indianapolis: Hackett Publishing, 1978.

Hafen, Brent Q., Keith J. Karren, Kathryn J. Frandsen, and N. Lee Smith. *Mind/Body Health*. Needham Heights, MA: Allyn and Bacon, 1996.

Halpern, Jodi. "What Is Clinical Empathy?" *Journal of General Internal Medicine* 18, no. 8 (August 2003): 670–74.

Harada, Sumako. *From the Crumbled City: Tanka and Haiku of the Kobe Earthquake.*

Hart, Gerald D. *Asclepius, the God of Medicine.* London, England: Royal Society of Medicine Press, 2000.

Hayes, John H., and Carl R. Holladay. *Biblical Exegesis.* Revised ed. Atlanta: John Knox Press, 1987.

Henderson, D. C., P. van de Velde, R. F. Mollica, and J. Lavelle. *The Crisis in Rwanda: Mental Health in the Service of Justice and Healing.* Cambridge, MA: Harvard Program in Refugee Trauma, 1996.

Hollingshead, August B., and Frederick C. Redlich. *Social Class and Mental Illness.* New York: John Wiley and Sons, 1958.

Holmes, Thomas, and Richard Rahe. "The Social Readjustment Rating Scale." *Journal of Psychosomatic Research* 11, no. 2 (August 1967): 213–18.

International Council of Scholars. *Encyclopedia of World Art.* London: McGraw Hill, 1961.

Jackson, Stanley. *Care of the Psyche: A History of Psychological Healing.* New Haven: Yale University Press, 1999.

Jolly, Alison. *Lucy's Legacy: Sex and Intelligence in Human Evolution.* Cambridge, MA: Harvard University Press, 1999.

Kaplan, Justin, ed. *Bartlett's Familiar Quotations.* Boston: Little, Brown, 1992.

Kelley, Susan D., L. McDonald, and R. F. Mollica. *Psychosocial and the Concrete Realities of Psychosocial Practice at the Field Level in Bosnia and Cambodia.* Report. Cambridge, MA: Harvard Medical School, July 2004.

Koenig, Harold, and Harvey Jay Cohen, eds. *The Link Between Religion and Health: Psychoneuroimmunology and the Faith Factor.* Cambridge: Oxford University Press, 2002.

Krakow, Barry, M. Hollifield, L. Johnston, et al. "Imagery Rehearsal Therapy for Chronic Nightmares in Sexual Assault Survivors with Posttraumatic Stress Disorder." *Journal of the American Medical Association* 286, no. 5 (2001): 537–45.

Lakoff, George, and Mark Johnson. *Philosophy in the Flesh: The Embodied Mind and Its Challenge to Western Thought.* New York: Basic Books, 1999.

Lawlor, D. A., and S. W. Hopker. "The Effectiveness of Exercise as an Intervention in the Management of Depression: Systematic Review and Meta-Regeression Analysis of Randomised Controlled Trials." *British Medical Journal* 322, no. 7289 (March 31, 2001): 763–66.

Lawrence, W. Gordon. *Introduction to Social Dreaming.* London, UK: Karnac, 2005.

LeDoux, Joseph E. "Emotion, Memory, and the Brain." *Scientific American*, special ed. (April 1, 2002): 62–71.

Levi, Primo. *Survival in Auschwitz and The Reawakening: Two Memoirs.* Translated by Stuart Woolf. New York: Summit Books, 1958.

MacQuarrie, Brian. "Reservation Where 10 Died Has Long Known Pain." *Boston Globe*, March 24, 2005, 1, 21.

Majno, Guido. *The Healing Hand.* 3rd ed. Cambridge, MA: Harvard University Press, 1982.

Mapother, E. "Mental Hygiene in Adults." *Journal of Roy San Institute* 3 (1929): 165–75.

Marshall, Grant N., Terry L. Schell, Marc N. Elliott, et al. "Mental Health of Cambodian Refugees 2 Decades after Resettlement in the United States." *Journal of the American Medical Association* 294, no. 5 (August 3, 2005): 571–79.

Martin, R. "Sense of Humor." In *Positive Psychological Assessment: A Handbook of Models and Measures*, edited by S. J. Lopez and C. R. Snyder. (Washington, DC: American Psychological Association, 2003): 313–26.

May, Herbert G., and Bruce M. Metzger, eds. *The New Oxford Annotated Bible with the Apocrypha.* New York: Oxford University Press, 1977.

Merton, Thomas. *Contemplative Prayer.* Introduction by Thich Nhat Hanh. New York: Doubleday, 1996.

Mollica, Richard F. "Invisible Wounds: Waging a New Kind of War." *Scientific American* 282, no. 6 (June 2000): 54–57.

———. "The Trauma Story." In *Post-Traumatic Therapy and Victims of Violence*, edited by F. M. Ochberg. New York: Brunner/Mazel, 1988.

———. "Traumatic Outcomes: The Mental Health and Psychosocial Effects of Mass Violence." In *Humanitarian Emergencies: The Medical and Public Health Response*, edited by J. Leaning, S. M. Briggs, and L. Chen. Cambridge, MA: Harvard University Press, 1999.

———. "Upside-Down Psychiatry: A Genealogy of Mental Health Services." In *Pathologies of the Modern Self: Postmodern Studies on Narcissism, Schizophrenia, and Depression*, edited by David Levin, 363–84. New York: New York University Press, 1988.

———, B. Lopes Cardozo, H. J. Osofsky, et al. "Mental Health in Complex Emergencies." *The Lancet* 364, no. 9450 (December 4, 2004): 2058–67.

———, et al. "The Effect of Trauma and Confinement on Functional Health and Mental Health Status of Cambodians Living in Thai-Cambodia Border Camps." *Journal of the American Medical Association* 270, no. 5 (August 4, 1993): 581–86.

———, A. E. Goldfeld, B. H. Pesavento, and S. V. Faraone. "The Physical and Psychological Sequelae of Torture: Symptomatology and Diagnosis," *Journal of the American Medical Association* 259, no. 18 (May 13, 1988): 2725–29.

———, and Y. Caspi-Yavin. "Measuring Torture and Torture-Related Symptoms." *Psychological Assessment: A Journal of Consulting and Clinical Psychology* 3, no. 4 (December 1991): 581–87.

———, and Russell R. Jalbert. *Community of Confinement*. Alexandria, VA: Committee on Refugees and Migrants, The World Federation for Mental Health, February 1989.

———, Y. Kikuchi, J. Lavelle, and K. Allden. *The Invisible Human Crisis: Mental Health Recommendations for Care of Persons Evacuated and Displaced by the Hanshin-Awaji (Kobe Earthquake)*. Harvard University and Waseda University, April 1995.

———, B. Lopes Cardozo, H. J. Osofsky, B. Raphael, A. Ager, and P. Salama. "Mental Health in Complex Emergencies." *Lancet* 364 (2004): 2058–67.

———, K. Rey, and M. Massaglia. "Longitudinal Study of Memory Consistency among Bosnian Refugees." Unpublished manuscript, 2005.

———, N. Sarajlić, M. Chernoff, et al. "Longitudinal Study of Psychiatric Symptoms, Disability, Mortality, and Emigration among Bosnian Refugees." *Journal of the American Medical Association* 286, no. 5 (2001): 546–54.

———, and Linda Son, "Cultural Dimension in the Evaluation and Treatment of Sexual Trauma." *Psychiatric Clinics of North America* 12, no. 2 (June 1989): 372–74.

Monroe, Michael, et al. "Primary Care Physician Preferences Regarding Spiritual Behavior in Medical Practice," *The Archives of Internal Medicine* 163, no. 22 (December 8, 2003): 2751–56.

Mydans, Seth. "Fear of Disease." *New York Times*. December 28, 2004, A1.

———. "Thai Villagers Haunted by Tsunami's Missing." *International Herald Tribune*, February 9, 2005, 2.

Osler, William. *Aequanimitas*. New York: Norton, 1963.

Polgreen, Lydia. "Painful Legacy of Darfur's Horrors." *International Herald Tribune*. February 12 and 13, 2005, 1 and 4.

Raphael, Beverly, and J. P. Wilson, eds. *Psychological Debriefing: Theory, Practice, and Evidence*. New York: Cambridge University Press, 2000.

Raymo, Chet. "Prying Open Darwin's 'Black Box.'" *Boston Globe*, July 19, 1999, C2.

Rousseau, Jean-Jacques. *On the Social Contract*. Translated by G. D. H. Cole. Mineola, NY: Dover, 2003.

Sappho. *Sappho: A New Translation.* Translated by Mary Barnard. Berkeley: University of California Press, 1958.

Satel, Sally, and Christina Hoff Sommers. "The Mental Health Crisis That Wasn't: How the Trauma Industry Exploited 9/11." *Reason* 37, no. 4 (August/September 2005): 48–55.

Simons, Marlise. "Officers Say Bosnian Massacre Was Deliberate." *New York Times International,* October 12, 2003.

Smith, Merrill, ed. *Warehousing Refugees: A Denial of Rights, A Waste of Humanity.* World Refugee Survey. Washington, DC: U.S. Committee for Refugees, 2004.

Smyth, J. M., A. A. Stone, A. Hurewitz, and A. Kaell. "Effects of Writing about Stressful Experiences on Symptom Reduction in Patients with Asthma or Rheumatoid Arthritis: A Randomized Trial." *Journal of the American Medical Association* 281, no. 44 (April 14, 1999): 1304–9.

Sophocles. *Philoctetes.* Translated by R. G. Ussher. Oxford, England: Aris & Phillips, 2001.

———. *Philoctetes.* Edited by T. B. L. Webster. Cambridge, England: Cambridge University Press, 2002.

Southwick, Steven M., Meena Vythilingam, and Dennis S. Charney. "The Psychobiology of Depression and Resilience to Stress: Implications for Prevention and Treatment." *Annual Review of Clinical Psychology* 1 (April 2005): 255–91.

Spiegel, David. "Healing Words: Emotional Expression and Disease Outcome." *Journal of the American Medical Association* 281, no. 14 (April 14, 1999): 1328–29.

Swedish Integration Board. "Rapport Integration." 2003.

Temkin, Owsei, and C. Lilian Temkin, eds. *Ancient Medicine: Selected Papers of Ludwig Edelstein.* Baltimore: Johns Hopkins Press, 1967.

Throckmorton, Burton H., Jr., ed. *Gospel Parallels: A Synopsis of the First Three Gospels.* 2nd ed. New York: Thomas Nelson and Sons, 1957.

Tutu, Desmond Mpilo. *No Future Without Forgiveness.* New York: Doubleday, 1999.

United States Department of Defense. "Transcript of Osama bin Laden Video Tape," December 13, 2001. http://www.defense/in.mil/news/Dec20011d20011213ubl.pfd.

Van der Kolk, B. A., M. S. Greenberg, S. P. Orr, and R. K. Pitman. "Endogenous Opioids, Stress Induced Analgesia, and Posttraumatic Stress Disorder." *Psychopharmacology Bulletin* 25 (1989): 417–21.

Vasari, Giorgio. *Lives of the Most Eminent Painters.* Edited by Marilyn A. Lavin and Mrs. Jonathan Foster. New York: Heritage, 1967.

Wenzlaff, Richard M., and Daniel M. Wegner. "Thought Suppression." *Annual Review of Psychology* 51 (2000): 59–91.

Wilson, Edward O. *Sociobiology: The Abridged Edition.* Cambridge, MA: Harvard University Press, 1980.

Winson, Jonathan. "The Meaning of Dreams." *Scientific American*, special ed. (April 1, 2002): 54–61.

Ytzhak. "Osama bin Laden Turns to Poetry." *Victoria Independent Media Center*, September 20, 2003. http://victoria.indymedia.org/news/2003/09/16949.php.

INDEX

adoption, birth mothers and, 61
Afghanistan, 64, 129, 132, 153
African Americans
    dummy personality and, 71
    slavery and, 71, 76, 202, 235
    terrorism and, 220
    treatment biases toward, 9
Alderman, Liz and Steve, 129–133
al-Qaeda, 74, 83–85, 86
altruism, 165–170, 186, 207, 211–212
amae, 218-220
Amduat (The Book of That Which Is in the World Beyond the Grave), 36
American Refugee Committee (ARC), 89
Amnesty International, 242
amygdala, 96, 97
Anatomy of Dependence, The (Doi), 218
animism, 176, 179
Argentina, 66, 76
artwork
    human tragedy represented in, 36, 77, 238–240
    importance of here and now in, 157–158

pain of healers and, 29–30, 48, 188–191
    trauma stories as, 121–125
Asclepius, 191
Astrachan, Boris, 215, 217
asylum policies, impact of, 174–175
Auschwitz, 110–111
Australia, asylum policies of, 174–175

Balamuth, Ron, 152
Barrett, Michael, 216
Bedlam Hospital (London), 13–14
Bennett, Douglas, 13–14, 194, 235–236
beta-endorphins, 95
betrayal, family solidarity and, 200–202
Bible, exegesis and, 16–17
bin Laden, Osama, 83–85
Bolanski, C., 25–26
Bosnia-Herzegovina, 48–61, 76, 125–128, 129, 156, 173–174
    black humor and, 123
    civil war and, 148–151
    cultural annihilation and, 65–66

Bosnia-Herzegovina (*continued*)
  ethnic cleansing in, 66, 149–150,
    152–153
  rape in, 140, 180
  Sarajevo siege (1992), 24–26,
    49–61, 64, 67, 94–95
  spirituality and, 178, 179,
    182–184
  Srebrenica massacre (1995), 76,
    77–78, 139, 149–150, 152–153,
    163, 165–166, 229, 244–245,
    246
brainwashing, 18
brain waves, 136–137
Brody, Robert, 206
Buddhist rituals, 41–42, 101, 114,
    138–139, 168–169, 182
Burundi, genocide in, 62

Cambodia, 129, 153, 240
Cambodian refugees, 8–24. *See also*
    Harvard Program in Refugee
    Trauma/Indochinese Psychiatry
    Clinic; Khmer Rouge regime;
    Site 2 refugee camp
  brainwashing and, 18
  dummy personality and, 68–72
  "The King Snake" fable, 43–46
  limits of psychiatric tools, 10–13
  new clinical approach for, 13–19
  oral history of Cambodian women,
    27–30, 37–48, 60, 107
  self-care instruction for, 194–208
cancer, 198, 205
Caravaggio (*Madonna die
    Palafrenieri*), 32–33
cardiovascular disease, 95, 145, 198
Cezanne, Paul, 157–158
Chile, 66, 76, 129, 153
  Pinochet's regime in, 40, 73,
    111–113, 228
Chippewa people, 152
concentration camps
  altruism in, 166

Khmer Rouge, 10–13, 73, 116–117,
    135–136, 177, 201–203, 225–226
  Nazi, 55–56, 65, 110–111
Congo, 104
cooperation
  altruism as, 165–170
  in self-healing process, 163–164,
    165
cortex, 96, 142
cortisol, 95
courage, in self-healing process,
    158–162
Cousins, Norman, 206
creativity, in trauma stories, 124
crimes against humanity, 66, 230
cultural annihilation, 64–72
  destruction of ordinary reality and,
    67–68
  dummy personality and, 68–72
  "ethnic cleansing," 66, 149–153, 235
  language and, 69–70
  nature of, 64
  origins of, 65–66
  sexual violence and, 66–67

damnatio memoriae (damnation of
    the memory), 75–78
Darfur, Sudan, 67
Dart, Raymond, 162–163
Darwin, Charles, 162
Dayton Peace Accords (1995), 48–49,
    174, 183–184
declarative memory, 96–97
dependency, obligation *versus*, 218–222
depression, 99–100
  humiliation and, 78–81, 122
  of refugees, 175
diabetes, 194
dihydroepiandrosterone (DHEA), 95
"disappeared" people, 76–78,
    149–150, 229
Doi, Takeo, 218
domestic violence, 63, 71–72, 209,
    235

dreams, 134–156
  collective sharing of, 147–155
  in connecting inner and outer
    worlds, 155–156
  failed memories and, 142–147,
    203–204
  negative roles of, 139–147
  nightmares, 134–138, 140–147, 150,
    152, 155–156, 203–204
  positive roles of, 136–139
  social relevance of, 155–156
  spirits and, 182, 183
  unconscious and, 135, 137

East Timor, independence from
    Indonesia (1999), 63, 174, 178,
    179
ego splitting, 68–72
Egypt, ancient, 36
electroencephalogram (EEG), 136
El Salvador, Catholic Church and,
    179
emotional memory, 96–97
empathy, 115–121, 244
  in bridging cultures, 119–121
  defined, 115
  healing impact of, 116–118,
    169–170, 223–224
  nature of, 115–116
  origins of concept, 115
  trauma stories and, 115–121, 128
endorphins, 199
ethnic cleansing, 66, 149–153, 235.
    See also cultural annihilation
ethnic identity, pride in, 196
exegesis, 15–19
exercise, in self-healing process,
    195–197, 209

failed memories, dreams and,
    142–147, 203–204
fear, 96, 122, 145–146
  of healers, 188–190, 244
fight or flight response, 95–97, 199

First Night custom (Ottoman
    Empire), 56
Franklin, Lynn, 61
French Revolution, 83
Freud, Sigmund, 135

genocide
  in Burundi, 62
  in Cambodia (1975-1979), 11, 23,
    24, 92, 99, 101, 194, 225–226
  in the Holocaust, 13, 31, 55–56, 65,
    110–111
  Native American, 150–152, 235
  in Rwanda, 62–63, 67–68, 73–74,
    121, 129, 159–161
Geta, 77
Greece, ancient, 34–35, 191–193, 234
Guatemala, 66
Guernica (Picasso), 239

Harada, Sumako, 120–121
Harvard Program in Refugee
    Trauma/Indochinese Psychiatry
    Clinic
  attempt to close, 214–218
  Bosnia trauma story, 48–61,
    125–128
  creation of beauty and, 105–109
  establishment of, 8–24
  expansion to full-time clinic,
    19–22
  mental health needs of refugees,
    10–13
  oral history of Cambodian women,
    27–30, 37–48, 60, 107
  phenomenological method and,
    14–15
healers. See also empathy;
    Harvard Program in Refugee
    Trauma/Indochinese Psychiatry
    Clinic; self-healing
  in ancient civilizations, 191–193
  drugs and, 14, 147, 223
  good prognosis and, 190–194

healers (*continued*)
    humanitarian relief efforts and,
        224–228, 236
    medical arrogance and, 222–224
    pain of, 29–33, 48, 49–61, 188–191,
        244
    questions for therapeutic reform,
        243–244
    requests for help with self-healing
        and, 26–27, 224–228
health. *See also* self-healing
    defining, 193
    global transformation of concept
        of, 193–194
    importance of, 57–58
heart disease, 95, 145, 198
Hera, 34–35
Hercules, 34–35
hippocampus, 96
Holmes, Thomas, 198–199
Holocaust, 13, 31, 55–56, 65,
    110–111
Honan, Kevin, 216
humane deterrence, 174, 226
humanitarian relief efforts, 224–228,
    236. *See also* International Red
    Cross; United Nations (UN)
human rights
    healing *versus,* 228–231
    laws concerning, 66, 85, 230
humiliation, 41–42
    components of, 78–81, 122
    creating sense of, 74–75
    damnation of the memory and,
        75–78
    as emotional state caused by
        violence, 63, 72–81, 148–149
    as motivation for violence, 56,
        81–87
    reversing feelings of, 170
    sexual, 75, 111–113
    work in healing of, 173
humor, 3, 123, 204–206
Hun Sen, 228

Hurricane Katrina (2005), 153, 156,
    174, 242–243, 246
Hutu, 62, 66, 67–68, 73–74
hypertension, 95, 145, 198

imagery techniques, for treating
    nightmares, 146–147
imagination, in trauma stories, 124
incitamento devozionale (call to
    devotion), 190
Indochinese Psychiatry Clinic. *See*
    Harvard Program in Refugee
    Trauma/Indochinese Psychiatry
    Clinic
Indonesia
    East Timor independence
        movement (1999), 63, 174, 178,
        179
    tsunami disaster (December, 2004),
        3, 4, 156, 164, 174, 237
insulin resistance, 95
International Red Cross, 65, 77–78,
    89
Interpretation of Dreams, The (Freud),
    135
Iraq, 18, 104, 129, 153, 171
Isaac of Stella, 42–43
Islamic Nation, 85
Italy, 153

Jalbert, Russell, 90
James, William, 15
Japan, Kobe earthquake (1995),
    119–121, 218–220
Jesus, 16–17, 29–30, 32–33, 189–190
Jolly, Alison, 164
journalists
    kidnapping and murder of, 65
    responses to tragedy, 3–4
journal writing, 61, 204
justice, social, 212–213, 228–231

Kapetanovic, Aida, 149–150
Karadzic, Radovan, 64

Khmer Rouge regime, 10–13, 20,
    23–24, 27–29, 38–42, 64, 66,
    68–70, 73, 82–83, 86, 88–89, 92,
    99, 101, 107, 113–114, 116–117,
    135–136, 160–162, 167–172, 174,
    177, 178–179, 182, 194, 198,
    200–203, 207, 225–226, 228–229
Kobe, Japan earthquake (1995),
    119–121, 218–220
Korean War, 18
Kosovo, 160
Kyoto treaty, 85

language, message of violence and,
    69–70
Laotian refugees, 73, 79
Lavelle, James, 9, 10
Lawrence, J. Gordon, 147–148
Lek, Rosa, 10
Levi, Primo, 110–111
life-world, 98
Lipps, Theodore, 115

Macedonia, 160, 161
Mandela, Nelson, 177
Marcus Aurelius Antonius Caracalla, 77
Mark the Greek, 16–17
May the Circle Be Unbroken
    (Franklin), 61
meditation, 200, 244
Merton, Thomas, 42–43
metabolic syndrome, 95
midbrain, 142
Mollica, Frank, 1–3
Mort du Loup, La (Death of the Wolf),
    80–81

Nakas, Bakir, 50–61, 94–95
Native Americans, 8
    ethnic cleansing and, 150–152, 235
    spirit intervention and, 182
Navajo, 182
Nazi concentration camps, 55–56, 65,
    110–111

Neoptolemus, 35
neuroscience
    dreams and, 145–146
    stress response and, 96–97
    thought suppression and, 141–142
New York City
    violence in public schools, 221–222
    World Trade Center terrorist
        attacks (2001), 26–27, 74, 76, 86,
        129–133, 164, 166, 177, 220–222,
        234, 239
nightmares, 134–138, 140–147, 150,
    152, 155–156, 203–204
Nikolic, Momir, 163
Nuruddin, Dervis Ahmed, 180
nutrition, in self-healing process,
    195–196, 209

obligation, dependency *versus*,
    218–222
Odysseus, 35, 47
Osler, William, 104–105
Ottoman Empire, First Night custom,
    56
Oz, Amos, 85–86

Palestine/Israel, 104
Paparo, Franco, 153
Peru, 76, 129
    Shining Path guerrillas, 236–237,
        238, 246
Peter C. Alderman Foundation, 129,
    131, 239
Peter C. Alderman Masterclass,
    129–133, 153–155, 223–224
phenomenological method, 14–19
Philoctetes (Sophocles), 34–35, 37, 47,
    175–176, 234, 240, 243
Picasso, Pablo, 239
Pinochet, Ugarte, 40, 73, 111–113, 228
Pol Pot, 23, 24, 38–42, 82–83, 86, 92,
    99, 101, 113–114, 135–136,
    171–172, 174, 178–179, 194, 198,
    202, 225–226, 228–229

posttraumatic stress disorder (PTSD),
    140–141, 147, 175, 221, 235, 245
prayer, 42–43, 181, 184, 200, 208
puppets, 107–108

racism, 220
Rahe, Richard, 198–199
rape. *See also* sexual violence
    betrayal and, 201
    conventional religious institutions
        and, 179–180
    First Night custom (Ottoman
        Empire), 56
    as instrument of terror, 55–56,
        66–67, 140, 180
    nightmares following, 147
    trauma stories and, 21
Raphael, 188–190, 191, 239, 244
rapid eye movement (REM) sleep,
    136–137
Red Lake reservation, 152
Redlich, Fritz, 9
refugees. *See also* Cambodian refugees
    asylum policies and, 174–175
    attitudes toward, 5
    basic health screenings, 9–10
    mental health needs of, 9, 10–13
    psychotropic drugs and, 14, 147
    Southeast Asian, 8–24
relaxation techniques, 200
religious intolerance, 64
Republika Srpska (Serb Republic),
    149, 153
resiliency, in self-healing, 94–95, 172,
    177, 202, 235–236, 245
revenge, humiliation and, 78–81, 122
Rome
    ancient, 75–77, 191–193
    modern, "art stop" in, 239–240
Rousseau, Jean-Jacques, 82–87
Rwanda, 153, 174, 178, 179, 230
    gacaca courts, 179
    genocide in, 62–63, 67–68, 73–74,
        121, 129, 159–161
    sexual violence in, 66

Sappho, 31
Sarajevo siege (1992), 24–26, 49–61,
    64, 67, 94–95
Sassetta (*Saint Thomas Aquinas at
    Prayer*), 29–30, 48
Schlesinger Library on the History of
    Women in America, 27
self-healing, 88–109. *See also* dreams;
    trauma stories
    altruism in, 165–170, 186, 207,
        211–212
    assisting nature's healing in,
        102–105, 245
    barriers to development of,
        103–105
    beneficial effects of, 243–244
    choice in, 157–162
    on collective level, 24–27, 147–187
    cooperation in, 163–164, 165
    courage in, 158–162
    creation of beauty and, 105–109
    dependency *versus,* 218–222
    in everyday life, 184–187
    exercise and, 195–197, 209
    family solidarity and, 200–202
    humanitarian relief efforts *versus,*
        224–228, 236
    humor in, 204–206
    journal writing in, 61, 204
    medical arrogance *versus,* 222–224
    medication as symbol of, 122
    moving from extreme to ordinary
        in, 208–212
    nutrition and, 195–196, 209
    at personal level, 22–27
    physical dimension of, 95–97, 123,
        155
    potential of, 124–125
    psychological dimension of,
        97–100, 123, 155
    requests for help with, 26–27,
        224–228
    research on, 235–236
    resiliency in, 94–95, 172, 177, 202,
        235–236, 245

as response to trauma, 4
role in recovery from trauma,
    105–109
self-care in, 22–27, 194–208
serious illness and, 184–187
social dimension of, 100–102, 123,
    147–155, 165–184, 206–208
as social force for the twenty-first
    century, 233–240
social justice and, 212–213
societal recovery and, 217–218
spirituality in, 175–184, 207–208,
    211–212
symbiosis in, 163–164
work in, 170–175, 207, 211–212
September 11 terrorist attacks (2001),
    26–27, 74, 76, 86, 129–133, 164,
    166, 177, 220–222, 234, 239
sexual violence, 43–46. See also rape
    conventional religious institutions
        and, 179–180, 207–208
    cultural annihilation and, 66–67
    dreams and, 140
    humiliation in, 75, 111–113
    as instrument of terror, 55–56, 63,
        229–230
    multiple implications of, 16
    stress reactions from, 197
shame
    sexual violence and, 45–46, 75,
        111–113
    trauma and, 30–33, 45–46, 55,
        234–235
shell shock, 235
Shining Path guerrillas (Peru),
    236–237, 238, 246
Site 2 refugee camp, 89–93, 98–99,
    100–103, 107, 167–170, 174,
    181–182, 224–230, 241–242
slavery. See also concentration camps
    African American, 71, 76, 202,
        235
    Angkor and, 82–83
social aspects of healing, 165–184,
    206–208

altruism in, 165–170, 186, 207,
    211–212
collective sharing of dreams,
    147–155
in everyday life, 184–187
family solidarity and, 200–202
human rights and, 228–231
maintaining a sick society,
    231–233, 246–247
in self-healing process, 100–102,
    123, 147–155, 165–184, 206–208
spirituality in, 175–184, 207–208,
    211–212
work in, 170–175, 207, 211–212
Social Contract (Rousseau), 82–83
social Darwinism, 162–164
social justice, 212–213, 228–231
Somalia, 174
Sophocles, 34–35, 37, 47, 175–176
South Africa, 40, 177, 228
Spain, 153–155
    Madrid terrorist railroad bombings
        (2004), 154–155
    Spanish Civil War, 239
Spencer, Herbert, 162
spirit possession, 10–13
spirituality
    ancient healers and, 192
    animism and, 176, 179
    Buddhist rituals and, 41–42, 101,
        114, 138–139, 168–169, 182
    conventional religious institutions,
        179–180
    medical and psychiatric attitudes
        toward, 181–184
    prayer and, 42–43, 181, 184, 200,
        208
    in self-healing process, 175–184,
        207–208, 211–212
    spirit intervention and, 181–182
Srebrenica
    massacre (1995), 76, 77–78, 139,
        149–150, 152–153, 163, 165–166,
        244–245, 246
    rebuilding of, 229, 231–233

Steere, Douglas V., 42
stigma
    of rape, 140
    trauma and, 30–33
storytelling. *See* trauma stories
stress response, 209
    fight or flight, 95–97, 199
    illness and, 95, 145, 194, 197–200
    nightmares and, 134–138, 140–147,
        150, 152, 155–156, 203–204
    posttraumatic stress disorder
        (PTSD), 140–141, 147, 175, 221,
        235, 245
stroke, 145
Sudan, 66, 67, 174
Supplemental Security Income (SSI),
    175
Survival in Auschwitz (Levi), 110–111
"survival of the fittest," 162, 163
Sweden, asylum policies of, 174–175
symbiosis, in self-healing process,
    163–164

Taliban, 64
Thailand, United Nations refugee
    camps, 20, 88–93, 98–99,
    100–103, 117, 167–170, 174,
    181–182, 224–230, 241–242
theta rhythms, 136–137
Thich Nhat Hanh, 159
thought suppression, 140, 141–142
Tor, Svang, 27–28, 194–195
Transfiguration, The (Raphael),
    188–190, 191, 239, 244
trauma. *See also* trauma stories
    cultural meaning of, 41–42, 55–56,
        60–61, 223
    moments of revelation and, 18–22
    multiple meanings of, 17–19
    pain of healer and, 30–33, 49–61
    of sexual violence, 43–46
    as term, 36–37
    treating psychological effects of
        torture, 21–22

trauma stories, 34–61, 110–133. *See
    also* trauma
    Bosnian, 48–61
    Cambodian oral history project,
        27–30, 37–48, 60, 107
    coaching with, 123–125
    cultural meaning of trauma, 41–42,
        55–56, 60–61, 223
    dreams and, 138
    empathy in, 115–121, 128
    factual accounting of events in,
        39–41, 50–55, 223
    good prognosis and, 190–191
    good stories, 125–133
    in healing process, 19–22, 37,
        59–61, 110–133, 237–238
    historical purpose of, 35–37
    listener-storyteller relationship and,
        47–48, 58–61, 222
    looking behind the curtain, 42–46,
        56–58, 222
    national archives for, 238–239
    nature of, 21
    as object of art, 121–125
    poor stories, 111–114, 133
    social role of, 245–246
    toxic stories, 123, 133, 246
Trimble, David, 85–86
Trois Freres, Les, France, cave
    paintings, 36
Trojan War, 34–35
truth commissions, 228–229
tsunami disaster (December, 2004), 3,
    4, 156, 164, 174, 237
Tu, Binh, 10
Tutsi, 62, 66, 73–74

Uganda, 76, 129, 153
United Nations (UN)
    Border Relief Operations
        (UNBRO), 88–89
    defining health, 193
    Education, Scientific, and Cultural
        Organization (UNESCO), 153

High Commissioner of Refugees, 5
human rights and, 230–231
refugee camps and, 20, 88–93,
    98–99, 100–103, 107, 117,
    167–170, 174, 181–182, 224–230,
    241–242
United States
    African Americans of, 9, 71, 76,
        202, 220, 235
    al-Qaeda and, 74, 76, 83–85
    Hurricane Katrina (2005), 153, 156,
        174, 242–243, 246
    Native Americans of, 8, 150–152,
        182, 235
    USS *Cole* bombing, 83–84
    World Trade Center terrorist
        attacks (2001), 26–27, 74, 76, 86,
        129–133, 164, 166, 177, 220–222,
        234, 239
Upper Paleolithic cave paintings, 36
upside-down psychiatry (Bennett),
    13–14, 194, 235–236
USS *Cole*, 83–84
utopia, quest for, 81–87

Vietnam War, 18, 31, 235. *See also*
    Cambodian refugees
    prisoners of war, 99–100
    Vietnamese refugees, 79–81
Vigny, Alfred de, 80–81
violence. *See also* genocide; rape;
    sexual violence; trauma; trauma
    stories
    as crack in the "cosmic egg," 5
    domestic, 63, 71–72, 209, 235
    exploiting horrors of, 5
    humiliation as emotion of, 63,
        72–81, 148–149
    humiliation as motive for, 56,
        81–87
    in New York City public schools,
        221–222
    quest for utopia and, 81–87
Virgin Mary, 32, 178

vis medicatrix naturae (healing power
    of nature), 102–103
Vischer, Robert, 115

Wegner, Daniel M., 141
Winson, Jonathan, 136–137
women. *See also* rape; sexual violence
    concept of health and women's
        movement, 193–194
    domestic violence and, 63, 71–72,
        209, 235
work
    nature of, 172–173
    in self-healing process, 170–175,
        207, 211–212
World Food Programme, 88–89
World Health Organization (WHO),
    193
World Trade Center terrorist attacks
    (2001), 26–27, 74, 76, 86,
    129–133, 164, 166, 177, 220–222,
    234, 239
World War I, 235
World War II, 25, 55, 162, 193, 230

Yang, Ter, 10
Yugoslavia, former, 182–184, 228,
    230. *See also* Bosnia-Herzegovina
    components of, 48–49
    Dayton Peace Accords (1995),
        48–49, 174, 183–184
    World War II and, 55